T0367615

The
BRANCH and
END TIME

DOUG ISRAEL

ARCHWAY
PUBLISHING

Archway Publishing books may be ordered through booksellers or by contacting:

Archway Publishing
1663 Liberty Drive
Bloomington, IN 47403
www.archwaypublishing.com
1-(888)-242-5904

ISBN: 978-1-4808-0467-8 (sc)
ISBN: 978-1-4808-0468-5 (e)

Library of Congress Control Number: 2013923019

Printed in the United States of America

Archway Publishing rev. date: 02/10/2014

This book is dedicated to all who seek the truth regarding the major themes of God's word, from the theologian to the lay person to the sceptic.

CONTENTS

INTRODUCTION

I am not a theologian. However, as a lay person I can see that there are very serious flaws in theologians' understanding of creation, salvation, and end time events. Theologians have used illogical reasoning to achieve their understanding of all three of these major themes. This illogical reasoning was necessitated due to their disbelief and mistranslation of important scriptures regarding these themes. As a result, their explanations of these themes are illogical and contradict God's Word. For example, theologians claim that the heavens and the earth and everything that is in them were created in the first six earth days, even though Genesis clearly reveals that God created the heavens and the earth an indefinite amount of time before He made the first earth day. This claim by theologians was necessitated by their mistranslation of Exodus 20:11. The following is the King James mistranslation of Exodus 20:11:

> For in six days the Lord made the heavens and the earth, the sea, and all that is in them, and rested on the seventh day: ———

In Exodus 20:11, what theologians haven't taken note of is that the same Hebrew word that is used for the heavens is used for the earth's sky or atmosphere, and the same Hebrew word that is used for the planet earth is used for the dry land. The following is a corrected translation of Exodus 20:11:

> For in six days Yahweh made the sky, and the dry land, and the sea, and everything that was in them, and rested on the seventh day; ——

So, according to Scripture, God created the heavens and the earth an indefinite amount of time before He made the first earth day, by causing the earth to rotate on its axis. It was an indefinite amount of time after God created the heavens and the earth that He made the earth's sky, dry land, sea, and all that was in them, during the first six earth days. It is shocking that over the centuries theologians haven't recognized and corrected their mistranslation of Exodus 20:11. Theologians should have noticed that in Exodus 20:11 the sea is redundant if the sky is translated as the heavens, and the dry land is translated as the earth. On the other hand, the sky, the dry land, and the sea describe the three states of matter of the planet which God filled with birds, land life forms, and sea creatures.

In order to properly understand creation, it is first necessary to understand why Genesis gives two accounts of the creation of humankind, but only one of these accounts forbidding them to eat of the tree of knowledge of good and evil. Theologians have no clue. In order to understand God's plan of salvation, it is first necessary to understand what happened at Jesus' conception, death, and resurrection that enables Jesus to give eternal life to whosoever believes in Him. Theologians have no clue. In order to properly understand end time events, it is first necessary to understand what event causes the resumption of the seventy weeks of years, and why that event enables Jesus to take His great power and begin to reign as the Almighty. Theologians have no clue. Forgive me for being so critical, but it is critical that theologians step up and become competent in these major themes of God's word.

Part I
UNVEILING THE TRUTH

Part I unveils the truth regarding some of the major themes of God's Word. These themes include: Creation, which includes when the heavens and the earth were created, and when humans were created; God's plan of salvation, which includes the purpose of Jesus' conception and death, what happens when a person is born again, and the time of the resurrection and rapture of believers; the seventy weeks of years regarding the people of Israel, which includes the event that interrupts the seventy weeks of years, and the event that causes the resumption of the seventy weeks of years; and God's revelation that He is one, which includes the concepts of the First, last ones, and Last.

To properly understand God's plan of salvation, we must also understand the seventy week of years and that God is one. The seventy weeks of years and the fact that God is one are intertwined with God's plan of salvation. The interruption and the resumption of the seventy weeks of years, and the First, last ones, and Last come into being due to the execution of God's plan of salvation.

God gives us some understanding of these major themes straight up, but the full truth of them must be discovered by logical analysis of Scripture. This takes an effort to search out the appropriate scriptures that reveal the truth regarding these themes. Unfortunately, theologians have not yet made the necessary effort to discover the full truth of these major themes of God's Word. There is not one of these themes that theologians have gotten correct. Their teaching on all of these major themes contradicts God's Word, and much of their understanding is derived from illogical reasoning.

Chapter One
CREATION

Most theologians incorrectly understand that the universe was created during the six days during which God made the earth's sky, dry land, sea, and everything that was in them. However Genesis 1:1—5 clearly reveals that the universe was created before God made the first earth day. We know that day and night come, because the earth rotates on its axis. God had created the universe, consisting of all the stars with their planets, before He separated the darkness from the light; by so doing He made the first earth day. Much of our confusion stems from the fact that "heaven" is used to describe all the stars and planets other than our planet (Genesis 1:1), but also the earth's atmosphere or sky (Genesis 1:6—8). In addition, "earth" is used to describe the whole planet (Genesis 1:1), but also the dry land (Genesis 1:9—10). From Genesis chapter one, we should know that in Exodus 20:11 "heaven" means the earth's atmosphere or sky, and "earth" means dry land.

> Exodus 20:11 (King James) For in six days the Lord made heaven and earth, the sea, and all that in them is, and rested on the seventh day: ——

A less confusing translation of Exodus 20:11 would be as follows:

Exodus 20:11 (D. Israel) For in six days Yahweh made the sky, and the dry land, and the sea, and all that was in them, and rested on the seventh day; ——

Therefore, according to Scripture, we know that the universe was created an indefinite amount of time before God made the first earth day, and before He made the earth's sky, dry land, seas, and all that was in them. As creationists point out, scientists had to made certain assumptions in order to make their calculation of the age of the universe. So, we don't know whether or not science is correct in its claim that the universe is billions of years old. What we do know is that Genesis chapter one does not contradict that claim. Genesis chapter one describes creation up to the end of the sixth earth day.

Genesis 1:1—31(King James)
1   In the beginning God created the heaven and the earth.
2   And the earth was without form, and void; and darkness was upon the face of the deep. And the Spirit of God moved upon the face of the waters.
3   And God said, Let there be light: and there was light.
4   And God saw the light, that it was good: and God divided the light from the of the darkness.
5   And God called the light Day, and the darkness he called Night. And the evening and the morning were the first day.
6   And God said, Let there be a firmament in the midst of the waters, and let it divide the waters from the waters.
7   And God made the firmament, and divided the waters which were under the firmament from the waters which were above the firmament: and it was so.
8   And God called the firmament Heaven. And the evening and the morning were the second day.

9 And God said, let the waters under the heaven be gathered together under one place, and let the dry land appear: and it was so.

10 And God called the dry land Earth; and the gathering together of the waters called he the Seas: and God saw that it was good.

11 And God said, Let the earth bring forth grass, the herb yielding seed, and the fruit tree yielding fruit after his kind, whose seed is in itself, upon the earth: and it was so.

12 And the earth brought forth grass, and herb yielding seed after his kind, and the tree yielding fruit, whose seed was in itself, after his kind: and God saw that it was good.

13 And the evening and the morning were the third day.

14 And God said, Let there be lights in the firmament of the heaven to divide the day from the night; and let them be for signs, and for seasons, and for days, and years:

5 And let them be for lights in the firmament of the heaven to give light upon the earth: and it was so.

16 And God made two great lights; the greater light to rule the day, and the lesser light to rule the night: he made the stars also.

17 And God set them in the firmament of the heaven to give light upon the earth,

18 And to rule over the day and over the night, and to divide the light from the darkness: and God saw that it was good.

19 And the evening and the morning were the fourth day.

20 And God said, Let the waters bring abundantly the moving creature that hath life, and fowl that may fly above the earth in the open firmament of heaven.

21 And God created great whales, and every living creature that moveth, which the waters brought forth abundantly, after their kind: and God saw that it was good.

22 And God blessed them, saying, Be fruitful, and multiply, and fill the waters in the seas, and let the fowl multiply in the earth.

23 And the evening and the morning were the fifth day.

24 And God said, Let the earth bring forth the living creature after his kind, cattle, and creeping thing, and beast of the earth after his kind: and it was so.

25 And God made the beast of the earth after his kind, and cattle after their kind, and every thing that creepeth upon the earth after his kind: and God saw that it was good.

26 And God said, Let us make man in our image, after our likeness: and let them have dominion over the fish of the sea, and over the fowl of the air, and over the cattle, and over all the earth, and over every creeping thing that creepeth upon the earth.

27 So God created man in his own image, in the image of God created he him; male and female he created he them.

28 And God blessed them, and God said unto them, Be fruitful, and multiply, and replenish the earth, and subdue it: and have dominion over the fish of the sea, and over the fowl of the air, and over every living thing that moveth upon the earth.

29 And God said, Behold, I have given you every herb bearing seed, which is upon the face of the earth, and every tree, in which is the fruit of a tree yielding seed; to you it shall be for meat.

30 And to every beast of the earth, and to every fowl of the air, and to every thing that creepeth upon the earth, wherein is life, I have given every green herb for meat: and it was so.

31 And God saw every thing that he had made, and, behold, it was very good. And the evening and the morning were the sixth day.

In Genesis 1:1 God created the universe, consisting of all the stars and planets, including our sun, earth, and moon. Verse two describes the condition of the earth before God made the dry land. The earth was without form and void, because water covered the entire surface; thus, there was no land to give definition. Darkness covered the deep, the water, because the sun's light could not penetrate the very thick water vapour cover. Verse two does not describe the result of Satan being cast from Heaven, as some believe.

In verse three, God gave the earth light by causing the very thick water vapour and cloud cover to thin enough for the sun's light to penetrate. In verse four, God made the first earth day, dividing the light from the darkness by causing the earth to rotate on its axis. In verses 6—8, God separated the thick water vapour and cloud from the surface water covering the earth; thus, God made the earth's atmosphere or sky. In verses 9—10, God gave form and definition to the earth by causing the dry land to appear.

In verses 14—19, God caused the thick water vapour and cloud around the earth to thin further, so that the stars, sun, and moon became visible from earth. In verses 26— 31, God created the first of two creations of humans, male and female, whose offspring are called the sons and daughters of men. The first creation of humankind were given permission to eat everything. There was no commandment not to eat from the tree of knowledge, because eating from it would have no effect on them. Unlike the second creation of humankind, the first creation of humankind were not given the breath of the Spirit of life. At that time, they were not given the potential to have eternal life.

God faced a problem of conflicting objectives when creating humankind. If God created only one couple, then their offspring would have to commit incest to reproduce. In Leviticus, God has told us that a parent is not to mate with his or her offspring, and that a brother and sister are not to mate (Leviticus 18:6—11). God considers incest to be wicked and lewd. If God created three or four couples, the number that repopulated the earth after the flood, then that problem would be solved. However, creating multiple couples creates a problem that doesn't exist with only one couple. God placed the tree of knowledge of good and evil in the garden of Eden for the purpose of creating temptation for Adam and Eve. Adam and Eve knew the consequence of their disobedience to God, but they chose to believe Satan rather than God. The problem with multiple couples is that if and when one couple sinned by eating from the tree of knowledge, then the temptation would be nullified to the other couples. The other couples would see the effect of eating on the couple that sinned; thus, they would not be tempted to eat from the tree of knowledge of good and evil.

In order to solve this problem of conflicting objectives, God decided to make two separate creations of humans separated by an indefinite period of time. The first creation of humankind consisted of multiple couples, in order that it wouldn't be necessary for their offspring to commit incest to reproduce. The first creation of humankind were created like the second creation with a body, soul and spirit. However, unlike the second creation of humankind, the first creation of humankind were not given the breath of the Spirit of life. Because the first creation of humankind were not given the breath of the Spirit of life, they were told that they could eat anything (Genesis 1:29—30). God did not command them not to eat from the tree of knowledge, because their eating from it would have no effect on them. They did not have the breath of the Spirit of life; therefore, they could not spiritually die the very day they ate (Genesis 2:16—17). The purpose of the first creation of humankind was to produce mates for the offspring of Adam and Eve. The offspring of the first creation of humankind were called the sons and daughters of men; whereas the offspring of Adam and Eve, the second creation of humankind, were called the sons and daughters of God.

Genesis 6:1—2 (King James)

1   And it came to pass, when men began to multiply on the face of the earth, and daughters were born to them,

2   That the sons of God saw the daughters of men that they were fair; and they took them wives of all which they chose.

Genesis 2:1—4 sums up God's work that He did both before and during the time He made the first six earth days, and describes the sanctification of the seventh day. Theologians incorrectly understand that Genesis 2:5—8 is a more detailed description of God's work that He did during the first six days, whereas it actually describes events after the seventh day.

Genesis 2:1—8 (D. Israel)

1   And the heavens and the earth were completed, and all their host.

2   And God ended His work which He made at the seventh day; and He rested in the seventh day from all His work which He had made.

3   And God blessed the seventh day and sanctified it, because He rested in it from all His work which God had created.

4   To be made, these things became the generations of the heavens and the earth, at them being created in the day of Yahweh God making the dry land and the sky.

5   And every shrub of the field was not yet on the earth, and every plant of the field had not yet sprung up, for Yahweh God had not caused it to rain on the earth.

6   And there was none of mankind that worked the ground, since a midst went up from the earth, and watered all the face of the ground.

7   Again Yahweh God formed the man of the dust of the ground, and He blew into his nostrils the breath of life; and the man became a living soul.

8   And Yahweh God planted a garden in Eden to the east, and there He put the man whom He formed.

Verse one sums up creation up to the end of the sixth earth day, including the creation of the heavens and the earth, which occurred an indefinite period of time before God made the first earth day by causing the earth to rotate on its axis. After God made the earth's dry land and sky, all the work that God created consisted of the different life forms that He created. These things that God created were the generations of the heavens and the earth. That is, all the different life forms were generated, were created, from the materials of the heavens and the earth.

All these life forms were created in the day, the five day period of time, that God had made the dry land and the sky; the period of time when the earth's environment became suitable to sustain all these different life forms (Gen. 1:6—10).

Verse five describes a point in time that all the shrubs and plants would have sprouted and appeared above the earth's surface had there been sufficient moisture. God made the earth's vegetation on the third earth day, and plants usually take at least a week and sometimes months to sprout and appear above the earth's surface. So, verse five describes an indefinite period of time after the seventh earth day. In verse six, God has presented us with another choice. Is this verse stating that there were no humans at this time, given that God had not yet created humans; or is this verse stating that none of humankind worked the ground, since it was well watered by a midst?

Standard translations have made the incorrect choice. Humankind working the ground could be translated technically correct as, "and there was not a man to till the ground," as the King James has; or it could be translated technically and appropriately correct as, "And there was none of mankind that worked the ground." The following translation of Genesis 2:6 has Strong's numbers for the Hebrew words.

2050a(120)	369	3807a(5647)
And mankind	there was none	that worked
def(127)	2050a(108)	5927
the ground,	since (a) midst	went up
4480(def)(776)	2050a(8248)	853 3605(6440)
from the earth	and watered	--- all (the) face

def(127)
(of) the ground.

Translators should have reasoned out that the two accounts of the creation of humankind are two different creations of humans, and that verse five is describing an indefinite period of time after the seventh earth day, an indefinite period of time after the creation of multiple couples of humans on the sixth earth day. Verse six describes an indefinite period of time after verse five, an indefinite period of time after not all the shrubs and plants were on the earth, a time when all the shrubs and plants were on the earth and thrived because of being well watered by a midst.

Verse seven describes the second creation of man, an indefinite period of time after the time of the land being well watered by a midst, that in turn was an indefinite period of time after the first creation of humankind. The second creation of humankind were given the breath of the Spirit of life from Yahweh God. They would have had eternal life, if they were obedient and had not eaten from the tree of knowledge of good and evil. Verse five describes the time when the ground had insufficient moisture for all the shrubs and plants to sprout, verse six describes the time when the entire surface of the ground was well watered by a midst and vegetation thrived, and verses 7-8 describe the time when the midst had dissipated to the extent that Adam and Eve took water from a river to work the garden of Eden (Gen. 2:9—15).

We should recognize that the two descriptions of the creation of humankind contained in chapters one and two of Genesis are two different creations, not two accounts of the same creation of them. The fact that God gave both male and female permission to eat everything they wanted in chapter one, but before Eve was created He told Adam not to eat from the tree of knowledge in chapter two tells us that these are two different creations of humankind. If the description of the creation of humans in chapter one was just a summary of chapter two's description, then what they were permitted to eat would have been omitted. If the description of the creation of humankind in chapter one is just a summary of the creation of humans in chapter two, then God couldn't tell them what they were permitted to eat without telling them what they couldn't eat. Otherwise, God telling them that they were permitted to eat anything becomes a lie.

In Genesis 2:7, God breathed the breath of life into Adam. This not only caused Adam to become a living being, like the first creation and all the animals (Genesis 6:17), but the act of blowing breath into Adam was for the purpose of giving Adam a portion of God's Spirit. Genesis 2:7 describes the giving of the breath of the Spirit of life to Adam, but because of eating from the tree of knowledge of good and evil both Adam and Eve spiritually died the very day they ate (Genesis 2:16—17). Because of the sin of Adam and Eve, all humankind is spiritually dead, and in this state can not have eternal life.

In Genesis 7:21—23, God revealed that unlike the rest of creation who were living souls, one group of creation not only were living souls having the breath of life, but also had the breath of the Spirit of life. Not understanding the difference, the King James fudged the translation of these verses by omitting "Spirit." What Genesis 7:22 is stating is that all of the group of humankind that had the breath of the Spirit of life were among all of humankind who died in the flood. This group of humankind that died consisted of all the descendants of Adam and Eve, except those who were in the ark.

Genesis 7:21—23 (D. Israel)

21 And all flesh died that moved on the earth: fowl, and cattle, and beast, and every swarming thing that swarms on the earth, and all mankind.

22 All who the breath of the Spirit of life was in his nostrils were among all who died on dry land.

23 So, every living thing was blotted out which was on the face of the land, from man to cattle to creeping things, and to the fowl of the sky; even they were wiped out from the earth; and only Noah was left, and those who were with him in the ark.

Even though the descendants of Adam and Eve had the breath of the Spirit of life, it was only a remnant of what Adam and Eve had before their fall. This is revealed in Malachi, which reveals that Adam had only a remnant of God's Spirit after the fall.

Malachi 2:15 (D. Israel) "And not one was brought forth, and a remnant of the Spirit was his. And what of the one? A godly seed was being sought. So take heed in your spirit, and with the wife of your youth do not deal treacherously."

2050a(3808)	259	6213
"And not	one	was brought forth,

2050a(7605)	7307	(3807a)pro
and (a) remnant	(of) (the) Spirit	(was) ---- his.

2050a(4100)	def(259)	1245
And what (of)	the one?	Was being sought

2233 430	2050a(8104)	preb(7307)pro
(a) seed godly.	So take heed	in your spirit,

2050a(preb)(802)	(5271)pro	408
and with (the) wife	(of) our youth	not

898
deal treacherously."

In Malachi, God warned against dealing treacherously or deceitfully with Him (Mal. 1:14—2:3). The penalty that God will render to the one who does this is that He will corrupt his seed. In Malachi 2:15, God gave an example of one who dealt treacherously with Him. Before the first son of God, Adam, had a child he dealt treacherously with God, by eating from the tree of knowledge of good and evil. Adam sought a godly seed, but the one he produced was corrupt. As a consequence of Adam's sin, God corrupted Adam's first child, Cain. Before any offspring was born to the first son of God, Adam, at a point in time that was after the fall, a remnant of God's Spirit indwelt him. Before the fall, Adam and Eve had a fuller measure of the breath of the Spirit of life, sufficient to give eternal life, if they hadn't dealt treacherously with God. Adam and Eve were not the first of humankind created by God, but they were the first son and daughter of God; they were the first having the breath of the Spirit of life.

In Malachi, God likewise warned husbands not to deal treacherously with their wives. It is implied that he who deals treacherously with his wife is in danger of having his seed corrupted by God. It is implied that he who acts treacherously is acting treacherously against his own spirit; thus, he is in danger of producing a corrupt offspring. Even though God corrupted Cain, Adam's first child, Cain had the opportunity to elevate his character by doing what is right. In Genesis 4:7, God is addressing Cain.

> Genesis 4:7 (D. Israel) "If you do well there is exaltation, but if you do not do well sin lies at the door; and his desire is toward you, but you must exercise dominion over him."

518 pro(3190)	7613	2050a(518)
"If you do well	(there is) exaltation,	but if

3808	pro(3190)	3807a(6607)	2403 7257
not	you do well	at (the) door	sin lies;

2050a(413)pro	(8669)pro	2050a(859)
and toward you	(is) his desire,	but you

pro(4910)	preb(pro
must exercise dominion	over him."

In Genesis 4:7, sin is a feminine noun, but his or its is masculine. So, this indicates it is not sin whose desire is toward he who is tempted, but Satan. Satan gets dominion over a person when that person gives in to temptation and sins. He who is tempted to sin must be strong and resist that temptation. God corrupted Adam's seed, Cain. However, that corruption wasn't to the extent that Cain couldn't have resisted his temptation to sin. As it turned out, Cain did not resist his temptation to sin, and killed his brother Abel.

Genesis 3:20 states that Eve would become the mother of all living. However, Eve was not the first mother of humankind. The multiple females of the first creation of humans had children an indefinite amount of time before the creation of Eve. This verse is a prophetic statement that refers to the type of life that Jesus offered to whosoever believes in Him.

John 11:25—26 (NAS)
25 Jesus said to her, "I am the resurrection and the life: he who believes in Me shall live even if he dies,
26 and everyone who lives and believes in Me shall never die. ..."

Jesus is describing the type of life in which whosoever is born into will never die; thus, upon this birth the believer in Jesus becomes one of the living who never dies, being a descendant of Eve. What Jesus is describing in John 11:25—26 is that whosoever believes in Him is made spiritually alive; and that the believer's spirit never dies, even upon the believer's physical death. Because Adam and Eve both had a remnant of the breath of the Spirit of life, Eve would become the mother of all the living. She would become the mother of all who pass out of the spiritual death of this life at being born again, and have the surety of being resurrected after physical death.

John 5:24 (NAS) "Truly, truly, I say to you, he who hears My word, and believes Him who sent Me, has eternal life, and does not come into judgment, but has passed out of death into life."

The women of the first creation of humans could not become the mothers of all the living, because they didn't have the breath of the Spirit of life. So, what becomes of those of the first creation of humankind and their descendants, those who didn't have the breath of the Spirit of life? Is their fate not to have the opportunity to receive eternal life? The first book of Peter reveals that Jesus' Spirit preached to the dead, to those who had lived up to the time of the flood. All humans after the flood had a remnant of the breath of the Spirit of life. So, the purpose of Jesus' preaching was to give those who had lived up to the time of the flood, and didn't have a remnant of the breath of the Spirit of life, the opportunity to believe and receive eternal life.

> I Peter 3:18—20 (D. Israel)
> 18 Because even Christ once suffered on account of sins, the righteous for the sake of the unrighteous, so that He might bring us to God; indeed being put to death in the flesh, but made alive in the Spirit;
> 19 in which also going to the spirits in prison He preached
> 20 to the formerly disobedient, when once waited the longsuffering of God to the days of Noah; to the ark being prepared in which a few, that is, eight souls were saved through water.

To sum up Scripture's account of creation, we must conclude that theologians have made two major mistakes. The first mistake was the inappropriate translation of Exodus 20:11. In this verse #8064 has been inappropriately translated as "heaven," whereas it should be translated as "sky" (Genesis 1:8); and #776 has been inappropriately translated as "earth," whereas it should be translated as "dry land" (Genesis 1:10). Genesis 1:1—5 clearly reveals that the heavens and the earth were created before God separated the light and the darkness in order to make the first earth day. The appropriate translation of this verse is:

> Exodus 20:11 (D. Israel) For in six days Yahweh made the sky, and the dry land, and the sea, and all that was in them; ——

This mistake has forced theologians to ignore the fact that God created the heavens and the earth before He made the first earth day. With this mistake, theologians must conclude incorrectly that the universe came into existence during the same week as the creation of humankind, whereas Genesis 1:1—5 clearly reveals that the universe was created an indefinite amount of time before the creation of the first earth day.

The second mistake that theologians have made is to incorrectly conclude that Adam and Eve were the first couple of humankind that God created. They incorrectly believe that it was necessary for Adam and Eve's offspring to commit incest in order to reproduce. They have failed to recognize the reason why God told humankind, male and female, in Genesis 1:29—30 that they were permitted to eat anything; whereas in Genesis 2:16—17 God told Adam not to eat from the tree of knowledge of good and evil. Theologians have failed to recognize that God chose to make two different creations of humankind separated by an indefinite period of time, in order to resolve conflicting objectives. The first creation of humankind were multiple couples, in order that their offspring did not have to commit incest in order to reproduce. Their ultimate purpose was to provide mates for the offspring of Adam and Eve. The second creation of humankind was a single couple, so that the fall of one couple wouldn't nullify the temptation of the tree of knowledge for other couples. Unlike the first creation of humankind, the second creation were created having the breath of the Spirit of life, having the potential for eternal life.

We do not know whether or not science is correct in its estimate that the universe is billions of years old. As creationists point out, science had to make certain assumptions to make this estimate. What we do know is that Scripture does not contradict this estimate. On the other hand, the estimate that humans have existed for millions of years seems to be incorrect, according to Scripture. From Bible genealogy, we know that Adam and Eve were created about 4000 BC; and Genesis 6:1—2 reveals that the descendants of the first creation of humankind began to be many or multiplied, at the time of the sons of God taking the daughters of men for wives. The sons of God describe the sons of Adam and Eve, whereas the daughters of men describe the female descendants of the first creation of multiple couples. It certainly wouldn't have taken million of years for the first creation of humankind to be many or multiplied. So, it appears from Scripture that science is incorrect in its estimate that humans have existed for millions of years. The estimate that science has for the time of the existence of the first human is flawed by the theory of evolution, which requires that humans have existed for millions of years in order to evolve. The majority of scientists have not yet deduced that all life forms were created.

Chapter Two
GOD'S PLAN OF SALVATION

We know that whosoever believes in Jesus has forgiveness of sins, and has eternal life. We also know that without the shedding of blood there is no atonement. So, we know that it was necessary for Jesus to die in order for us to receive eternal life. What we don't know is why death was necessary to achieve atonement; thus, why it was necessary for Jesus to die. God's plan of salvation would be fathomless to humans if it weren't for His Word, but God has revealed His plan of salvation within His Word. Nevertheless, God has set forth His plan in His Word in such a manner that requires us, first to believe key scriptures, and then to properly and logically analyze His Word. God has placed important information regarding His plan of salvation, here a little and there a little throughout His Word. By so doing, He has prevented His plan of salvation from being distorted by scribes and theologians.

However, God is still waiting for us to search out, believe, and understand His amazing and logical plan of salvation as set forth in His Word. At the present time, the church is content to believe an illogical theory that tries to explain God's plan of salvation. Some of the scriptures that reveal God's plan of salvation have been distorted by mistranslation, but remain intact in the original Hebrew. All that remains is for humans to make the effort to understand and believe. God's plan of salvation as revealed in the Bible is yet to be discovered by Christians, Jews, and Muslims. Even though all three faiths claim belief in at least some portions of God's Word, they all have rejected or mishandled the scriptures that reveal how God achieves salvation for whosoever believes in Jesus.

To understand God's plan of salvation, it is first necessary to understand what happened at Jesus' conception, death, and resurrection. In addition, we should understand what will happen at the resumption of the seventy weeks of years, because of what happened at Jesus' conception, death, and resurrection. The following scriptures will give us this understanding.

> I Thessalonians 5:23 (NAS) Now may the God of peace Himself sanctify you entirely, and may your spirit and soul and body be preserved complete, without blame at the coming of our Lord Jesus Christ.

Most theologians don't believe such scriptures as I Thessalonians 5:23, that indicate that humankind consists of both a soul and a spirit. Most incorrectly believe that the soul and the spirit are synonyms. If we do not believe that we have both a soul and a spirit, we can not understand God's plan of salvation. Our disbelief that we have both a soul and a spirit has caused a domino effect, that causes disbelief of other important scriptures.

John 1:18 gives us insight into what happened at Jesus' conception.

> John 1:18 (NAS) No man has seen God at any time; the only begotten God, who is in the bosom of the Father, He has explained Him.

However, we don't believe that Jesus is the only begotten God, most translations having changed "the only begotten God" to "the only begotten Son." Our problem with Jesus being the only begotten God stems from the fact that the Word was God from the days of eternity, an eternity before the time of Jesus' conception. So, how could Jesus be begotten God at the time of His conception, given that the Word was already God? What we fail to acknowledge is that Scripture indicates that the soul is separate and distinct from the spirit, and that flesh consists of both the body and the soul. So, given that the body is conceived and that the Word was already God, that means that at the time of Jesus' conception the Word who was God emptied Himself of God (Phil. 2:6-7), emptied Himself of the Holy Spirit, and became flesh (John 1:14), became Jesus' soul. Therefore, at the time of Jesus' conception, Jesus' live righteous Spirit was conceived; and because Jesus was the Son of Yahweh God, Jesus' conceived Spirit made Him God, the only begotten God.

Psalm 22:30 gives us insight into what happened at Jesus' death and resurrection.

> Psalm 22:30 (D. Israel) All those going down to the dust will bow before Him, even His soul not being revived. A seed will serve Him, he will declare concerning the Lord to a generation.

Psalm 22:30 with Strong's numbers:

3807a(6440)pro	3766	3605
Before Him	will bow	all

(3381)pl	6083
those going down	(to) (the) dust,

2050a(5315)pro	3808	2421	
even His soul	not	being revived.	(A)

2233	(5647)pro	pro(5608)
seed	will serve Him,	he will declare

3807a(136)	3807a(1755)
concerning the Lord.	to (a) generation.

The first part of Psalm twenty-two describes Jesus' death on the cross. Psalm 22:30 then states that all who die will bow before Yahweh God, even Jesus' soul that was not revived. Unfortunately, many of the scriptures that deal with God's plan of salvation have been mistranslated, including Psalm 22:30. This verse reveals that Jesus' soul was not restored to life at Jesus' resurrection. It also reveals that Jesus' soul would be restored to life as a seed; that is, through the process of conception and birth. It indicates that when Jesus' soul is restored to life as a seed, that he will declare to a generation concerning the Lord. So, from Psalm 22:30, we know that the resurrected Jesus consists of His glorified spiritual body and His Spirit, but not His soul.

We know from the gospels that Jesus died on a Friday and was resurrected on Sunday. Before Jesus' death He stated that He would be killed and raised up the third day.

Matthew 17:22—23 (NAS)
22 And while they were gathering together in Galilee, Jesus said to them, "The Son of Man is going to be delivered into the hands of men;
23 and they will kill Him, and He will be raised on the third day." ——

When we describe a second event occurring a certain number of days after a first event, we must count the day of the first event as the first day. This allows for the possibility of the second event occurring on the same day as the first event. So, Jesus' death on a Friday and His resurrection on Sunday fits Jesus' statement, that He would be raised up the third day. Friday was the first day, Saturday was the second day, and Sunday was the third day

However, Jesus gave a different time frame regarding His soul. He revealed that His soul would be taken out of Sheol, the heart of the earth, on Monday afternoon.

Matthew 12:40 (NAS) for just as Jonah was three days and

three nights in the belly of the sea monster, so shall the Son of Man be three days and three nights in the heart of the earth.

We don't believe Matthew 12:40, because we know that Jesus was in a tomb for less than two days and two nights. However, Matthew 12:40 is not referring to Jesus' body being in a tomb on the surface of the earth. It is referring to Jesus' soul being in Sheol in the heart of the earth. In order for Jesus' soul to be in the heart of the earth for three days and three nights, that means he came out of the heart of the earth on Monday afternoon, given that Jesus died on Friday afternoon. Jesus' soul was taken out of Sheol, the place of the dead, by the resurrected Jesus on Monday afternoon. Psalm 116:3—6 describes Jesus' soul in Sheol. Psalm 116:7 then describes the resurrected Jesus telling His soul to return to his rest, to return to Heaven. And in Psalm 116:8—9, Jesus' soul describes being restored to life, which will occur in the latter years.

Psalm 116:3—9 (D. Israel)
3 The cords of death encompassed me, the straits of Sheol found me;
4 trouble and sorrow I have found; therefore, on the name of Yahweh I call: "I pray, Yahweh, deliver my soul."
5 Yahweh is gracious and righteous, and our God is merciful; Yahweh watches over the simple.
6 I have been brought low, but because of me He saves.
7 Return, My soul, to your rest, for Yahweh will deal bountifully on account of you.
8 Because You delivered my soul from death, my eyes from tears, and my feet from stumbling,
9 I walk before Yahweh in the lands of the living.

Jesus' soul will be restored to the land of the living as a seed, restored in the latter years into the tribe of Joseph. Jesus' soul restored to life in the latter years is he who is called the Branch (Jeremiah 23:5—6;

Zechariah 3:8—9; 6:11—13). The Branch will become the Davidic King at his reunification with Jesus, at the resumption of the seventy weeks of years.

Jeremiah 23:5—6 (D. Israel)

5   "Behold, days are coming," says Yahweh, "that I will raise up to David a righteous Branch; and a King will reign and prosper, and will do justice and righteousness in the earth.

6   In His days Judah will be saved, and Israel will dwell safely; and this will be His name by which He will be called, Yahweh our righteousness."

Jesus who was from the tribe of Judah was a shoot from the stem of Jesse; whereas the Branch is a branch from the roots of Jesse, and is from the tribe of Joseph.

Isaiah 11:1 (D. Israel) And a shoot will come forth from the stem of Jesse, and a branch from his roots will bear fruit.

Although we believe that the Messiah was a shoot from the stem of Jesse, we don't believe that the Messiah will also be a branch from the roots of Jesse; as described in Isaiah 11:1, and as confirmed in Genesis 49:22—24. Christians believe that the Messiah was a shoot from the stem of Jesse, because Jesus was a descendant of Jesse, being from the tribe of Judah. However, we don't understand how the Messiah will also be a branch from the roots of Jesse. We don't yet understand that Jesus' soul is not part of the resurrected Jesus. We don't yet understand that Jesus' soul re-enters life as a seed into the tribe of Joseph, being a branch from the roots of Jesse. The root, the ancestor, of Jesse that Jesus' soul will be from is Jacob. And the branch from the ancestor that he will be from is Jacob's son Joseph.

Genesis 49:24 is another scripture that has been mistranslated by theologians. Some translations have put brackets around, "from there will be the Shepherd, the Stone of Israel." They have fudged this verse with brackets in an attempt to make the Shepherd and Stone of Israel not come from the tribe of Joseph, given that Jesus was from the tribe of Judah. However, Genesis 49:22—24 correctly reveals that the Messiah is also from the tribe of Joseph. Jesus' soul will re-enter life into the tribe of Joseph, being a branch from the roots of Jesse, before being reunited with the resurrected Jesus at the resumption of the seventy weeks of years. At being reunited with Jesus, the Branch will once again be Jesus, the Shepherd and Stone of Israel.

Genesis 49:22—24 (D. Israel)
22 "Joseph will be a fruitful branch, a fruitful branch on account of a spring;
23 his branches will go over the wall, and the masters of arrows will vex him, and shoot at and hate him;
24 but his bow will abide with strength, and the arms of his hands will be agile from the hands of the Mighty One of Jacob; from there will be the Shepherd, the Stone of Israel, —"

Jesus' soul will re-enter life as a sinner, as described in Isaiah, the Branch being born of normal parents. The Branch will have the sickness of being a sinner, just as all of humankind.

Isaiah 53:10—11 (D. Israel)
10 But Yahweh will be pleased to crush Him, to make Him sick. When you make his soul guilty, he will see his seed, he will prolong his days, and the pleasure of Yahweh will prosper in his hands.
11 From the work of his soul he will see; he will be satiated with his knowledge.

In Isaiah 53:10, standard translations have inappropriately translated the Hebrew word #818 meaning "guilty" as the Hebrew word #817 meaning "guilt offering." These Hebrew words have the same consonantal spelling, with different vowels; but the vowels were not included in the original text.

When the Branch becomes a born again Christian, the stone the builders rejected becomes the head of the corner.

> Psalm 118: 22—23 (D. Israel)
> 22 The stone the builders rejected became the head of the corner;
> 23 this was from Yahweh, it is marvellous in our eyes.

Psalm 118:22 is spoken by an anonymous contemporary of the Branch. He gains understanding of God's plan of salvation by believing the teaching given by the Branch. Jesus was rejected by the builders, the Jewish priests, for confirming to them that He was the Son of God. So, the Branch's contemporary will understand that the stone rejected by the builders is the resurrected Jesus, consisting of Jesus' glorified spiritual body and His Spirit, those parts of Jesus that were conceived the Son of God; and he will understand that the corner or corner stone is he who existed before Jesus' conception as the Word; who became Jesus' soul, and in the latter years becomes the Branch's soul. So, he will understand that when the Branch became a born again Christian, the stone rejected by the builders became the head of the corner, just as Jesus became the head of each member of His church at each being born again (Ephesians 1:22—23).

In Psalm eighty-five, the Branch reveals that before glory, before God, can dwell in the land of Israel, the Branch must be reunited with the resurrected Jesus. The Branch who has sprung up from the earth is symbolized by truth and peace, whereas Jesus who looks down from Heaven is symbolized by mercy and righteousness.

> Psalm 85:10—11 (D. Israel)
> 10 That glory may dwell in our land, mercy and truth must meet together, righteousness and peace must kiss.

11 Truth has sprung up from the earth, and righteousness looks down from Heaven.

Standard translations have destroyed these verses by incorrectly linking, "That glory may dwell in our land," to the previous verse.

To properly understand God's plan of salvation, we must recognize and understand the event that will cause the resumption of the seventy weeks of years of Daniel.

Daniel 9:24—26 (D. Israel)

24 "Seventy weeks will be divided concerning your people and concerning your holy city, to finish the transgression and to seal up sins, even to make atonement for iniquity; then to bring in everlasting righteousness, and to seal up vision and the prophet, and to anoint the most holy place.

25 Therefore, know and understand, from the issuing of the word to restore and rebuild Jerusalem until the Messiah, the Ruler, will be seven weeks and sixty-two weeks. It will be rebuilt with plaza and ditch, even in the distress of the times.

26 And after the sixty-two weeks the Messiah will be cut off, and there will be nothing for Him. —"

Micah reveals the event that caused the interruption of the weeks of years, and also the event that will cause the resumption of the seventy weeks of years.

Micah 5:2—3 (D. Israel)

2 "And you, Bethlehem Ephrathah, small at being among the thousands of Judah, out of you He will go forth for Me to become ruler in Israel; and His goings forth have been from ancient times, from the days of eternity.

3 Therefore, He will give them up until the time when she who travails has brought forth; then the rest of His brothers will return to the sons of Israel."

It is easy to see that the one who comes forth from Bethlehem refers to Jesus. And it should be easy to understand that Jesus gave up the nation of Israel at His death, and it was Jesus' death that provided the atonement necessary for the age of grace or church age. So, it should be easy to understand that it was Jesus' death that caused the interruption of the seventy weeks of years regarding the people of Israel. Micah reveals that Jesus will once again take up the nation of Israel at the birth of a child. Even though Micah doesn't identify the mother or the child, we should be able to understand that it is this birth that will cause the resumption of the seventy weeks of years, because it will be at this birth that Jesus will once again take up the nation of Israel. The birth of this child will restart the clock of the seventy weeks of years that stopped a few hours into the seventieth week of years at Jesus' death.

The book of Revelation further describes the birth of this child, and reveals that the child that is born is Jesus, who is born to the nation of Israel.

Revelation 12:1—5 (NAS)

1 And a great sign appeared in heaven: a woman clothed with the sun, and the moon under her feet, and on her head a crown of twelve stars;

2 and she was with child; and she cried out, being in labor and in pain to give birth.

3 And another sign appeared in heaven: and behold, a great red dragon having seven heads and ten horns, and on his heads were seven diadems.

4 And his tail swept away a third of the stars of heaven, and threw them to earth. And the dragon stood before the woman who was about to give birth, so that when she gave birth he might devour her child.

5 And she gave birth to a son, a male child, who is to rule all the nations with a rod of iron; and her child was caught up to God and to his throne.

How can this be? How can Jesus be born once again, during the end time? This birth of Jesus does not describe Jesus' natural birth at Bethlehem to Mary, but His super-natural birth on Mount Zion to the nation of Israel. Jesus' super-natural birth is the reunification of the Branch with the resurrected Jesus. It is the reunification of he who was Jesus' soul with Jesus' glorified spiritual body and Spirit. The reunification of Jesus' soul and Spirit is depicted as Jesus' birth, because the same thing happens at Jesus' super-natural birth as happened at His natural birth. That is, at Jesus' natural birth Jesus' soul who was the Word was united with Jesus' conceived body and Spirit, whereas at Jesus' super-natural birth Jesus' soul who has become the soul of the Branch is reunited with that which was his body and Spirit, the resurrected Jesus.

The reunification of Jesus' soul and Spirit at Jesus' super-natural birth will occur immediately after Jesus comes out of the midst of the church.

II Thessalonians 2:7—8 (D. Israel)
7   For the mystery of lawlessness already works; only He is re-
    straining him now until He comes out of the midst.
8   And then the lawless one will be revealed, whom the Lord will
    consume with the Spirit of His mouth, and will destroy by the
    appearance of His coming;

Theologians have fudged the translation of II Thessalonians 2:7, changing "comes out of the midst" to "is taken out of the way." This verse is referring to the fact that Jesus who is in the midst of the church (Rev. 1:13;1:20) is restraining the Antichrist, until He comes out of the midst of the church to indwell the Branch's spirit. When Jesus comes out of the midst of the church, the church age is over, even though the church will not yet be raptured. When Jesus indwells the spirit of the Branch at Jesus' super-natural birth, the Jewish dispensation of the seventy weeks of years will resume. During the church age, salvation is achieved by grace through belief in Jesus. During the remainder of the seventy weeks of years, salvation will be achieved by being judged to have been obedient to the law.

The nation of Israel will be in pain to give birth to Jesus at His super-natural birth. That is, she will be in metal anguish in her struggle to understand and accept Jesus as her Messiah. The Jewish priests rejected Jesus as Israel's Messiah at the end of the sixty-ninth week of years of Daniel 9:25, and cried out to Pilate for Jesus' death. A few hours later Jesus died, a few hours into the seventieth week of years. The Jewish priests will accept Jesus as Israel's Messiah on Mount Zion, and they will cry out to God for Jesus' super-natural birth. They will cry out for the reunification of the Branch with the resurrected Jesus. They will cry out, "Bind the sacrificial feast with cords, even to the horns of the alter."

Psalm 118:26—27 (D. Israel)

26 Blessed is he who comes in the name of Yahweh; we have blessed you from the house of Yahweh.

27 God is Yahweh, and He has given light to us. Bind the sacrificial feast with cords, even to the horns of the alter.

The sacrificial feast symbolizes Jesus' soul who has become the Branch's soul, whereas the blood smeared on the horns of the alter symbolizes Jesus' life giving Spirit. On the day of atonement, the goat of the sin offering symbolizes Jesus who died in order to provide atonement for whosoever believes in Him (Leviticus 16:9). The sacrificial feast of the sin offering is described in Leviticus 4:1—10, and consists of the fat that covers the inwards of the slain goat, as well as the kidneys and the lobe of the liver (Leviticus 4:8—9). The blood of the slain goat for the sin offering was smeared on the horns of the alter of sweet incense before Yahweh (Leviticus 4:7). The people of Israel will have been given light by Yahweh through the Branch, he who comes in Yahweh's name. They will have been given understanding of God's plan of salvation.

Just before Jesus' death, He addressed the people of Jerusalem, and stated that their house was being left desolate; and that they would not see Him again until they say, Blessed is he who comes in the name of the Lord.

Matthew 23:37—39 (NAS)

37 "O Jerusalem, Jerusalem, who kills the prophets and stones those who are sent to her! How often I wanted to gather your children together, the way a hen gathers her chicks under her wings, and you were unwilling.

38 Behold, your house is being left desolate!

39 For I say to you, from now on you shall not see Me until you say, "Blessed is He who comes in the name of the Lord!"

In these verses, Jesus was not referring to the time of His triumphant entry into Jerusalem, which occurred earlier (Matthew 21:9). Jesus was looking ahead to the time described in Psalm 118:26—27. He was referring to the time of the Branch's glorification, the time of the reunification of His soul and Spirit. At being reunited with the resurrected Jesus, the Branch will be Jesus; thus, the people of Jerusalem will see Jesus at that time. However, this sighting of Jesus will be brief, in that He will shortly thereafter be raptured to the throne of God (Rev. 12:5).

In Psalm 2:7, Jesus describes His super-natural birth, and reveals that it occurs on the day that he is anointed with Yahweh's Spirit on Mount Zion. This anointing will occur immediately after Jesus' super-natural birth, and immediately before His rapture to the throne of God (Rev. 12:5). Jesus was baptized with the fullness of Yahweh's Spirit, the Holy Spirit, during His first advent; but at Jesus' death and separation of His soul and Spirit, Jesus ceased from being anointed with Yahweh's Spirit. However, immediately after Jesus' super-natural birth, He once again will be anointed with the fullness of Yahweh's Spirit; thus, He will once again be as Yahweh the Almighty. Standard translations have destroyed Psalm 2:6 by inappropriately translating #5258 as "set," rather than as "anointed."

Psalm 2:1—9 (D. Israel)

1   Why do the nations rage, and the peoples ponder a vain thing?

2   The kings of the earth will take their stand; yea, the rulers take counsel against Yahweh and against His anointed.

3   "Let us tear apart their bands, and throw from us their cords."

4   He abiding in the heavens laughs; the Lord will mock at them.

5   Then He will speak to them in His anger; yea, in His wrath He will terrify them.

6   "Yea, I anointed My King on Zion, My holy mountain."

7   "I will declare concerning the statute of Yahweh: He said to Me, 'You are My Son, today I have begotten You.

8   Ask of Me and I will give the nations as Your inheritance, even the ends of the earth as Your possession.

9   You will break them with a rod of iron; You will dash them as a potter's vessel.'"

Psalm 2:1—9 is spoken from a point in time that is after the Branch's glorification, but before Jesus' second advent. The nations will be enraged against God, due to Him anointing Jesus on Mount Zion, immediately after the Branch's glorification. They will ponder a vain thing. They will make plans to defeat God in battle at Jesus' second advent.

The blessing of becoming the ruler of the nations was originally given to Jacob. Genesis 27:29 describes this blessing.

Genesis 27:29 (D. Israel) "May the nations serve you, and the peoples bow to you; become the ruler of your brothers, and may your mother's sons bow to you; may those who curse you be cursed, and may those who bless you be blessed."

Jacob passed this blessing on to both Judah (Genesis 49:10) and Joseph (Genesis 49:26); given that Jesus was from the tribe of Judah, and the Branch is from the tribe of Joseph.

Genesis 49:26 (D. Israel) "The blessings of your father have prevailed over the blessings of my progenitors; as far as the summit
of the everlasting hill they will be for the head of Joseph, and for
the crown of the head of the prince of his brothers."

The Branch will receive this blessing at his glorification when he goes
up to the summit of the everlasting hill, the mountain of Yahweh,
and stands up in Yahweh's holy place. Psalm twenty-four describes the
Branch going up on the everlasting hill to receive this blessing. However,
standard translations have destroyed Psalm twenty-four. In Psalm 24:6,
the Branch is addressed as Jacob, because the blessing of standing up in
Yahweh's place and becoming ruler of the nations was originally given to
Jacob. At standing up in Yahweh's place at his glorification, the Branch
will first be reunited with the resurrected Jesus, and then anointed with
the fullness of Yahweh's Spirit; and then raptured to the throne of God.
At being anointed with the fullness of Yahweh's Spirit, the Branch who
will have become Jesus will become as Yahweh. After being anointed
with the fullness of Yahweh's Spirit, he will be raptured to the throne of
God through the everlasting doors of Heaven as Yahweh, the King of
glory.

Psalm 24:3—10 (D. Israel)

3   Who will go up upon the mountain of Yahweh, and who will
    stand up in His holy place?

4   One who will have clean hands and a pure heart, who will not
    have lifted up his soul to vanity, and will not have sworn to
    deceit.

5   He will lift up the blessing from Yahweh, and righteousness
    from the God of his salvation.

6   This one a generation will seek, those who will seek your face,
    Jacob.

7   Lift up your heads, O gates, and be lifted up, O everlasting
    doors, and the King of glory will come in.

8 Who is the King of glory? Yahweh powerful and mighty, Yahweh mighty in battle.

9 Lift up your heads, O gates, and be lifted up, O everlasting doors, and the King of glory will come in.

10 Who is He, this King of glory? Yahweh of hosts, He is the King of glory.

When it is time for the Branch to be glorified, God will command that he go up on Mount Zion and declare, "Behold your God!" At making this declaration the Branch will be glorified, and once again become Jesus at being reunited with Him. The Branch is told to go up on Mount Zion to Himself, given that the resurrected Jesus was his body and Spirit at Jesus' first advent, and Jesus' Spirit will once again indwell him at his glorification.

> Isaiah 40:9 (D. Israel) Go up upon the high mountain to Yourself, bearer of good news to Zion. Lift up your voice with strength, bearer of good news to Jerusalem. Lift up, do not fear, say to the cities of Judah, "Behold your God!"

When we understand the scriptures that reveal what happens to Jesus' soul after Jesus' death, we can understand the existence of the Branch. We can understand that the Branch is he who is restored to life into the tribe of Joseph as a seed having Jesus' soul; who is born a sinner, but who becomes a born again Christian; and who will be reunited with the resurrected Jesus at the resumption of the seventy weeks of years. At being reunited with Jesus at Jesus' super-natural birth, he once again will be Jesus. He who was the Word, who became Jesus' soul, who became the Branch's soul, will once again become Jesus' soul. In the book of Revelation at Jesus' second advent, Jesus is called the Word of God, and is wielding the sword of His spirit.

Revelation 19:13—15 (NAS)

13 And He is clothed with a robe dipped in blood; and His name is called the Word of God.

14 And the armies which are in heaven, clothed in fine linen, white and clean, were following Him on white horses.

15 And from His mouth comes a sharp sword, so that with it He may smite the nations; and He will rule them with a rod of iron; and He treads the wine press of the fierce wrath of God, the Almighty.

At the time of the Branch's glorification, God will command that the Branch gird on his sword. God will command the Branch's reunification with Jesus, his glory and his majesty.

Psalm 45:3—6 (D. Israel)

3 Gird your sword on your thigh, Mighty One, your glory and your majesty.

4 And in Your majesty prosper; ride on the matter of truth and meekness and righteousness, and Your right hand will teach You fearful things.

5 Your arrows are sharp — peoples fall under You — in the heart of the enemies of the King.

6 Your throne, O God, is forever and ever; a scepter of uprightness is the scepter of Your kingdom.

So, now we know what happened at Jesus' conception, death and resurrection, and what will happen at the resumption of the seventy weeks of years. Can we now understand why Jesus' death gives eternal life to whosoever believes in Him? We know that Jesus like all humankind had both a soul and a spirit. We also know that it was Jesus' soul who existed before Jesus' conception as the Word, and that Jesus' Spirit was conceived at the time of His conception. We also know that Jesus' soul and Spirit were separated at Jesus' death, and were not reunited at

Jesus' resurrection. And we know that Jesus' soul and Spirit will be reunited at the resumption of the seventieth week of years, which will end the church age or age of grace. What now?

What if we believed I John 3:9, which states that he who is born of God is not able to sin, because God's seed abides in him.

> I John 3:9 (J. P. Green) Everyone who has been begotten of God does not sin, because His seed abides in him, and he is not able to sin, because he has been born of God.

Is this verse serious? Even born again Christians sometimes fail and sin. But hold on, we are told that the born again believer does not sin, because God's seed abides in him. The seed of God consists of the parts of Jesus that were conceived at Jesus' conception, those parts being Jesus' body and Spirit. So it is the resurrected Jesus, consisting of Jesus' glorified spiritual body and His Spirit that indwells the believer. When we believe that humans consist of both a soul and a spirit, we can understand how the seed of God indwelling the believer's spirit can cause the believer's spirit to be unable to sin. We can understand that it is the believer's spirit that is born again, and it is the believer's soul that is still capable of sin. Jesus' live righteous Spirit indwelling the believer's spirit gives the believer eternal life. In addition, Jesus' righteous Spirit indwelling the believer's spirit provides a righteous vessel for Yahweh's Spirit, the Holy Spirit, to indwell. He who has Jesus indwelling his spirit also has Yahweh's Spirit indwelling his spirit. He who does not have the Son, neither has the Father. But he who has the Son, also has the Father (I John 2:23).

So, Jesus conception was necessary in order that Jesus' live righteous Spirit be conceived. And Jesus' death was necessary in order to separate Jesus' life giving Spirit from His soul, in order to free His Spirit to indwell the believer's spirit, and in so doing give him eternal life. Without the shedding of blood, there is no atonement. On the day of atonement it was the blood of the slain sin offering, that made atonement for the sins of the people of Israel. The reason why the blood of the animal made atonement was because the life of the flesh is in the blood (Leviticus 17:11). Blood is symbolic of Jesus' life giving Spirit. Jesus shed His blood to make atonement for our sins. Jesus shed His blood to give us His life giving Spirit. Atonement means that which cleanses, and it also means that which covers. When Jesus' righteous Spirit indwells the believer's spirit, He cleanses the believer's spirit of all sin, and at the same time He covers the sins of the believer's soul to his born again spirit. And by so doing, He creates a righteous vessel for the indwelling of the Father's Holy Spirit. Jesus is in the born again believer's spirit, and the Father is in Jesus (John 17:23).

In Romans, Paul confirms that it is Jesus indwelling the believer that makes the believer's spirit righteous, even unable to sin. Jesus is our righteousness.

Romans 8:9—10 (NAS)
9   However, you are not in the flesh but in the Spirit, if indeed the Spirit of God dwells in you. But if anyone does not have the Spirit of Christ he does not belong to Him.
10   And if Christ is in you, though the body is dead because of sin, yet the spirit is alive because of righteousness.

Most theologians don't believe Romans 8:9—10, in that they believe that the Spirit of Christ means the Holy Spirit. However, it is not he who does not have the Holy Spirit doesn't belong to God. It is he who does not have Jesus' Spirit. If you do not have the Son, neither do you have the Father, and you do not belong to God. He who has the Son, also has the Father (I John 2:23). He who is indwelt by Jesus, the seed of God, also has the Father, because it is Jesus' righteous Spirit that creates a righteous vessel for Yahweh's Holy Spirit to indwell.

The born again believer is not only forgiven his sins, but he is justified; he is made righteous. Isaiah 53:12 is a two-legged double-step. Leg one describes the destiny of Jesus' Spirit after His death, whereas leg two describes the destiny of Jesus' soul after Jesus' death. Jesus justifies the born again believer, because the resurrected Jesus, the seed of God, indwells the believer's spirit and makes the believer's spirit righteous. To be justified means to be made righteous. The born again believer is justified, because his spirit is made righteous, even unable to sin. Standard translations have destroyed Isaiah 53:12.

Isaiah 53:12 (D. Israel)
leg 1 step 1   My righteous Servant will justify many,
leg 2 step 1   but their iniquities he will bear.
leg 2 step 2   Therefore, I will divide to him with the many, and he will divide the spoil with the strong; because he will have stripped bare his soul to death, and will be counted with transgressors;
leg 1 step 2   even the sin of many He will lift up, and for transgressors He will reach the mark.

Jesus, the seed of God, indwells the believer's spirit and lifts up, removes the sin of the believer's spirit. Jesus reaches the mark of being without sin for the believer, by making the believer's spirit incapable of sin.

The Branch will bear the sins of humankind, in that he will be born of normal parents; thus, he will be born a sinner. However, God will divide to him with the many when he is born again (Psalm 118:22). The Branch will be justified, just as the many who are born again. After Jesus' second advent, the Branch who will have become Jesus will divide the spoil taken from those nations defeated at the battle of Armageddon. The Branch will be counted with transgressors. This is not referring to Jesus being crucified with two thieves, transgressors of the Roman state. It is referring to after the stripping bare of His soul to death, when Jesus' soul becomes the Branch's soul. At being the soul of the Branch, he who was Jesus' soul will be a sinner; thus, he will be counted with transgressors of God.

For centuries we have accepted the nonsense of the Satisfaction Theory, that incorrectly and illogically explains the purpose of Jesus' death. There are various forms of the Satisfaction Theory, which basically states that the purpose of Christ's death was to satisfy justice, was to pay the debt or penalty of humankind's sins. However, even many theologians admit that the Satisfaction Theory is logically flawed. Nevertheless, the Satisfaction Theory remains the foundation of the church's understanding of the purpose of Jesus' death. There are three major logical objections to the Satisfaction Theory, not counting the fact that it contradicts Scripture's portrayal of God's plan of salvation. The first objection is that if the purpose of Christ's death was to satisfy justice, was to pay the debt of humankind's sins, then Jesus was over qualified for the job. We know that Jesus qualified to be the sacrifice for sin, because He was without sin. He was the unblemished lamb. However, the vilest sinner would be just as qualified to bear punishment as Jesus, for the degree of righteousness of a person has nothing to do with his ability or suitability to bear punishment. The second objection is that if the purpose of Christ's death was to satisfy justice, was to pay the penalty of mankind's sins, then the Father could not have resurrected Jesus. Jesus would have had to remain dead for all eternity in payment of the penalty for sin, the penalty of eternal death. The third objection is that if the purpose of Christ's death was to satisfy justice, was to pay the penalty of mankind's sins, then God could no longer punish sin, since Jesus would have already taken that punishment. In fact, the Satisfaction Theory makes the asking of forgiveness unnecessary, since a debt that has been paid requires no asking of forgiveness.

Scripture reveals that the purpose of Jesus' death was not to execute judgment for the sins of humankind, but for the exact opposite purpose. The beginning of Isaiah chapter forty-two contains a two-legged double-step. Leg one refers to Jesus during His first advent, whereas leg two refers to Jesus during His second advent. Standard translations have poorly translated, "He will bring forth judgment to faithfulness."

Isaiah 42:1—4 (D. Israel)

"Behold My Servant, I will uphold Him; My elect in whom My soul is pleased.

leg 1 step 1 I will put My Spirit upon Him.

leg 2 step 1 He will bring forth justice to the nations.

leg 1 step 2 He will not cry out, and will not cause His voice to be heard in the street. He will not break a crushed reed, and He will not quench a smouldering wick. He will bring forth judgment to faithfulness.

leg2 step 2 He will not be disheartened or crushed, until He has established justice in the earth. And the coastlands will wait expectantly for His law."

The most significant thing that Jesus did during His first advent was to bring forth judgment to faithfulness at His death. At Jesus' death, He brought forth the judgment of God that was already upon humankind, to the faithfulness of God to whosoever believes in Jesus. At the fall of Adam and Eve, God executed judgment upon them, causing them to die on the very day they fell (Genesis 2:17). They did not physically die, but they became spiritually dead. Thereafter spiritual death has been transmitted to all humankind. Jesus' death freed His life giving Spirit to indwell and make righteous the spirit of whosoever believes in Him. God is faithful to bring forth His judgment that is upon all humankind to whosoever believes in Jesus. God is faithful to bring to life the believer's spirit, which was dead on account of the fall of Adam and Eve. Because Jesus' live righteous Spirit indwells the spirit of the believer, the believer's spirit is made alive and righteous; and the believer has the surety of eternal life.

Chapter Three
THE SEVENTY WEEKS OF YEARS

The prophecy of Daniel 9:24—27 has been called the most important in the Bible. It foretells the time of the coming of the Messiah and the fact that He will be cut off, will be killed. In addition, when it has been properly translated, it reveals that the seventy weeks of years that have to do with the Jewish people will be divided. The age of grace or church age is sandwiched between two parts of the seventy weeks of years.

Daniel 9:24—27 (D. Israel)

24 "Seventy weeks will be divided concerning your people and concerning your holy city, to finish the transgression and to seal up sins, even to make atonement for iniquity; then to bring in everlasting righteousness, and to seal up vision and the prophet, and to anoint the most holy place.

25 Therefore, know and understand, from the issuing of the word to restore and rebuild Jerusalem until the Messiah, the Ruler, will be seven weeks and sixty-two weeks. It will be rebuilt with plaza and ditch, even in the distress of the times.

26 And after the sixty-two weeks the Messiah will be cut off, and there will be nothing for Him. And the people of a coming ruler will destroy the city and the sanctuary. And its end will be with a flood, and until the end a war of desolation is determined.

27 And he will confirm a covenant with many for one week, and in the middle of the week he will cause the sacrifice and offering to cease. —"

The decree to restore and rebuild Jerusalem is described in Nehemiah chapter two. We are told that in the twentieth year of king Artaxerxes in the month of Nissan, he grants Nehemiah permission to restore and rebuild Jerusalem. So, the issuing of the decree would have occurred either in 445 or 444 BC, depending on the method used to calculate the reign of Artaxerxes. However, the fact that Jesus died on a Friday Passover indicates that the correct year is 444 BC. When the date of Jesus' death is calculated using the sixty-nine weeks of years from 445 and 444 BC, we land on Monday April 12th for Passover 32 AD, but on Friday April 1st for Passover 33 AD. These dates are calculated using the modern Gregorian calendar. Most understand that the seventy sevens are seventy times seven years, which equals four hundred and ninety years, and that the years consist of three hundred and sixty days each.

Theologians have made three significant errors in their understanding of Daniel 9:24—27. The first error is inappropriately translating #2852 as "determined" or "decreed," rather than as "divided." We should recognize that by translating #2852 as decreed or as determined, we include the entire list of events described in Daniel 9:24 within the seventy weeks of years that are concerning the Jewish people. However, we should also recognize that the finishing of transgression, the sealing up of sin, and the atoning for iniquity have to do with the age of grace, not the Jewish dispensation. The instant Jesus died atonement was made, and the age of grace or church age started. No atonement was made while Jesus suffered on the cross until He died, for without the shedding of blood, without death, there is no atonement (Lev. 17:11; Heb. 9:22). The reason that there was no atonement until Jesus' death is because it was at His death, that His Spirit was freed from His soul to indwell and make righteous the spirit of the believer; and in so doing, Jesus makes atonement.

The second error that theologians have made is understanding that the arrival of the Messiah at sixty-nine weeks of years was at Jesus' triumphant entry into Jerusalem, five days before His death. With this understanding, they include the five days from Jesus' triumphant entry until His death within the age of grace, leaving a full seventieth week of years to be completed in the future. This should be recognized as illogical reasoning. For not only does these five days belong to the Jewish dispensation, but it should be recognized that it was Jesus' death that created the separation between the Jewish dispensation and the age of grace, not Jesus' triumphant entry into Jerusalem. The correct understanding is that the Messiah's appearance at the end of sixty-nine weeks of years occurs on the morning of the day of His death, at His confirmation before the Jewish priests that He is the Son of God, and then before Pilate that He is the King of the Jews. Since there were a few hours between His confirmation and his death, the seventieth week of years that is yet to be fulfilled will actually be a few hours short of a full week of years. The time between His confirmation and His death is the first part of the seventieth week of years.

If the end of the sixty-ninth week of years occurred at Jesus' triumphant entry, the seventieth week of years yet to be fulfilled would be short five days of a full week of years. However, the book of Revelation reveals that the seventieth week of years still has $(1260)2 = 2520$ days remaining to be fulfilled. The two witnesses of the book of Revelation are Old Testament type prophets who start their ministries at the beginning of the resumption of the seventy weeks of years, and end their ministries at the mid-point of the seventieth week of years.

Revelation 11:3 (NAS) "And I will grant authority to my two

witnesses, and they will prophesy for twelve hundred and sixty
days, clothed in sackcloth."

They end their ministries at the sealing up of vision and the prophet
(Daniel 9:24); at that time, the mystery of God will be finished as He
proclaimed to His prophets.

> Revelation 10:7 (NAS) but in the days of the voice of the sev-
> enth angel, when he is about to sound, then the mystery of God
> is finished, as He preached to His servants the prophets.

Many have assumed that the decree to rebuild Jerusalem was given
on the first of Nissan 444 BC, and have calculated that date to be March
5, 444 BC, Julian calendar. This would line up with the sixty-ninth
week of years falling on Jesus' triumphant entry, if it occurred four days
before Jesus' death. However, it is uncertain whether or not the first
of Nissan occurred on March 5, 444 BC, Julian calendar. We should
actually understand that the decree was issued on March 7, 444 BC,
Gregorian calendar, because this date lines up with the sixty-ninth week
of years falling on April 1, 33 AD, Gregorian calendar, the day of Jesus'
death.

The third error that theologians have made is accepting an illogical
starting point for the resumption of the seventy weeks of years; they
incorrectly understanding that the resumption occurs at the start of the
seven year covenant of Daniel 9:27. Theologians are completely blind
to the fact that it is actually the reunification of Jesus soul and Spirit,
that causes the resumption of the seventy weeks of years. Just as it was
the separation of Jesus' soul and Spirit at His death, that caused the
separation of the seventy weeks of years, it will be the reunification of
Jesus' soul and Spirit at His super-natural birth that will cause the resumption of the seventy weeks of years. As stated in Micah 5:3, He will
give them up until the time when she who is in labor has brought forth.
Jesus gave up the nation of Israel at His death, but will take them up

again at His super-natural birth. Immediately after Jesus' super-natural birth, He will be anointed with Yahweh's Spirit and will be caught up to the throne of God, bringing in His everlasting righteous reign (Rev. 12:5). The nation of Israel will give birth to a child on whose shoulders will be the government, and He will uphold it with justice and righteous (Isaiah 9:7). He will seek justice and be prompt in righteousness (Isaiah 16:5). Jesus will have taken His great power and will have begun to reign, once again becoming the Almighty by being anointed with the fullness of Yahweh's Spirit, immediately after His super-natural birth on Mount Zion (Psalm 2:6—7). Jesus will have changed from being the Almighty who was and who is to come (Rev. 1:8), to being the Almighty who is and who was and who is to come.

Revelation 1:8 is spoken by Jesus from the point in time of the book of Revelation being given to the apostle John. At this point in time, Jesus is not anointed with the fullness of Yahweh's Spirit. Jesus was anointed with the fullness of Yahweh's Spirit from His baptism until His death. And Jesus will once again be anointed with the fullness of Yahweh's Spirit, immediately after Jesus' super-natural birth at the resumption of the seventy weeks of years. In addition, at the point in time of Revelation 1:8 the rapture has not occurred, but Jesus will come on the clouds at the rapture (Mat. 24:29—31). So, in Revelation 1:8, Jesus is the Almighty who was and who is to come.

Revelation 1:7—8 (D. Israel)

7 Behold, He is coming with the clouds, and every eye will see Him, even those who pierced Him; and all the tribes of the earth will mourn over Him. Yes indeed. Amen.

8 "I am the First and the Last," says the Lord God who is, "even who was and who is to come, the Almighty."

Revelation 11:17 is spoken from the point in time of the seventh trumpet, a point in time that is after He has taken His great power at once again becoming the Almighty, and a point in time that is after He has come on the clouds at the rapture; thus, in Revelation 11:17 Jesus is the Almighty who is and who was, having already come on the clouds at the rapture.

> Revelation 11:17—18 (D. Israel)
> 17 "We give You thanks, Lord God, the Almighty, who is and who was, because You have taken Your great power and have begun to reign.
> 18 And the nations were enraged, and Your wrath came, and the time has come for the dead to be judged and to give reward to Your servants, to the prophets and to the saints and to those who fear Your name, the small and the great; and to destroy those who destroy the earth."

The nations will be enraged, when Jesus takes His great power at being anointed with the fullness of Yahweh's Spirit, at the resumption of the seventy weeks of years (Psalm 2:1—6). God's wrath comes immediately after the rapture at the sixth seal (Rev. 6:12—17). God's wrath will change from testing to judgment at the seventh trumpet. At that time, He will judge the dead; not the physically dead, but the spiritually dead. At the time of the third bowl of wrath, a point in time that is also after the rapture, Yahweh God is also described as He who is and who was. At this time, Yahweh has already come on the clouds at the rapture. He will already have come at the rapture, because Jesus will be as Yahweh the Almighty at that time.

> Revelation 16:5 (NAS) And I heard the angel of the waters saying, "Righteous art Thou, who art and who wast, O Holy One, because Thou didst judge these things;"

Note that the King James has adulterated Revelation 16:5 by adding "and shalt be," and Revelation 11:17 by adding, "and art to come."

Atonement refers to the cleansing of sin, and it also refers to the covering of sin. These two meanings of atonement are described in Daniel as finishing the transgression, and as sealing up sins. Jesus' death accomplished both these things for the born again believer. The instant a Christian is born again the transgression of his spirit is finished. This is accomplished by Jesus, the seed of God, by Him indwelling the believer's spirit (I John 3:9). As Isaiah 53:12 states, "and for transgressors He will reach the mark." The mark that Jesus reaches for transgressors of God is the mark of making the believer's spirit to be without sin. Jesus justifies the believer, makes him righteous, by causing the believer's spirit to be incapable of sin by means of indwelling him. Even though the believer's soul is still capable of sin, the sins of his soul are covered; they are sealed up from the believer's righteous spirit, due to the indwelling of Jesus. These two aspects of atonement given to the Christian create a righteous vessel for the Spirit of the Father, the Holy spirit, to indwell. Thus, the instant Jesus died the veil of the temple was torn in two, signifying the interruption of the Jewish dispensation and the start of the age of grace. For the instant Jesus died, atonement for the believer was provided, and the born again Christian could enter the presence of God.

The remaining portion of the seventy weeks of years will be divided from the age of grace in order to bring in everlasting righteousness, and to seal up vision and the prophet, and to anoint the most holy place; these three events marking the resumption, mid-point, and end of the seventieth week of years. In order that these three events occur, the church age must end and the second portion of the seventy weeks of years must start; for Jesus must come out of the midst of the church to be reunited with His soul, in order that Jesus' everlasting righteous reign begin. The seventy weeks of years were divided a few hours into the seventieth week of years at Jesus' death, and will be resumed at Jesus' supernatural birth and the beginning of Jesus' everlasting righteous reign, a few hours into the seventieth week of years.

Vision and the prophet will be sealed up at the mid-point of the seventieth week of years. This will occur at the end of the 1260 day ministry of the two witnesses (Rev. 11:3), which will occur just before the seventh trumpet sounds. The two witnesses are Old Testament type prophets who start their ministry when Jesus comes out of the midst of the church, at the resumption of the seventy weeks of years. The end of the seventy weeks of years will be marked by the anointing of the most holy place, at the time of its being made right from the actions of the little horn, the Antichrist.

Daniel 8:11—14 (D. Israel)

11 And even to the commander of the host it magnified itself, and the regular sacrifice was taken from Him, and the place of His sanctuary was thrown down.

12 And the host and the regular sacrifice was given over by reason of transgression; and it practiced and prospered.

13 Then I heard a holy one speaking, and another holy one said to that particular holy one who spoke, "Until when will be the vision of the regular sacrifice and the transgression making desolate, making both the holy place and the host a trampling place?"

14 And he said to me, "Until two thousand and three hundred evenings and mornings, then the holy place will be made right."

Daniel 8:17 (D. Israel) —— "Understand, son of man, that the vision pertains to the time of the end."

We don't believe that the vision of the 2300 days pertains to the time of the end, not understanding that the seven year covenant is not the seventieth week of years. We don't yet understand that it is the birth of the child described in Micah 5:3 and Revelation 12:5, that causes the resumption of the seventieth week of years, and not the start of the seven year covenant between the nation of Israel and the Antichrist. We know from Daniel 12:11 that the regular sacrifice is stopped 1290 days before Jesus' second advent, at the end of the seven year covenant; and it can be assumed that the making right of the holy place must occur at or before the anointing of the most holy place, at the end of the seventieth week of years (Daniel 9:24). Therefore, the seven year covenant can not be the seventieth week of years, given that there is only 1290 days from the stopping of the regular sacrifice to the end of the seven year covenant, not 2300 days. Daniel 8:11—17 is a key scripture that gives us the chronological relationship between the seven year covenant and the seventieth week of years. Assuming that the anointing of the most holy place is the completion of the making right of the holy place, then the seventieth week of years will start 360 days(7) – 2300 days = 220 days before the stopping of the regular sacrifice and the setting up of the abomination of desolation, which occurs 1230 days into the seven year covenant. So, the seventieth week of years will start 1230 – 220 = 1010 days after the start of the seven year covenant.

Theologians don't yet understand why the sixty-nine weeks of years, from the issuing of the decree until the Messiah, has been described as seven weeks and sixty-two weeks. The most popular speculation is that the seven weeks of years marks the completion of the rebuilding of Jerusalem, the city of Jerusalem being destroyed by Babylon in 586 BC. However, it seems inappropriate that the time of the completion of the rebuilding of Jerusalem would be included in the prediction of the time of the coming of the Messiah. The seven weeks of years should have something to do with when the Messiah and Ruler makes His appearance. Indeed, it can be shown that the seven weeks of years actually marks the first prophetic Jubilee year after the issuing of the decree in 444 BC to rebuild Jerusalem, which in turn gives us an anchor point in time for calculating the time of the coming of the Messiah and King of Israel.

Many have speculated that Jesus was born in a Jubilee year, given that a Jubilee year is a year of celebration and release from debt and bondage. Jesus came that we might be free from the bondage of sin. However, those trying to show that Jesus was born in a Jubilee year incorrectly tried to line up Jesus' birth with the solar Jubilee cycle, that started at Israel's entry into the promised land; whereas God uses the 360 day "prophetic year," and reset the Jubilee at the destruction of

Jerusalem in 586 BC. At Israel's exodus out of Egypt, God gave the people of Israel a calendar consisting of twelve months having thirty days each. It was the Jewish priests who added a month when necessary to make the calendar line up with the solar year. However, God has always kept His 360 day/year calendar.

The destruction of Jerusalem in 586 BC is described in II Chronicles 36:19—21, and indicates that the land enjoyed its Sabbaths all the days of its desolation.

> II Chronicles 36:19—21 (NAS)
> 19 Then they burned the house of God, and broke down the wall of Jerusalem and burned all its fortified buildings with fire, and destroyed all the valuable articles.
> 20 And those who had escaped from the sword he carried away to Babylon; and they were servants to him and his sons until the rule of the kingdom of Persia,
> 21 to fulfill the word of the Lord by the mouth of Jeremiah, until the land had enjoyed its Sabbaths. All the days of its desolation it kept sabbath until the seventy years were complete.

The seventy years described in II Chronicles 36:21 refers to the seventy prophetic years that the nations would serve Babylon (Jeremiah 25:11—12). There were several phases of the Jewish exile to Babylon, the first being in 605 BC. However, II Chronicles 36:19—21 only describes the exile at the destruction of Jerusalem in 586 BC. The reason for only describing the year 586 BC was to identify 586 BC as the first Sabbath year rest of the fifty year cycle. The land didn't start to enjoy its Sabbaths at the beginning of the seventy years in 608 BC at the defeat of Assyria by Babylon, but in the year 586 BC at the destruction of Jerusalem. As Chronicles states, the land kept its Sabbaths all the years of its desolation, until the completion of the seventy years. In other words, the land kept its Sabbaths all the years from the destruction of Jerusalem in 586 BC, until the end of the rule of Babylon at the rule of Persia in 539 BC.

If 586 BC is the first Sabbath rest year of a fifty year Jubilee cycle, it should line up with seven weeks of years after the issuing of the decree to restore and rebuild Jerusalem. If the seven weeks of years marks the first prophetic Jubilee year after 444 BC, it would occur 7(7) = 49 prophetic years after 444 BC. Converting 49 prophetic years into solar years we get: 49 years(360 days/365.2422) = 48.3 solar years. So, the first prophetic Jubilee year after 444 BC occurred in 444 BC – 48 = 396 BC. To confirm that 396 BC is a prophetic Jubilee year, it is necessary to calculate the first prophetic Jubilee year after 586 BC, which is the first Sabbath year rest of a set of seven Sabbath rest years followed by a Jubilee year. So, the first prophetic Jubilee year after 586 BC would be 50 – 7 = 43 prophetic years after 586 BC. Converting 43 prophetic years to solar years we get: 43 years(360 days/365.2422 days) = 42.38 solar years. So, the first prophetic Jubilee year after 586 BC occurred in 586 BC – 42 = 544 BC. If 396 BC is a prophetic Jubilee year the difference between 544 BC and 396 BC should be equally divisible by 50 when converted to prophetic years rounded off to the nearest year. The difference between 544 BC and 396 BC is 148 solar years, which equals 148 solar years(365.2422/360) =150.16 prophetic years. So, this confirms that 396 BC is a prophetic Jubilee year, being the first prophetic Jubilee year after the decree to rebuild Jerusalem. To determine the year of Jesus' birth all we have to do is select the prophetic Jubilee year that fits the time period of His birth. Eight more prophetic Jubilee years from 396 BC fits the time period for Jesus' birth. Converting 8(50) = 400 prophetic years into solar years we get: 400 prophetic years(360/365.2422) = 394.26 solar years. When we subtract 394 solar years from 396 BC we get 2 BC for Jesus birth.

Daniel's prophecy predicted the Messiah's appearance at His death to be sixty-nine weeks of years after the decree, which equals 69(7) = 483 prophetic years. Daniel's prophecy indicates that Jesus was born 7(7) + 8(50) = 449 prophetic years after the issuing of the decree in 444 BC; and indicates that Jesus died 7(69) – 449 = 34 prophetic years after His birth. So, Daniel's prophecy indicates that Jesus died on His prophetic year birthday. There is a very good reason why Jesus died on His birthday according to God's prophetic calendar. We could say that it was Jesus' fate to die on His prophetic year birthday. It seems appropriate that Jesus was not only born in a Jubilee year, but also on the day of release of a Jubilee year (Leviticus 25:9—11). And as Daniel 9:24 indicates, the Messiah's death was for the purpose of making atonement for iniquity. So, it was not only appropriate that Jesus die on the day of atonement according to God's calendar, but it was His fate.

The day of release of a Jubilee year occurs on the same day as the annual day of atonement. Even though Jesus was born in September and died in April, His birth and death were on the same day of God's calendar, because the prophetic year regresses from September to April over a period of thirty-four prophetic years. It was appropriate that Jesus died on Passover according to the Jewish calendar, but it was Jesus' fate that He died on the day of atonement according to God's prophetic year calendar. The goat for Yahweh that was slain on the day of atonement symbolized Jesus (Leviticus 16:7—9). Jesus died to make atonement for whosoever believes in Him. Knowing that Jesus died on His prophetic year birthday, we can calculate the date of His birth. All we have to do is convert the thirty-four prophetic years between Jesus' birth and death into days, and count backwards from His death on April 1, 33 AD. So, thirty-four prophetic years equals 34(360) = 12,240 days; including eight leap year days between 2 BC and 33 AD, and subtracting 12,240 days from April 1, 33 AD we get September 26, 2 BC as the date of Jesus' birth. Until recently it was thought that Jesus' birth had to be before 4 BC, due to the understanding that Herod died in 4 BC, and the knowledge that Herod was a ruler at the time of Jesus' birth. However, recently it has been discovered that Herod probably died in 1 BC.

The year 2 BC for Jesus' birth fits with the information provided by Luke. Luke 3:23 states that Jesus was beginning to be about thirty at the time of His baptism. When a person begins to be about thirty means that he is almost thirty. So, if Jesus was born on September 26, 2 BC, He would begin to be about thirty in the summer of 29 AD. We are told in

Luke 3:1—3 that John the Baptist started his ministry in the fifteen year of the reign of Tiberius Caesar. It has been determined that year would either be 28 or 29 AD, depending on the method that was used to determine the year of Tiberius' reign. So, Jesus beginning His ministry in 29 AD lines up with the information given by Luke.

There is disagreement as to whether there were three or four Passovers during Jesus' ministry. If Jesus started His ministry in 29 AD after the Passover of that year, there would be four Passovers during His ministry, given that Jesus was crucified at the Passover of 33 AD. As indicated in John 6:4, Passover is considered to be "the feast of the Jews." John 5:1 could be translated as "a feast of the Jews," or it could be translated as "the feast of the Jews." So, there is disagreement as to whether this feast is a Passover. However, we don't have to rely on the uncertainty of the translation of John 5:1, to determine the number of Passovers during Jesus' ministry. We can calculate that there were actually four Passovers during Jesus' ministry, the fourth being at His crucifixion. The determination of four Passovers during Jesus' ministry can be calculated from Jesus' parable in Luke.

Luke 13:6—9 (NAS)

6   And He began telling this parable: "A certain man had a fig tree which had been planted in his vineyard; and he came looking for fruit on it, and did not find any.

7   And he said to the vineyard-keeper, 'Behold, for three years I have come looking for fruit on this fig tree without finding any. Cut it down! Why does it even use up the ground?'

8   "And he answered and said to him, 'Let it alone, sir, for this year too, until I dig around it and put in fertilizer;

9   and if it bears fruit next year, fine; but if not, cut it down.'"

It is not hard to see that the man in the parable having the vineyard is Jesus, and that the fig tree is the nation of Israel. Jesus made four trips to Jerusalem falling in consecutive years, and on His fourth trip He spoke to a fig tree causing it to die (Mat. 21:18—19). The death of the fig tree symbolizes the spiritual death of the nation of Israel, given that Israel had rejected Jesus, the giver of life; and thus could bear no fruit. Jesus' first yearly trip to Jerusalem would have been the Passover of 30 AD (John 2:13—23); Jesus second yearly trip would have been the disputed Passover of 31 AD (John 5:1); Jesus third yearly trip to Jerusalem was the Feast of Dedication in 32 AD, Jesus did not come to Jerusalem for the Passover of 32 AD (John 6:4); Jesus fourth yearly trip to Jerusalem was the Passover of 33 AD, the year He caused the fig tree to die and the year of His death.

The following table lays out the calculation for Jesus' birth, counting back thirty-four prophetic years or 12,240 days from Jesus' death. Jesus died on the day of atonement of a prophetic year, and was born thirty-four prophetic years before His death on the prophetic day of atonement, which in the year of His birth was also the day of release of a prophetic Jubilee year. When we calculate a future date a certain number of days after a known date, we don't tally the day of the known date, but tally the day of the future date. Similarly, when we work backwards from a know date, we don't tally the known date, but tally the past date. The known date for Jesus' death is April 1, 33 AD, Gregorian calendar. Subtracting 12,240 days from this date we come to September 26, 2 BC for Jesus birthday.

don't tally April 1 33 AD	0	days in 15 AD	365
days in March 33 AD	31	days in 14 AD	365
days in February 33 AD	28	days in 13 AD	365
days in January 33 AD	31	days in 12 AD (leap yr.)	366
days in 32 AD (leap yr.)	366	days in 11 AD	365
days in 31 AD	365	days in 10 AD	365
days in 30 AD	365	days in 9 AD	365
days in 29 AD	365	days in 8 AD (leap yr.)	366
days in 28 AD (leap yr.)	366	days in 7 AD	365

days in 27 AD	365	days in 6 AD	365
days in 26 AD	365	days in 5 AD	365
days in 25 AD	365	days in 4 AD (leap yr,)	366
days in 24 AD (leap yr.)	366	days in 3 AD	365
days in 23 AD	365	days in 2 AD	365
days in 22 AD	365	days in 1 AD	365
days in 21 AD	365	days in 1 BC	365
days in 20 AD (leap yr.)	366	days in December 2 BC	31
days in 19 AD	365	days in November 2 BC	30
days in 18 AD	365	days in October 2 BC	31
days in 17 AD	365	days in September 2 BC,	
days in 16 AD (leap yr.)	366	to and including Sept. 26	5

total 12,240 days

We can also calculate the date of Jesus' birth starting from the month of Nissan in 444 BC, Jewish calendar. Most have assumed that the decree was issued on Nisan 1, 444 BC, which was supposedly March 5, 444 BC according to the Julian calendar. The date that lines up for Jesus' death is March 7, 444 BC, Gregorian calendar. The following is the calculation for Jesus' birth on September 26, 2 BC, then going on to the date of His death on April 1, 33 AD, Gregorian calendar. Jesus was born 7(7) + (50 prophetic years/Jubilee)8 Jubilees = 449 prophetic years after March 7, 444 BC. Converting 449 prophetic years unto days we get: 449(360 days) = 161,640 days.

days in March 444 BC	24	days in January 2 BC	31
days in April 444 BC	30	days in February 2 BC	28
days in May 444 BC	31	days in March 2 BC	31
days in June 444 BC	30	days in April 2 BC	30
days in July 444 BC	31	days in May 2 BC	31

days in August 444 BC	31	days in June 2 BC	30
days in September 444 BC	30	days in July 2 BC	31
days in October 444 BC	31	days in August 2 BC	31
days in November 444 BC	30	days in September 2 BC	26
days in December 444 BC	31		

total 269 days

total 299 days

The total years from 443 to 3 BC is 441 solar years, including both 443 and 3 BC; 441 solar years (365 days/year) = 160,965 days. There are 107 leap years during this period of time. A leap year occurs in every year divisible by four including 400 BC; but not including 300, 200, or 100 BC, according to the rules of the Gregorian calendar. So, from March 7, 444 BC to September 26, 2 BC is: 299 + 160,965 + 107 + 269 = 161,640 days. We can go on from Jesus birth on September 26, 2 BC to His death on April 1, 33 AD. The time from March 7, 444 BC to April 1, 33 AD is 69(7) = 483 prophetic years; 483 prophetic years(360 days/prophetic year) = 173,880 days. When we subtract the days from March 7, 44 BC to September 26, 2 BC we get: 173,880 − 161,640 = 12,240 days. This is the same number of days that we calculated between Jesus' birth and death by working backwards from April 1, 33 AD.

It takes an effort to understand that the seven weeks of years of Daniel 9:25 is an indicator for the date of Jesus' birth. God wants us to put an effort into understanding His Word. It is good that we can understand how to calculate both the date of Jesus' birth and death from Daniel 9:25. Pointing out how to calculate these dates magnifies God's Word. However, it is even more important that we understand why and when the seventy weeks of years were divided, and why and when they will resume. We should understand that Micah 5:2—3 reveals that Jesus gave up the nation of Israel at His death, which caused the interruption of the seventy weeks of years; and that it reveals that Jesus will once again take up the nation of Israel when she who is in labor brings forth a child, which will cause the resumption of the seventy weeks of years. We should understand that Revelation 12:5 reveals that she who is in labor is the nation of Israel, and the child she brings forth is Jesus. We should understand that this is not Jesus' natural birth at Bethlehem to Mary, but Jesus' super-natural birth on Mount Zion to the nation of Israel.

The seventy weeks of years were divided at Jesus' death, because Jesus death caused the separation of Jesus' Spirit from His soul, which freed His Spirit to make atonement for the believer by indwelling and making righteous his spirit; thus, the age of grace or church age began. The seventy weeks of years will resume at Jesus' super-natural birth, because at that time Jesus will come out of the midst of the church to be reunited with His soul, by means of indwelling the spirit of the Branch who is born having His soul; thus, the age of grace or church age will end. The seventy weeks of years were divided at Jesus' death at Him being rejected by Israel as her Messiah and King, whereas the seventy weeks of years will resume at Jesus' super-natural birth at Jesus being accepted by Israel as her Messiah and King. We should understand that it will be the reunification of Jesus' soul and Spirit at Jesus' super-natural birth, that will bring in everlasting righteousness, Jesus' everlasting righteous reign. We should understand that immediately after Jesus' super-natural birth, Jesus will once again be anointed with the fullness of Yahweh's Spirit; thus, He will reign as Yahweh the Almighty.

Chapter Four
THE RAPTURE

Most pastors avoid any detailed teaching on the rapture, due to the church's confusion on the subject. Some Christians think that the Bible indicates a pre-tribulation rapture, some a mid-tribulation rapture, and still others think that the rapture will occur at the end of the tribulation. Even though Christians are confused as to when the rapture occurs, the Bible is clear and unified as to when it will occur. The Bible contains six sets of scriptures that indicate when the rapture will occur. In the Old Testament, the prophets of Joel, Daniel, and Zechariah described the time of the rapture. In the New Testament, the apostle Paul described the time of the rapture, and Jesus described the time of the rapture in the gospels and in the book of Revelation. These six sets of scriptures are in agreement as to when the rapture will occur, some being more exact than others. It should be an embarrassment to the church that it has not made the necessary effort to search out and understand these scriptures. Given the number of scriptures that describe the time of the rapture, the church should be able to understand them, and be unified as to when the rapture occurs.

Second Thessalonians chapter two contains the first of six key scriptures that reveal the time of the rapture.

II Thessalonians 2:1—8 (D. Israel)

1   Now we request you, brethren, concerning the coming of our Lord Jesus Christ, and our gathering together to Him,

2   that you not be quickly shaken in mind, nor be troubled; not by a spirit, nor by a message, nor by a letter, as by us, as that the day of Christ is at hand.

3   Let no one by any means deceive you, since it will not come unless the falling away comes first, and the man of sin is revealed, the son of destruction;

4   who opposes and exalts himself over all that is called God or object of worship, so that he sits in the temple of God as God.

5   Do you not remember that while I was still with you, I told you these things?

6   And what restrains him now you know, for him to be revealed in his time.

7   For the mystery of lawlessness already works; only He is restraining him now until He comes out of the midst.

8   And then the lawless one will be revealed, whom the Lord will consume with the Spirit of His mouth, and will destroy by the appearance of His coming;

Paul began chapter two of II Thessalonians by correcting an error in understanding. Some Christians had incorrectly understood that the rapture, the day of Christ, was at hand. So, Paul clarified that the day of Christ would not come before the end time falling away, nor before the revealing of the Antichrist. Some Greek manuscripts have the day of the Lord instead of the day of Christ. From the context, it seems clear that the correct rendering is the day of Christ. For Paul used the day of Christ to refer to the rapture (II Cor. 1:14; Phil. 1:6; 1:10; 2:16), whereas he used the day of the Lord to refer to the day of God's wrath.

The day of God's wrath is the period of time that stretches from immediately after the rapture to Jesus' second advent. The only time Paul used the term the day of the Lord is in I Thessalonians 5:2—3, and it can be seen that it describes a time of destruction.

Those who believe that the rapture will occur before the start of the seven year covenant have used II Thessalonians 2:1—8 to try to prove their point. However, these verses indicate that the rapture will occur after the start of the seven year covenant, and probably after the start of the great tribulation. In II Thessalonians 2:1—8, it is revealed that the day of Christ, the rapture, would not occur before the Antichrist is revealed. And we are told that the Antichrist will be revealed after Jesus comes out of the midst, out of the midst of the church. Jesus comes out of the midst of the church at His reunification with His soul at the resumption of the seventy weeks of years. From Daniel 8:11—17 and Daniel 12:11, we know that the seventieth week of years begins (360 days)(7) – 2300 days = 220 days before the stopping of the regular sacrifice and the setting up of the abomination of desolation; these events occurring 1230 days into the seven year covenant. So, the rapture can not occur until after 1230 – 220 = 1010 days after the start of the seven year covenant.

In II Thessalonians 2:1—8, we are told that the Antichrist will be revealed by sitting in God's temple in Jerusalem, displaying himself as God. The great tribulation starts at the setting up of the abomination of desolation (Mat. 24:15—21), which occurs 1230 days into the seven year covenant (Dan. 12:11). The abomination of desolation is an image of the beast (Rev. 13:14—15), the Antichrist becoming the beast by means of being indwelt by the demon from the abyss (Rev. 17:8). Because the regular sacrifice is removed at the same time as the setting up of the abomination of desolation, it appears that the making of the image is pre-planned, so that it can be set up at the capture of the temple. Jerusalem does not fall to the Antichrist until 1260 days into the covenant, but the temple comes under the Antichrist's control at or before 1230 days into the covenant. And most likely the Antichrist will display himself as God on the same day as the setting up of his image in the temple. So, this would place the time of the rapture to be after the start of the great tribulation, which would be after 1230 days into the covenant.

The gospels contain the second of six key scriptures which reveal the time of the rapture. In Matthew chapter twenty-four, Jesus' disciples asked Him, What will be the sign of Your coming, and the end of the age? In Matthew 24:4—31, Jesus then describes a series of end time events that lead to His coming on the clouds at the rapture of the church.

Matthew 24:4—31 (D. Israel)

4   And Jesus answering said to them, "See that not any mislead you.

5   For many will come in My name, saying, I am the Christ, and will mislead in various ways.

6   And you will be hearing of wars and rumors of wars; see that you are not troubled, for it is necessary for all these things to happen, but that is not yet the end.

7   For nation will rise up against nation, and kingdom against kingdom, and there will be famines, and pestilences, and earthquakes in various places.

8   And all these things are the beginning of birth pains.

9   Then they will deliver you up to tribulation, and they will kill you, and you will be hated by all nations for My name's sake.

10 And then many will stumble, and will deliver up one another, and will hate one another.

11 And many false prophets will arise, and will mislead many.

12 And because lawlessness will be multiplied, the love of many will become cold.

13 But the one who endures to the end, this one will be delivered.

14 And this gospel of the kingdom will be preached in all the world for a witness to the nations, and then the end will come.

15 Therefore, when you see the abomination of desolation standing in the holy place, spoken by Daniel the prophet, let the one reading understand,

16 then let the one in Judea flee to the mountains;

17 let the one on the housetop not come down to take a thing from his house;

18 and let the one in the field not turn back to take his garment.

19 But woe to those who are with child, and to those who nurse in those days.

20 And pray that your flight not occur in winter, nor on the Sabbath.

21 For then will be great tribulation, such as has not occurred from the beginning of the world until now, nor by no means will occur.

22 And if those days were not shortened, not any flesh would be saved; but because of the elect those days will be shortened.

23 Then if anyone says to you, Behold, here is the Christ, or there; do not believe him.

24 For false christs and false prophets will arise, and will show great signs and wonders, so as to mislead, if possible, even the elect.

25 Behold, I have told you beforehand.

26 Therefore, if they say to you, Behold, He is in the desert, do not go out; Behold, He is in the private rooms, do not believe it.

27 For just as lightning comes forth from the east, and flashes as far as the west, even so will be the coming of the Son of Man.

28 For wherever the corpse may be, there the vultures will gather.

29 And immediately after that tribulation of those days the sun will be darkened, and the moon will not give its light, and the stars will fall from the sky, and the powers of the heavens will be shaken.

30 And then the sign of the Son of Man will appear in the sky, and then all the tribes of the earth will mourn, and they will see the

Son of Man coming on the clouds of the sky with power and
great glory.

31 And He will send His angels with the great sound of a trumpet,
and they will gather together His elect from the four winds,
from one end of the sky to the other."

Matthew chapter twenty-four describes two different times of tribulation. The first tribulation is described in Matthew 24:9 in which
Christians are delivered up to tribulation and are killed. This is the tribulation of the fifth seal, as described in Revelation 6:9—11. The second
tribulation is described in Matthew 24:15—21, which is described as
the great tribulation. Both of these times of tribulation start at the same
time, at the setting up of the abomination of desolation, 1230 days into
the seven year covenant (Mat. 24:15—21; Daniel 12:11). However, the
tribulation of the fifth seal will end at the sixth seal, whereas the time of
the great tribulation will continue until being cut short by Jesus' second
advent at the end of the seven year covenant. Theologians have interpreted the tribulation of verse twenty-nine to be the great tribulation,
whereas it actually refers to the tribulation of the fifth seal. In Matthew
chapter twenty-four, the great tribulation is referred to as occurring in
"those days" (vs. 19; vs. 22). So, in Matthew 24:29—31, the signs in
the heavens and then the rapture will occur immediately after the tribulation of the fifth seal (vs. 9), and within "those days" of the great
tribulation.

Any doubt as to which tribulation is being referred to in verse
twenty-nine can be resoled by referring to Revelation 6:12—17. Both
Matthew chapter twenty-four and Revelation chapter six describe the
sun and moon being darkened and the stars falling from the sky. In
Revelation, these signs in the heavens occur during the sixth seal, the
event that occurs immediately after the tribulation of the fifth seal. The
sixth seal occurs well before the end of the great tribulation, which ends
at the seventh bowl of wrath at Jesus' second advent. So, from Matthew
chapter twenty-four we know that the rapture will occur immediately

after these signs in the heavens, which will occur immediately after the tribulation of the fifth seal of Christians being delivered up to tribulation. Revelation 6:12—17 confirms that the rapture will occur immediately after the tribulation of the fifth seal, indicating that the rapture will occur during the sixth seal.

Many incorrectly use Zechariah chapter twelve as confirmation that Jesus coming on the clouds in Matthew 24:30 and in Revelation 1:7 is referring to Him coming at His second advent.

Zechariah 12:10 (NAS) "And I will pour out on the house of David and on the inhabitants of Jerusalem, the Spirit of grace and of supplication, so they will look on Me whom they have pierced; and they will mourn for Him, as one mourns for an only son, and they will weep bitterly over Him, like the bitter weeping over a first-born."

Revelation 1:7—8 (D. Israel)

7 Behold, He is coming with the clouds, and every eye will see Him, even those who pierced Him; and all the tribes of the earth will mourn over Him. Yes indeed. Amen.

8 I am the First and the Last, says the Lord God who is, even who was and who is to come, the Almighty.

Zechariah chapter twelve describes the day of Yahweh, which stretches from immediately after the rapture until Jesus' second advent. The siege of Jerusalem mentioned in Zechariah 12:2 does not occur at Jesus' second advent, but is completed just as the day of Yahweh starts at the mid-point of the seven year covenant. It will be at the start of the day of Yahweh that the people of Israel will mourn over Jesus, those left behind at the rapture. The reason that the armies of the nations come to Jerusalem at Jesus' second advent is not to capture Jerusalem. Jerusalem will have already been captured (Rev. 11:2). The armies of the nations will come to Jerusalem at Jesus' second advent in an attempt to do a vain thing; they will come in an attempt to defeat God in battle (Psalm 2:1—6).

Revelation 1:7—8 is spoken from the point in time of the book of Revelation being given to John. At this point in time, Jesus is the First and the Last, the Almighty who was and who is to come; given that He is not anointed with Yahweh's Spirit at this time, and He has not yet come at the rapture. On the other hand, Revelation 11:17 is spoken from the point in time of the seventh trumpet.

> Revelation 11:17 (D. Israel) We give You thanks, Lord God, the Almighty, who is and who was, because You have taken Your great power and have begun to reign.

At this point in time, Jesus is the First and the Last, the Almighty who is and who was; given that He has once again taken His great power at once again being anointed with Yahweh's Spirit, and He has already come on the clouds at the rapture at the sixth seal. If Zechariah 12:10, Matthew 24:30, and Revelation 1:7 were referring to Jesus coming at His second advent, then in Revelation 11:17 Jesus would be the First and the Last, the Almighty who is and who was and who is to come; given that at the seventh trumpet He has not yet come at His second advent.

Revelation 6:12—17 is the third of six key scriptures which reveal the time of the rapture.

Revelation 6:12—17 (NAS)

12 And I looked when He broke the sixth seal, and there was a great earthquake; and the sun became black as sackcloth made of hair, and the whole moon became like blood;

13 and the stars of the sky fell to the earth, as a fig tree casts its unripe figs when shaken by a great wind.

14 And the sky was split apart like a scroll when it is rolled up; and every mountain and island were moved out of their places.

15 And the kings of the earth and the great men and the commanders and the rich and the strong and every slave and free man, hid themselves in the caves and among the rocks of the mountains;

16 and they said to the mountains and to the rocks, "Fall on us and hide us from the presence of Him who sits on the throne, and from the wrath of the Lamb;

17 for the great day of their wrath has come; and who is able to stand?"

Revelation 6:12—17 compliments Matthew 24:4—31. It agrees with Matthew 24:4—31 that the rapture will occur after the tribulation of the fifth seal, and after the signs in the heavens. The sixth seal occurs after the tribulation of the fifth seal, and the rapture will occur immediately after these signs in the heavens, and immediately before the wrath of Yahweh and the Lamb. We know that those who are justified through belief in Jesus will be delivered from the coming wrath of God.

Romans 5:9 (NAS) Much more then, having now been justified by His blood, we shall be saved from the wrath of God through Him.

So, from Revelation 6:12—17, we know that the rapture must occur during the sixth seal. It will occur immediately after the signs in the heavens (Rev. 12:12—13), and immediately before the coming wrath of God (Rev. 12:16—17). Revelation 7:9—14 describes the raptured church in Heaven, that has come out of the great tribulation during the sixth seal.

Revelation 7:9—14 (NAS)

9 After these things I looked, and behold, a great multitude, which no one could count, from every nation and all the tribes and peoples and tongues, standing before the throne and before the Lamb, clothed in white robes, and palm branches were in their hands;

10 and they cry out with a loud voice, saying, "Salvation to our God who sits on the throne, and to the Lamb."

11 And all the angels were standing around the throne and around the elders and the four living creatures; and they fell on their faces before the throne and worshipped God,

12 saying, "Amen, blessing and glory and wisdom and thanksgiving and honor and power and might, be to our God forever and ever. Amen."

13 And one of the elders answered, saying to me, "These who are clothed in the white robes, who are they, and from where have they come?"

14 And I said to him, "My lord, you know." And he said to me, "These are the ones who come out of the great tribulation, and they have washed their robes and made them white in the blood of the Lamb."

Joel chapter two contains the fourth of six key scriptures which reveal the time of the rapture.

Joel 2:30—32 (D. Israel)

30 "And I will give signs in the heavens and on earth, blood, fire, and columns of smoke.

31 The sun will be turned into darkness, and the moon into blood, before the great and awesome day of Yahweh comes."

32 And it will be that all who have called on the name of Yahweh will be delivered, when on Mount Zion and in Jerusalem there will be an escape, as Yahweh has said, even among those left whom Yahweh will call.

Standard translation have poorly translated verse thirty-two.

2050a(1961)	3605	834	7121
And it will be (that) all		who will have called	

preb(8034)   3068   4422
on (the) name (of) Yahweh,   will be delivered,

3588   pre(2022) 6726   2050a(preb)(3389)
when   on Mount Zion   and in Jerusalem

1961   6413   prek(834)   559   3068
will be (an) escape,   as   has said Yahweh,

2050a(preb)(8300)pl   834   3068   7121
even among those left   whom Yahweh will call.

Like Matthew 24:29 and Revelation 6:12—13, Joel 2:30—31 describes the end time darkening of the sun and the moon. Matthew 24:29-31 describes these signs in the heavens as occurring immediately after the tribulation of the fifth seal, and immediately before Jesus' coming on the clouds to rapture the church. Revelation 6:12—17 describes these sings in the heavens as occurring during the sixth seal, and immediately before the coming of the wrath of God. Joel describes these signs in the heavens as occurring before the coming of the great and awesome day of Yahweh. The day of Yahweh or the day of the Lord is the period of time that stretches from immediately after the rapture of the church until Jesus' second advent; and it is the day of the wrath of God.

In Joel 2:32, we are told that all who have called on the name of Yahweh will be delivered, before the coming of the great and awesome day of Yahweh. They will be delivered from the day of Yahweh, the day of the wrath of God, at the rapture of the church. In addition, we are told that those who are left in Jerusalem will be provided an escape. An escape from what? We know from Daniel 12:11 that the tribulation of the fifth seal will begin 1230 days into the seven year covenant. We also know that at 1260 days into the seven year covenant the Antichrist will capture Jerusalem (Rev. 11:2), and that some of the people will flee into the wilderness at this time (Rev. 12:14). So, this indicates that the sixth seal and the rapture will also occur at the mid-point of the seven year covenant, at the same time that Jerusalem is being captured by the Antichrist, and some of the people of Israel escape from him by fleeing into the wilderness.

So, Joel 2:30—32 compliments the first three key scriptures which reveal the time of the rapture. It indicates that the rapture will occur after the signs in the heavens, but before the coming of the day of Yahweh; the day of the wrath of God being the period of time that stretches from immediately after the rapture of the church, until Jesus' second advent. In addition, Joel 2:30—32 indicates that the rapture will occur at the mid-point of the seven year covenant. It will occur at the same time as the capture of Jerusalem by the Antichrist, and the escape of some of the people of Jerusalem who are left behind at the rapture.

Zechariah 14:1—5 is the fifth of six key scriptures which reveal the time of the rapture. Zechariah 14:1—5 is a two-legged triple-step in which leg one refers to events at the beginning of the day of Yahweh, whereas leg two refers to events at the end of the day of Yahweh. Because theologians have failed to recognize that Zechariah 14:1—5 is a two-legged triple step, they have made two major mistakes regarding it. They incorrectly understand that Jerusalem's spoil refers to the things taken from the people of Jerusalem at its capture, whereas it refers to the things that the people of Jerusalem take from the nations that are defeated at Jesus' second advent. In addition, theologians incorrectly understand that Jesus as Yahweh splits the Mount of Olives at the time of His second advent, whereas Jesus splits the mount of Olives at the mid-point of the seven year covenant.

Zechariah 14:1—5 (D. Israel)
leg 1 step 1 Behold, the day of Yahweh comes;
leg 2 step 1 and your spoil will be divided in your midst.
leg 1 step 2 For I will gather all the nations against Jerusalem to battle. And the city will be captured, and the houses will be plundered, and the women ravished. And half

the city will go out into exile, but the rest of the people will not be cut off from the city.

leg 2 step 2 And Yahweh will go out and fight against those nations, according to the day of His fighting in the day of battle.

leg 1 step 3 And on that day His feet will stand on the Mount of Olives which is in front of Jerusalem on the east; and the Mount of Olives will split from its middle, from the east even to the west, a very great gorge. And half of the mountain will move northward, and half of it south. And you will flee by the gorge of My mountains, for the gorge of My mountains will reach to Azel. And you will flee as you fled before the earthquake in the days of Uzziah king of Judah.

leg 2 step 3 And Yahweh will come. My God, all the holy ones will be with you.

Both leg one and leg two are in reverse chronological order. Leg one refers to events at the beginning of the day of Yahweh, and the chronological order of leg one is:

1 Yahweh's feet stand on the Mount of Olives causing it to split, and giving an avenue of escape for those in Jerusalem who are left behind at the rapture of the church.

2 Jerusalem is captured by the Antichrist at the mid-point of the seven year covenant.

3 The day of Yahweh comes. The day of Yahweh, the day of the wrath of God, comes immediately after the rapture of the church.

We know that leg one is in reverse chronological order from Revelation 6:12—13, which reveals that a great earthquake occurs just before the signs in the heavens, which occur immediately before Jesus

coming on the clouds to rapture the church. The great earthquake is
the splitting of the Mount of Olives. So, the splitting of the Mount of
Olives occurs on the day that the day of Yahweh comes (Zech. 14:4),
but actually before it comes. That is, on the day that the day of Yahweh
starts the Mount of Olives will split, then the signs in the heavens will
occur, then Jesus will come on the clouds to rapture the church, and
then the day of Yahweh will start, the day of the wrath of God. The day
of Yahweh will stretch from immediately after the rapture of the church
until Jesus' second advent. The chronological order of leg two is:

1 Yahweh comes with all the holy ones.
2 Yahweh fights against the nations that gather against Him, at
   the battle of Armageddon at Jesus' second advent.
3 The people of Jerusalem who join Jesus who has become Yahweh
   will divide their spoil, the spoil that is taken from the nations
   that gathered against them at Jesus' second advent.

Zechariah confirms that which is indicated in Joel 2:30—32, that
there will be an escape for those in Jerusalem who are left behind at
the rapture. Zechariah reveals that this escape will be caused by Jesus
splitting the Mount of Olives, and at this time Jerusalem will be captured. And we know from Revelation 11:2 that Jerusalem is captured
by the Antichrist at the mid-point of the seven year covenant, and from
Revelation 12:14 that the people of Israel flee from the Antichrist at the
mid-point of the seven year covenant, at 1260 days into the seven year
covenant.

So, Zechariah 14:1—5 with the help of Revelation 6:12—17 reveals that the rapture will occur on the day that the day of Yahweh begins, just before it begins, and the rapture will be sandwiched between
the splitting of the Mount of Olives and the start of the day of Yahweh.
This means that the rapture will occur simultaneously or almost simultaneously to the capture of Jerusalem, since the capture of Jerusalem is
also sandwiched between the splitting of the Mount of Olives and the

start of the day of Yahweh. And since the capture of Jerusalem and the escape of those left behind will occur 1260 days into the seven year covenant, we know that the rapture of the church also occurs 1260 days into the seven year covenant.

Daniel chapter twelve contains the sixth of six key scriptures, which reveal the time of the rapture of the church.

Daniel 12:1—7 (D. Israel)

1 "And at that time Michael will stand up, the great prince who stands for the sons of your people; and there will be a time of distress such as has not occurred since there has been a nation up to that time; and at that time your people will be delivered, everyone found written in the book.

2 And many of those sleeping in the dust of the ground will awake, some to everlasting life, and some to disgrace and everlasting contempt.

3 And those who have insight will shine as the brightness of the firmament; and those who turn many to righteousness as the stars forever and ever.

4 But you, Daniel, shut up these words and seal the book until the time of the end; many will go to and fro, and knowledge will be multiplied."

5 Then I Daniel looked, and behold, two others were standing, one on this side of the bank of the river, and one on the other side of the bank of the river.

6 And one said to the man clothed in linen, who was on the waters of the river, "Until when is the end of these wonders?"

7 And I heard the man clothed in linen, who was on the waters of the river, when he lifted up his right hand and his left hand toward the heavens, and swore by He who lives forever that it will be at a time, times, and a half; and when he has finished shattering the power of the holy people, all these things will be completed.

Daniel 12:1 lists three events in chronological order that occur during the time of the end. Those event are:

1   Michael stands up.
2   There occurs a time of great distress, such as has never occurred up to that time.
3   Everyone found written in the book of life will be delivered at the rapture.

The chronological order is broken in verse two at the waking of those who sleep in the dust. For Paul revealed that the dead are resurrected and raptured immediately before the rapture of those who are alive at the time of Jesus coming on the clouds at the rapture (I Thess. 4:15—17). Michael stands up immediately after Jesus' super-natural birth (Rev. 12:5—7), which occurs 1010 days into the seven year covenant; the time of great distress, the great tribulation, will start 1230 days into the seven year covenant; and the rapture will occur 1260 days into the seven year covenant. Those who believe in a pre-tribulation rapture are forced to disbelieve Daniel 12:1. They have not made the necessary effort to search out and understand and believe the six sets of scriptures that agree as to when the rapture will occur, and which indicate that the rapture will occur within the great tribulation, just before the coming of the wrath of God.

In Daniel 12:6, the question is asked, Until when is the end of these wonders? The end of these wonders is the last event that is listed in chronological order in verse one, that being the delivering of everyone at the rapture whose name is found written in the book of life. In Daniel 12:7, the answer of when the end of these wonders will be is that it, the rapture, will occur after a time, times, and half a time, and as soon as the Antichrist (Daniel 11:40—45) has finished shattering the power of the people of Israel. It is understood that a time, times, and a half a time refers to three and a half years, consisting of 360 days each. The power of the people of Israel will be shattered by the Antichrist when he captures Jerusalem, and the people of Israel flee into the wilderness.

So, Daniel 12:1—7 reveals that the rapture will occur 3.5(360) = 1260 days into the seven year covenant, occurring at the same time as the capture of Jerusalem and the fleeing of the people of Jerusalem who were left behind. Joel 2:30-32, Zechariah 14:1—5, and Daniel 12:1—7 are all in agreement that the rapture will occur at the mid-point of the seven year covenant. However, there is some uncertainty as to which day the rapture actually will occur. It could occur on the last half of the twelve hundred and sixtieth day of the seven year covenant, or it could occur on the first half of the twelve hundred and sixty first day of the seven year covenant. When these two times are rounded off to the nearest day, they both equal 1260 days. Jesus said that only the Father knows the day of His coming to rapture the church (Matthew 24:32—36). However, when the seven year covenant starts, we will know within two days as to when the rapture will occur. The rapture will occur either on the twelve hundred and sixtieth or the twelve hundred and sixty first day of the seven year covenant.

Theologians are confused as to when the rapture will occur. However, Scripture is clear as to when the rapture will occur. The time of the rapture should unify the church, not confuse it. Every theologian should correctly understand when the rapture will occur, given that six different scriptures all indicate that the rapture will occur at the mid-point of the seven year covenant. The agreement as to the time of the rapture as described by Joel, Daniel, Zechariah, Paul, and Jesus should be used to magnify God's word. As it stands, it is an embarrassment that the church still can not understand the scriptures, that describes the time of the rapture. So, when will our theologians step up and get the time of the rapture correct? Perhaps if enough lay people learn, then theologians will be compelled to learn the scriptures that reveal the time of the rapture.

Chapter Five
YAHWEH IS ONE AND THE FIRST AND THE LAST

Both the Jewish and Muslim faiths stumble over the fact that God is one. The Christian faith has some understanding, in that it understands that God being one has to do with Jesus being one with the Father. However, the Christian faith is confused as to how Jesus is one with the Father, and doesn't understand the concepts of the First, last ones, and Last. Deuteronomy has introduced us to the fact that Yahweh is one.

Deuteronomy 6:4 (D. Israel)

8085　3478　3068　　(430)pro　3068　　259
"Hear, Israel, Yahweh (is) our God, Yahweh (is) one."

Because God is one, both the Jewish and Muslim faiths reject Jesus' claim of being God. They also reject Jesus' claim of being the Son of God, since if He was the Son of God that would mean He was God. In fact, the Jewish priests used Jesus' confirmation to them that He was the Son of God, to have Him delivered over to the Roman authority to death (Mat. 26:63—64).

Both the Jewish and Muslim faiths are blind to the fact that God being one implies something more than that there in only one God. Jesus affirmed the fact that God is one.

> Mark 12:29 (D. Israel) And Jesus answered him, "The foremost of all the commandments is, Hear, Israel, the Lord is our God, the Lord is one,…"

Furthermore, Jesus claimed that He was one with God the Father.

> John 10:30 (NAS) "I and the Father are one."

In addition, Jesus gave us insight into how He is one with Yahweh God.

> John 14:6—11 (NAS)
> 6 Jesus said to him, "I am the way, and the truth, and the life, no one comes to the Father, but through Me.
> 7 "If you had known Me, you would have known My Father also; from now on you know Him, and have seen Him."
> 8 Philip said to Him, "Lord, show us the Father, and it is enough for us."
> 9 Jesus said to him, "Have I been so long with you, and yet you have not come to know Me Philip? He who has seen Me has seen the Father; how do you say, 'Show us the Father'?
> 10 "Do you not believe that I am in the Father, and the Father is in Me? The words that I say to you I do not speak on My own initiative, but the Father abiding in Me does His works.
> 11 "Believe Me that I am in the Father, and the Father is in Me; otherwise believe on account of the works themselves."

Jesus became one with Yahweh when the fullness of Yahweh's Spirit, the Holy Spirit, abided in Him. Jesus became one with the Father at His baptism with the fullness of God's Spirit (Mat. 3:16-17). Jesus again claimed His oneness with Yahweh by giving for Himself the name "I am," the name that Yahweh gave for Himself in Exodus 3:14.

John 8:58 (NAS) Jesus said to them, "Truly, truly, I say to you, before Abraham was born, I am."

It was Jesus soul who was the Word, and who was in oneness with Yahweh before Jesus' conception, from eternity. The Word was one with Yahweh due to being indwelt with the fullness of Yahweh's Spirit, before emptying Himself of God's Spirit at becoming flesh, at becoming Jesus' soul (Phil.2:5-7).

Zechariah gives us further insight into the oneness of Yahweh, indicating that Yahweh is not always one. That is, Zechariah indicates that the Word and then Jesus are not always in full oneness with Yahweh. Standard translations have poorly translated Zechariah 14:9.

Zechariah 14:9 (D. Israel) And Yahweh will be King over all the earth. In that day Yahweh will be one, and His name one.

2050a(1961)   3068   4428 5921 3605   def(776)
And will be Yahweh King over   all   the earth.

preb(3117) 1931 1961   3068 259
   In day   that will be Yahweh one

2050a(8034)pro   259
and His name   one.

At Jesus' second advent, Yahweh will be King over all the earth, and will be one with Jesus who will be King over all the earth. In that day Yahweh will be one and His name one. That is, Yahweh will be one with Jesus, due to Jesus being anointed with the fullness of Yahweh's Spirit. In that day, Jesus' name will be one with Yahweh's name, both Jesus and Yahweh being called Yahweh at Jesus' second advent (Zechariah 14:5).

However, Jesus is not always one with Yahweh. Indeed, there are two periods of time when Jesus is not in full oneness with Yahweh. These periods of time occur when Jesus is not indwelt with the fullness of Yahweh's Spirit. The first period of time occurred at Jesus' conception when the Word emptied Himself of Yahweh's Spirit and became flesh, became Jesus' soul. So, Jesus was not one with Yahweh from His conception to His baptism with Yahweh's Spirit at the start of His ministry. The second period of time in which Jesus is not one with Yahweh stretches from Jesus' death, until immediately after Jesus' super-natural birth. Immediately after Jesus' super-natural birth, He is once again anointed with Yahweh's Spirit; thus, He is once again one with Yahweh. Yahweh described this anointing in Psalm chapter two, which occurs on Mount Zion at the resumption of the seventy weeks of years.

> Psalm 2:6 (D. Israel) "Yea, I anointed My King on Zion, My holy mountain."

In Psalm 2:7, Jesus confirms that His anointing by Yahweh's Spirit occurs on the day of His super-natural birth.

> Psalm 2:7 (D. Israel) "I will declare concerning the statute of Yahweh: He said to Me, 'You are My Son, today I have begotten You.'"

Once we understand how Jesus is one with Yahweh, and the fact that Jesus is not always one with Yahweh, we can understand the concepts of the First, last ones, and Last. Yahweh introduced the concepts of the First and last ones in Isaiah 41:4. Unfortunately, theologians have mistranslated this important verse, not understanding these concepts.

> Isaiah 41:4 (D. Israel) "Who wrought and did this, calling forth the generations from the beginning? I, Yahweh, am the First and with the last ones; I am He."

Then in Isaiah 44:5, Yahweh describes the First and the last ones; and in Isaiah 44:6-7, He describes the First and the Last.

Isaiah 44:1—8 (D. Israel)

1 And now listen, Jacob My servant, even Israel: I have chosen him.

2 Thus says Yahweh, your maker and former from the womb, "He will help you. Do not fear, My servant Jacob, even Jeshurun, I have chosen him.

3 For I will pour out water upon the thirsty, and floods upon dry ground; I will pour My Spirit upon your seed, and My blessing upon your offspring.

4 And they will spring up in among grass, as willows by streams of water.

5 This one will say, 'I am for Yahweh'; and this one will call out in the name of Jacob; and this one will write with his hand for Yahweh, and be named by the name of Israel."

6 Thus says Yahweh, the King of Israel and his redeemer, Yahweh of hosts: "I am the First and I am the Last, and apart from Me there is no God.

7 And who is as I am? He will proclaim and declare it; and He will set it in order for Me, from My placing the people of old. And things to come, even which will come, They will declare concerning them.

8 Do not fear nor be afraid; from that time will I not cause you to hear? —"

Like Isaiah 41:4, theologians have mistranslated sections of Isaiah 44:1—8, due to not understanding the concepts of the First, last ones, and Last. In Isaiah 44:1—2, Yahweh describes the Branch, one of the last ones, who will help the nation of Israel in regards to the latter year pouring out of God's Spirit (Genesis 49:25). Both Yahweh (Rev. 21:6) and Jesus (Rev. 22:13) claim to be both the First and the Last. Both

Yahweh and Jesus were the First, Yahweh the Almighty, from the time of Jesus' baptism with Yahweh's Spirit at Jesus' first advent until Jesus' death. During this period of time, they are both Yahweh the Almighty, because they are in oneness due to Jesus being baptized with the fullness of Yahweh's Spirit, the Holy Spirit. At Jesus' death, Jesus ceased from being anointed with the fullness of Yahweh's Spirit; thus, ceased from being as Yahweh. Both Yahweh and Jesus will be the Last, Yahweh the Almighty, immediately after the reunification of Jesus with the Branch; at Jesus once again being anointed with the fullness of Yahweh's Spirit. The last ones are Jesus' Spirit and soul from the time of Jesus' death until being reunited at the resumption of the seventy weeks of years at Jesus' super-natural birth, and then being anointed with the fullness of Yahweh's Spirit.

In Isaiah 44:5, God describes the First by stating that He would say He was for Yahweh. This is a description of Jesus during His first advent, who said He came to do the will of the Father (John 6:38). Then Isaiah 44:5 describes one of the last ones, one who will call out in the name of Jacob. This is a description of the resurrected Jesus who calls out to the church in the name of Jacob (Rev. chapters two and three). Jesus calls out in the name, the authority of Jacob, because the blessing of being set over the nations was originally given to Jacob (Genesis 27:29); and then it was passed on to Judah (Genesis 49:10). Then Isaiah 44:5 describes the other last one, one who will write for Yahweh, being named Israel. This is a description of the Branch who is born with he who was Jesus' soul.

In Isaiah 44:6, Yahweh stated that apart from Him there is no God. However, Jesus is also God by definition, due to being the Son of God. Even though Jesus is not always in full oneness with Yahweh, He is always with Yahweh, never deviating into sin. And during the times that Jesus is the First and the Last, Jesus is as Yahweh the Almighty, due to being anointed with the fullness of Yahweh's Spirit. In Isaiah 44:7, Yahweh asks the question, Who is as I am? Yahweh then describes He who is as He is. He first describes Jesus during His first advent, who declared that He was as Yahweh (John 14:6—11). Yahweh then describes

Jesus after His second advent, who will set the world in order for Him at that time (Isaiah 9:6—7). Then Yahweh reveals that Jesus as both the First and the Last will declare concerning things to come.

In Isaiah 44:8, Yahweh again tells the nation of Israel not to fear, not to fear the Branch whom Yahweh has chosen to help Israel. Yahweh then asks the question, Will I not cause you to hear at that time? The people of Israel will hear the words of the book written by the Branch for Yahweh, which in turn will cause them to hear Yahweh's words as contained in Scripture. The Branch's book is pointed out in Isaiah 29:18.

Isaiah 29:17—19 (D. Israel)

17 Is it not a little while and Lebanon will be turned into a fruitful field, and the fruitful field will be reckoned as a forest?

18 And in that day the deaf will hear the words of a book, and the eyes of the blind will see out of gloom and out of darkness.

19 And the humble in Yahweh will increase joy, and the poor of mankind will rejoice in the Holy One of Israel;

The spiritual wilderness of Israel will be turned into a fruitful field at the latter year pouring out of God's Spirit. The book written by the Branch for Yahweh will cause the people of Israel to hear and understand God's words as contained in Scripture. As a result, the people of Israel will understand God's plan of salvation, and worship God with the truth of His plan of salvation. And as a result of this understanding and worship, God will pour out His Spirit upon those who worship Him with the truth of His plan of salvation.

Isaiah 32:13—14 describes the time of Israel going into captivity to Babylon, and Isaiah 32:15 describes Israel becoming a fruitful field at the latter year pouring out of God's Spirit.

Isaiah 32:13—15 (D. Israel)

13 The thorn and the brier will come up on the ground of My people, even on all the joyful houses of the jubilant city.

14 For the palace will be abandoned, the crowd of the city deserted; hill and watchtower will be for dens for a long duration, a joy of wild donkeys, the pasturage of flocks;

15 until the Spirit is poured out on us from on high, and the wilderness becomes a fruitful field, and the fruitful field is reckoned as a forest.

The Branch's book will magnify the law, the Old Testament (Isaiah 42:21), causing the people of Israel to hear and understand God's words as contained in the law. The Branch will be deaf to God's voice at the time of being sent to Israel; but he is able to be God's messenger, due to seeing into God's plan of salvation. Isaiah 42:19—21 is a two-legged double-step, in which leg one refers to the nation of Israel, and leg two refers to the Branch.

Isaiah 42:19—21 (D. Israel)

leg 1 step 1   Who is blind yet My servant,

leg 2 step1   or deaf as My messenger I send?

leg 1 step 2   Who is blind as he who is at peace, even blind as the servant of Yahweh? You have seen many things, but have not taken heed.

leg 2 step 2   His ears are open, but he can not hear; Yahweh is pleased on account of his righteousness; he magnifies the law and makes it honorable.

In the book of Revelation, both Jesus and Yahweh are described with regard to being the First and the Last. The descriptions of each differ depending on the point in time in which they are being described. In Revelation 1:8, Jesus describes Himself from the point in time of the apostle John, a point in time in which He is not anointed with the fullness of Yahweh's Spirit.

Revelation 1:7—8 (D. Israel)

7   Behold, He is coming with the clouds, and every eye will see Him, even those who pierced Him; and all the tribes of the earth will mourn over Him. Yes indeed. Amen.

8   "I am the First and the Last," says the Lord God who is, "even who was and who is to come, the Almighty."

At the point of time of Jesus speaking Revelation 1:8, He is the Lord God who is. He is also the First who was, being Yahweh the Almighty from His baptism with the fullness of Yahweh's Spirit at His first advent until His death. And He is also the Last who is to come, once again becoming Yahweh the Almighty, at being anointed with the fullness of Yahweh's Spirit immediately after His super-natural birth. Jesus will come with the clouds as Yahweh the Almighty at the rapture of the church (Matthew 24:30).

Matthew 24:30—31 (D. Israel)

30   "And then the sign of the Son of Man will appear in the sky, and then all the tribes of the earth will mourn, and they will see the Son of man coming on the clouds of the sky with power and great glory.

31   And He will send forth His angels with the great sound of a trumpet, and they will gather together His elect from the four winds, from one end of the sky to the other."

Revelation 1:4 describes Yahweh the Almighty from the point on time of the apostle John, a point in time in which Yahweh's Spirit does not anoint Jesus.

Revelation 1:4 (NAS) John to the seven churches that are in Asia: Grace to you and peace, from Him who is and who was and who is to come; and from the seven Spirits who are before His throne;

At this point in time, like all points in time, Yahweh is Yahweh the Almighty who is. And He is the First who was; Yahweh being the First as well as Jesus at Jesus' first advent, due to Jesus being anointed with the fullness of Yahweh's Spirit, from Jesus baptism with Yahweh's Spirit until Jesus' death. And Yahweh is the Last who is to come; Yahweh being the Last as well as Jesus, due to Jesus once again being anointed with the fullness of Yahweh's Spirit, immediately after Jesus' super-natural birth; after which time Yahweh comes on the clouds to rapture the church, given that Jesus is at that time Yahweh, due to being anointed with the fullness of Yahweh's Spirit.

In Revelation 11:17, Jesus is described from the point in time of the seventh trumpet, a point in time that is after He has once again been anointed with the fullness of Yahweh's Spirit; and a point in time that is after He has come on the clouds to rapture the church.

Revelation 11:17—18 (D. Israel)

17 "We give You thanks, Lord God, the Almighty, who is and who was, because You have taken Your great power and have begun to reign.

18 And the nations were enraged, and Your wrath came, and the time has come for the dead to be judged and to give reward to your servants, to the prophets and to the saints and to those who fear Your name, the small and the great; and to destroy those who destroy the earth."

At this point in time, Jesus is no longer the Last who is to come. At this point in time, Jesus is the Last, Yahweh the Almighty who is, having already come at the rapture at the sixth seal. At this point in time, Jesus is still the First who was, being Yahweh Almighty from His baptism with Yahweh's Spirit until His death at His first advent.

Revelation 16:5 describes Yahweh the Almighty, from the point in time of the third bowl of wrath, a point in time that is after He has once again anointed Jesus with the fullness of His Spirit; and a point in time that is after Jesus as Yahweh has come with the clouds at the rapture.

> Revelation 16:5 (NAS) And I heard the angel of the waters saying, "Righteous art Thou, who art and who wast, O Holy One, because Thou didst judge these things";

At this point in time, Yahweh in no longer the Last who is to come. He is the Last, Yahweh the Almighty who is, having already come at the rapture at the sixth seal; having already come at the rapture due to Jesus being anointed with the fullness of His Spirit. And at this point in time, Yahweh is still the First who was. At this point in time, Yahweh is the First as well as Jesus, due to Jesus being baptized with the fullness of His Spirit during Jesus' first advent. Note that the King James has adulterated Revelation 11:17 by adding "and art to come," and has adulterated Revelation 16:5 by adding "and shalt be." This can be determined by recognizing that Jesus and Yahweh have already come with the clouds at the sixth seal at the rapture (Mat. 24:29—31; Rev. 6:12—17).

Revelation 11:17—18 gives us insight into the timing of Jesus taking His great power, taking His great power by means of Him once again becoming Yahweh the Almighty. Revelation 11:17—18 is spoken from a point in time that is just after the sounding of the seventh trumpet, and gives a list of end time events in chronological sequence, which start with Jesus taking His great power.

event 1 Jesus takes His great power and once again becomes Yahweh the Almighty, at the resumption of the seventy weeks of years, about eight months before the mid-point of the seven year covenant.

event 2 Jesus begins to reign immediately after taking His great power, at being caught up to the throne of God (Rev. 12:5).

event 3 The nations are enraged because of Jesus being anointed by Yahweh's Spirit on Mount Zion, the taking of His great power (Psalm 2:1—6). As a result of their rage they will ponder a vain thing. They will take counsel to defeat God in battle at Jesus' second advent.

event 4 God's wrath comes immediately after the rapture of the church, at the mid-point of the seven year covenant at the sixth seal (Rev. 6:12—17).

event 5 The time for the judgment of the dead comes at the sounding of the seventh trumpet. Similar to Matthew 8:22, the dead are not the physically dead, but the spiritually dead. The day of God's wrath is divided into two sections, the hour of testing and the hour of judgment. The hour of testing stretches from immediately after the rapture at the sixth seal to the hour of judgment (Rev. 14:7). The hour of testing ends when it is concluded that none of humankind in need of repentance have repented as a result of the plagues of the trumpets of the hour of testing (Rev. 9:20—21). The hour of judgment stretches from the seventh trumpet to the end of the seven year covenant.

event 6 The time to give reward to God's servants occurs during the hour of judgment, probably at the marriage of the Lamb (Rev. 19:7—9).

event 7 The destroying of those who destroy the earth will occur throughout the hour of judgment, and in particular at Jesus' second advent.

Revelation 11:17 describes the fact that Jesus as the Almighty has taken His great power, and that the nations were enraged. The fact that Jesus takes His great power suggests that before He takes His great power He is not the Almighty. This event is more fully described in Psalm chapter two, which clarifies that the taking of His great power occurs at His anointing by Yahweh's Spirit. And in fact, Psalm two reveals that His anointing with the fullness of Yahweh's Spirit occurs on the day of His birth; not His natural birth at Bethlehem, but His super-natural birth on Mount Zion.

Psalm 2:1—9 (D. Israel)

1   Why do the nations rage, and the peoples ponder a vain thing?

2   The kings of the earth will take their stand; yea, the rulers take counsel against Yahweh and against His anointed.

3   "Let us tear apart their bands, and throw from us their cords."

4   He abiding in the heavens laughs; the Lord will mock at them.

5   Then He will speak to them in His anger; yea, in His wrath He will terrify them.

6   "Yea, I anointed My King on Zion, My holy mountain."

7   "I will declare concerning the statute of Yahweh: He said to Me, 'You are My Son, today I have begotten You.

8   Ask of Me and I will give the nations as Your inheritance, even the ends of the earth as Your possession.

9   You will break them with a rod of iron; you will dash them as a potter's vessel.'"

Jesus' anointing on Mount Zion at the resumption of the seventy weeks of years will not be a secret to the nations. As Isaiah chapter forty describes, at the time of the Branch's glorification the Branch is directed to go up to Mount Zion to Himself, to Jesus who was the Branch's Spirit. The Branch is commanded to declare to the people of Israel, "Behold your God!" At declaring, Behold your God, the Branch will be reunited with Jesus and be Jesus; and then he as Jesus will be anointed with the fullness of Yahweh's Spirit, before being raptured to the throne of God (Rev. 12:5).

Isaiah 40:9 (D. Israel) Go up upon the high mountain to Yourself, bearer of good news to Zion. Lift up your voice with strength, bearer of good news to Jerusalem. Lift up, do not fear, say to the cities of Judah, "Behold your God!"

Part I gives understanding of some of the major themes of God's Word. In order for a theologian to be competent, he must have a good

understanding of these major themes. Unfortunately, we must conclude that at the present time we have no competent theologians. So,
will theologians ever become competent and properly teach the major
themes of God's Word? Will theologians ever teach the truth concerning
creation? Will theologians ever teach the truth of God's plan of salvation? Will theologians ever teach the truth concerning the seventy weeks
of years, and the event that causes the resumption of the weeks of years?
Will theologians ever teach the truth concerning how Yahweh is one,
and how both Jesus and Yahweh are the First and the Last.? Perhaps they
will when a sufficient number of lay persons learn the truth; then the
balance of power will shift, and theologians will be obliged to teach the
truth. May God reward those theologians who sacrifice themselves, by
teaching the truth before the balance of power shifts.

Part II
THE BRANCH IN SCRIPTURE

Part II gives commentaries on most of the obvious scriptures that are regarding the Branch. There are more verses in the Old Testament that refer to the Branch, than refer to Jesus at His first advent. However, many of the scriptures that testify of the Branch have been poorly translated by the various translations, often blotting out the record of his existence. The compilation of scriptures and commentaries of "The Branch In Scripture" are intended to reveal the Branch's existence in Scripture, and in so doing help reveal the truth of God's plan of salvation that is recorded in His Word. May God open His Word to you.

THE HEBREW TRANSLATIONS

Due to the fact that Bible translators don't recognize the identity of the Branch, it was unavoidable that they made serious errors in their translations regarding the Branch. So, the serious student of God's Word should have access to the original Hebrew text. In Hebrew there are no verb tenses of past, present, or future. The translator must translate the Hebrew verb into the most appropriate English tense based on the context. Hebrew vowels were not included in the original inspired writing, but were added much later by the Masoretes. And since some Hebrew words have the same consonantal spelling as others, differing only in their vowels, it is possible for the Masoretes to have given the wrong vowels to some words; thus, changing some words into others. Although this error is rare, there are a few important instances of it, so the translator must be cautious not to take the vowels as necessarily correct.

It is often asked, what is the best translation of the Bible? While it is true that some translations are better, generally speaking, than others, the ardent student can find errors in all the translations. The serious student should have access to the original Hebrew and Greek texts to resolve the best rendering of verses in question. The original Hebrew and Greek texts are the best. One doesn't have to be a Hebrew or Greek scholar to understand the original texts, especially with the excellent reference books available. The following reference books are sufficient to give the lay person quick understanding of the original Hebrew text of the Old Testament.

1   an interlinear Hebrew/English Bible
    When selecting an interlinear Bible make sure that Strong's
    numbers are given above each Hebrew word. This gives quick
    access to the meaning of each Hebrew word by looking it up in
    a Hebrew/English dictionary or lexicon, that also uses Strong's
    numbers.

2   a Hebrew lexicon (a Hebrew/English dictionary)
    Again, make sure it uses Strong's numbers for easy reference.

3   a Hebrew concordance with Strong's numbers
    A Hebrew concordance lists each occurrence of most of the
    Hebrew words. It also categorizes the various verb forms.

The following is a list of the abbreviations used to indicate prefixes and
suffixes attached to Hebrew words.

def	definite article
int	interrogative indicator
pl	plural
preb	preposition indicated by the Hebrew letter beth
prek	preposition indicted by the Hebrew letter kaph
pro	pronoun

GENESIS 27:29

Genesis 27:29 (D. Israel) "May the nations serve you, and the peoples bow to you; become the ruler of your brothers, and may your mother's sons bow to you; may those who curse you be cursed, and may those who bless you be blessed."

Genesis 27:29 describes the blessing of becoming the ruler of the nations that was bestowed upon Jacob. This blessing was passed on to both Judah (Genesis 49:10), and Joseph (Genesis 49:26); given that Jesus was from the tribe of Judah, and the Branch is from the tribe of Joseph.

Genesis 49:10 (NAS) "The scepter shall not depart from Judah, nor the ruler's staff from between his feet, until Shiloh comes, and to him shall be the obedience of the peoples."

Genesis 49:26 (D. Israel) "The blessings of your father have prevailed over the blessings of my progenitors; as far as the summit of the everlasting hill they will be for the head of Joseph, and for the crown of the head of the prince of his brothers."

GENESIS 49:22-26

22 "Joseph will be a fruitful branch, a fruitful branch on account of a spring;

23 his branches will go over the wall, and the masters of arrows will vex him, and shoot at and hate him;

24 but his bow will abide in strength, and the arms of his hands will be agile from the hands of the Mighty One of Jacob; from there will be the Shepherd, the Stone of Israel,

25 from the God of your father, and he will help you; then together with the Almighty, even He will bless you with the blessings of the heavens above, the blessings of the deep lying below, and the blessings of the breasts and the womb.

26 The blessings of your father have prevailed over the blessings of my progenitors; as far as the summit of the everlasting hill they will be for the head of Joseph, and for he crown of the head of the prince of his brothers."

Genesis 49:22—26 is spoken by Jacob just before his death. Jacob describes the blessing from God given through him to Joseph. Standard translations have poorly translated verses 24-25.

2050a(3427)	preb(386)	(7198)pro
but will abide with strength		his bow,

2050a(6339)	(2220)pl	(3027)pro
and will be agile (the) arms (of) his hands		

4480(3027)pl   46   3290
from (the) hands (of) (the) Mighty (One) (of) Jacob;

4480(8033)   7462   68
from there (will be) (the) Shepherd, (the) Stone (of)

3478
Israel,

    4480(410)   (1)pro   2050a(pro)(5826)
from (the) God (of) your father, and he will help you;

    2050a(854)   7706
then together with (the) Almighty

2050a(pro)(1288)(pro)   (1293)pl
even He will bless you (with) (the) blessings (of) (the)

8064   4480(5920)   (1293)pl   8415
heavens from above, (the) blessings (of) (the) deep

7257   8478   (1293)pl
that lies beneath, (and) (the) blessings (of) (the)

(7699)pl   2050a(7356)
breasts   and (the) womb.

In verse twenty-four, the King James and NAS have put brackets around, "from there will be the Shepherd, the Stone of Israel," in an attempt to change the meaning of these verses. The translators could see that these verses state that the Messiah, the Shepherd and Stone of Israel, is from the tribe of Joseph; but chose to fudge God's Word rather than believe it. Our theologians need to change their understanding to line up with the Word of God, not change the Word of God to line up with their understanding. Unfortunately, the poor translation of these verses in not an isolated case. Most of the scriptures that are regarding the Branch contain translation errors of similar gravity. Some of the mistranslated scriptures are done in ignorance, whereas others are intentional fudging of God's Word.

Isaiah 11:1 confirms that the Messiah will not only be a descendant of Jesse, but also a descendant of a branch from an ancestor of Jesse that will bear fruit.

Isaiah 11:1 (D. Israel) And a shoot will come forth from the stem of Jesse, and a branch from his roots will bear fruit.

Jesus was the shoot from the stem of Jesse, being a descendant of Jesse from the tribe of Judah. The Branch is the branch from the roots of Jesse, being a descendant of Jacob, the root of Jesse; and being of the branch of Joseph, Jacob's son. It is the Branch who is born into the tribe of Joseph, born having Jesus' soul. So, how does the Branch bear fruit? We know from Isaiah 53:11 that the Branch will see from the work of his soul, and be satiated with his knowledge. We know from Psalm 91:16 that God will cause him to see into God's salvation. We know from Psalm 116:12—14 that the Branch will vow to God to lift up the cup of salvation and offer it to the people of Israel. We know from Isaiah 55:4—5 that the Branch will be a witness to the people, and will call a nation to God that he does not know, the nation of Israel. We know from Isaiah 42:19—21 that the Branch will magnify the law. In addition, we know from Psalm 45:1 that the Branch's work for God will be writing for Him. So, we can deduce that the Branch will bear fruit by seeing into God's salvation, and then becoming a teacher-evangelist of God's salvation. The end result of the Branch's work for God is that he will bear fruit, in that many world wide will understand God's salvation and will turn to God by believing in Jesus. However, as Genesis 49:22 indicates, the biggest reason that the Branch will bear fruit will be on account of a spring, the spring of God's Spirit. The Branch will be instrumental in the latter year pouring out of God's Spirit, which will result in a rapid growth of the church.

Verse twenty-three states that the masters of arrows will vex the Branch, and shoot at and hate him. The masters of arrows are not archers, masters of arrows being an analogy for teachers. This analogy is formed from the Hebrew word # 3384 which can mean to shoot arrows; or it can mean to teach, to shoot out words to make a point. The Branch's work for God, his teaching and theology, will contradict and threaten the teaching of theologians. So, the reaction by some theologians to the Branch will be to critique, hate, and oppose him. The Branch describes the opposition to his words in Psalm fifty-six.

> Psalm 56:5 (D. Israel) All the day they wrest my words; all their thoughts are against me for evil.

However, it will be with God's help that the Branch will bear fruit, and with God's help that his bow will remain strong and agile to rebuff his critics.

Verse twenty-five states that the Shepherd, the Stone of Israel, will help Israel. Scripture reveals that the Branch will help the nation of Israel understand God's plan of salvation; and he also will be instrumental in the latter year pouring out of God's Spirit on the nation of Israel, and all the nations. In Isaiah forty-four, God reveals that He has chosen the Branch to help Israel, and that the Branch will write for Yahweh (Isaiah 44:5); and indicates that the Branch will be instrumental in God pouring out His Spirit.

> Isaiah 44:1—5 (D. Israel)
> 1 And now listen, Jacob My servant, even Israel: I have chosen him.
> 2 Thus says Yahweh, your maker and former from the womb, "He will help you. Do not fear, My servant Jacob, even Jeshurun, I have chosen him.

3 For I will pour out water upon the thirsty, and floods upon dry ground; I will pour My Spirit upon your seed, and My blessing upon your offspring.

4 And they will spring up in among grass, as willows by streams of water.

5 This one will say, 'I am for Yahweh'; and this one will call out in the name of Jacob; and this one will write with his hand for Yahweh, and be named by the name of Israel."

In verse twenty-six, translators have made "hill" plural, whereas the Hebrew text is singular. This seemingly small fudging of God's word completely changes the meaning of this verse. The everlasting hill refers to Mount Zion, the hill on which the Branch will receive the blessing that was originally given to Jacob. The Branch will receive the blessing of Jacob at his glorification, the blessing of becoming the ruler of the nations. Psalm twenty-four describes the Branch receiving the blessing of Jacob, by standing up in Yahweh's holy place on the everlasting hill, the mountain of Yahweh.

Psalm 24:3—6 (D. Israel)

3 Who will go up upon the mountain of Yahweh, and who will stand up in His holy place?

4 One who will have clean hands and a pure heart, who will not have lifted up his soul to vanity, and will not have sworn to deceit.

5 He will lift up the blessing from Yahweh, and righteousness from the God of his salvation.

6 This one a generation will seek, those who will seek your face, Jacob.

The Branch is addressed as Jacob in Psalm 24:6, because the blessing of becoming ruler of the nations was originally given to Jacob (Genesis 27:29). Yahweh is the ruler of the nations. He who receives the blessing of becoming ruler of the nations must become as Yahweh to receive the blessing. At the Branch's glorification at being reunited with Jesus, he will once again be Jesus, and Jesus will then be anointed with Yahweh's Spirit; thus, Jesus will then once again be as Yahweh, the King of glory. Psalm 24:7—10 sings of the Branch's entrance into the everlasting doors of Heaven at his rapture, after he has become Jesus and after he has become the King of glory.

Psalm 24:7—10 (D. Israel)

7 Lift up your heads, O gates, and be lifted up, O everlasting doors, and the King of glory will come in.

8 Who is the King of glory? Yahweh powerful and mighty, Yahweh mighty in battle.

9 Lift up your heads, O gates, and be lifted up, O everlasting doors, and the King of glory will come in.

10 Who is He, this King of glory? Yahweh of hosts, He is the King of glory.

LEVITICUS 16:9-10

9 "And Aaron shall bring the goat on which fell the lot for Yahweh, and shall make it a sin offering.

10 And the goat on which fell the lot for the complete removal shall be made to stand alive before Yahweh to make atonement upon it, to send it away to the wilderness for the complete removal."

The goat for Yahweh symbolizes Jesus. Jesus shed His blood in order to make atonement for the sins of whosoever believes in Him. We know from Leviticus 16:30 that the purpose of Israel's day of atonement was to cleanse the people of their sins. Jesus' death enabled His Spirit to indwell the believer's spirit, cleansing the believer of his sins. Jesus' Spirit makes righteous the spirit of the believer, making the believer's spirit unable to sin (I John 3:9). It is the believer's soul that is still capable of sin. In verse ten, standard translations have incorrectly translated the goat of the complete removal as the scapegoat.

2050a(def)(8163)	834	5927	(5921)pro	def(1486)
"And the goat	which	fell	on it	the lot

3807a(5799)
for (the) complete removal

5975	2416	3807a(6440)	3068
shall be made to stand	alive	before	Yahweh

3807a(3722)   (5921)pro 3807a(7971)   (853)pro
to make atonement   upon it, to send away   ----- it

3807a(5799)   def(4057)
for (the) complete removal (to) the wilderness."

So, what does the goat for the complete removal represent? We know from Exodus 30:10 that the purpose of the sin offering, the goat for Yahweh, was to make atonement for Israel's sins. We know from Leviticus 17:11 that without the shedding of blood there is no atonement. So, how can the goat for the complete removal make atonement, given that he is released alive? The atonement accomplished by the goat for the complete removal is a result of the shed blood of the goat for Yahweh, for the goat for the complete removal symbolizes Jesus' soul after being separated from Jesus' Spirit at His death. Without the shedding of the blood of the goat for Yahweh, there would be no goat for the complete removal, for without the shedding of Jesus' blood there would be no separation of Jesus' soul and Spirit at Jesus' death.

At Jesus' death, Jesus' soul descended to Sheol (Psalm 116:3; Matthew 12:40), but was taken out of Sheol to Heaven the day after Jesus' resurrection (Psalm 116:7; Matthew 12:40). Jesus' soul stood before Yahweh in Heaven on account of the atonement provided at Jesus' death. Then in the latter years, Jesus' soul will be born into the tribe of Joseph, for the complete removal of the sin of the believer at the resurrection and rapture. At the resumption of the seventy weeks of years, the Branch who will have been born having Jesus' soul will be reunited with his Spirit, and thus once again become Jesus' soul; and then through Jesus God will perfect the believer at the resurrection and rapture. At the resurrection and rapture, not only will the believer's spirit be perfect, but also both his body and soul. It is Jesus' soul born into the tribe of Joseph who testifies to the fact that God will perfect believers through him. After the Branch's glorification, he will once again be Jesus, and through Jesus God will perfect the works of His hands at the resurrection and rapture.

Psalm 138:8 (D. Israel) Your right hand, Yahweh, will perfect through me; Yahweh, Your mercy will be for everlasting. You will not forsake the works of Your hands.

Jesus died once to cleanse us of our sins. However, there are two phases in which His death atones, cleanses us from sin. The first phase occurs when a Christian is born again, and his spirit is indwelt by Jesus; thus, making the Christian's spirit righteous, even unable sin. The second phase will occur through the Branch after he becomes Jesus. It will occur at the resurrection and the rapture, when the believer's body and soul are perfected for eternal life. In like manner, it was because of the shed blood of the goat for Yahweh, that the goat for the complete removal is able to atone for sin by being released alive. The Jewish teachers must have had difficulty with releasing alive the goat for the complete removal. How could it atone for their sins without its blood being shed? Accordingly, the Jewish teachers later interpreted "a land cut off," or "a land of separation," as meaning a precipice from which the goat was to be thrown.

The goat for the complete removal was to stand before Yahweh, and the peoples sins placed on its head. Then the goat for the complete removal was to be sent into the wilderness for the complete removal of sin (Lev. 16:10). However, before the goat for the complete removal was sent into the wilderness, it would bear the peoples sins to a land cut off (Lev. 16:22). These things are symbolic of things that happen to Jesus' soul who becomes the Branch's soul, through whom the consequence of the sin of believers is completely removed. First Jesus' soul stands before Yahweh in Heaven, after being taken out of Sheol after Jesus' resurrection. Then in the latter years Jesus' soul will be restored to life, bearing our sins (Isaiah 53:12).

Isaiah 53:12 (D. Israel) My righteous servant will justify many, but their iniquities he will bear. —

That is, he will be born a sinner. Jesus' soul will be made sick with the sickness of sin at his re-entry into the land of the living as the Branch's soul.

Isaiah 53:10 (D. Israel) But Yahweh will be pleased to crush
Him, to make Him sick. When You make his soul guilty, he
will see his seed, he will prolong his days, and the pleasure of
Yahweh will prosper in his hands.

Jesus, He who knew no sin, was given sin that we might become the
righteousness of God in Him.

II Corinthians 5:21 (D. Israel) For He not knowing sin, for the
sake of us He gave sin, that we might become the righteousness
of God in Him.

That is, Jesus soul was given sin in order that we might obtain the righteousness of God by Jesus' Spirit, by means of His Spirit indwelling us.
Jesus' soul restored to life as the Branch will bear our sins to a land cut
off from the nation of Israel. Then at the time of the Branch's ministry
he will be sent as God's messenger to the wilderness, the wilderness of
Israel. Israel will be considered by God as a wilderness at the time He
sends the Branch to her. The meaning of wilderness, #4057, not only
means an uninhabited place, but is also used figuratively for fruitlessness.

The Branch will be sent to Israel and will be instrumental in changing Israel from being unfruitful to being fruitful (Isaiah 29:17—18),
at the time of the latter year poring out of God's Spirit (Isaiah 32:15).
Thus, the Branch from the roots of Jesse will bear fruit (Isaiah 11:1),
the branch of Joseph will be fruitful (Genesis 49:22—24). At the end of
the Branch's ministry to Israel, he will go up to Mount Zion to be glorified; he will go up to be reunited with Jesus, and to be anointed with
the fullness of Yahweh's Spirit; and then raptured to the throne of God
(Rev. 12:5). Less than a year later at the resurrection and rapture of the
church, he will return to earth as Jesus and as Yahweh to perfect and rapture believers, completely removing the consequence of sin for believers.

PSALM TWO

1 Why do the nations rage, and the peoples ponder a vain thing?
2 The kings of the earth will take their stand; yea, the rulers take counsel against Yahweh and against His anointed.
3 "Let us tear apart their bands, and throw from us their cords."
4 He abiding in the heavens laughs; the Lord will mock at them.
5 Then He will speak to them in His anger; yea, in His wrath He will terrify them.
6 "Yea, I anointed My King on Zion, My holy mountain."
7 "I will declare concerning the statute of Yahweh: He said to Me, 'You are My Son, today I have begotten You.
8 Ask of Me and I will give the nations as Your inheritance, even the ends of the earth as Your possession.
9 You will break them with a rod of iron; You will dash them as a potter's vessel.'"
10 So now, kings, act wisely; be instructed, judges of the earth.
11 Serve Yahweh with fear, and rejoice with trembling.
12 Kiss the Son lest He be angry and you perish from the way, for His anger may shortly be kindled. Blessed are all those seeking refuge in Him.

Standard translation have destroyed verse six by inappropriately translating the Hebrew word with Strong's number 5258 as "set" or as "installed," whereas it should be translated as "anointed."

2050a(589)	5258 (4428)pro 5921 6726	2022
"Yea, I	anointed My King on	Zion, mountain

(6944)pro
My holy."

This error in translation is due to not understanding the identity of the Branch. The writers of the New Testament, as a general rule and with the exception of the book of Revelation, were not given their words by God. On the other hand, it can be seen that the Old Testament, and particularly the books of the prophets and much of the book of Psalms, are words given by God. The New Testament writers didn't claim that their writing was given them by God. For example, in Acts 1:1 Luke reveals that the book of Acts is a letter written by him to Theophilus, and that he had made the first report to Theophilus, the book of Luke. However, some of the contents of the books of the New Testament can be seen to be coming from God, in that they contain knowledge that only God would possess. Of course, much of the gospels are quotations of what Jesus spoke, Jesus being God who spoke the words He was given to speak by God the Father.

God caused the New Testament writers to see into his plan of salvation up to a point. However, the modern church has regressed in understanding even from the incomplete understanding of the apostles John and Paul. These apostles understood that humans have both a soul and a spirit. They understood that Jesus became a life giving Spirit at His death, and that it is Jesus' Spirit indwelling the believer's spirit that justifies, makes righteous the believer. They understood that it is Jesus' Spirit that causes the believer's spirit to be unable to sin. However, John and Paul didn't see as far into God's plan of salvation as God causes the Branch to see. They didn't understand that in order for Jesus' Spirit to indwell the believer it was necessary for Jesus' soul and Spirit to be separated from each other through death. And so, they didn't understand that the resurrected Jesus consists of His glorified spiritual body and

His Spirit, but not His soul. They didn't understand that Jesus' soul will re-enter life during the latter years, through the process of conception and birth into the tribe of Joseph. And they didn't understand that Jesus' soul and Spirit must be reunited in the last days at the resumption of the seventy weeks of years. So, because of their incomplete understanding, the New Testament writers often made mistakes concerning Old Testament references to the Branch, not recognizing his identity.

The New Testament writers used Psalm 2:1-2 as a reference to those who gathered against God at Christ's crucifixion (Acts 4:25—26), and used Psalm 2:7 as a reference to Christ's birth at Bethlehem (Acts 13:33; Hebrews 1:5; 5:5). However, it is easy to see that Psalm two refers to the rebellion of the nations in the last days, not to the events of the crucifixion. In addition, by recognizing the identity of the Branch, it can be seen that verse seven doesn't refer to Jesus' natural birth at Bethlehem, but to His super-natural birth on Mount Zion. On the day of Jesus' super-natural birth, the reunification of His soul and Spirit, the Father will say to the Branch who will have become Jesus, "You are My Son, today I have begotten You." On that day, Jesus will not only be reunited with his soul, but He will once again be anointed with the fullness of the Father's Spirit, the Holy Spirit. On that day, Jesus will change from being the Almighty who was and who is to come, to being the Almighty who is, and who was, and who is to come.

Jesus was the Almighty during the ministry of His first advent, because the fullness of the Holy Spirit was upon Him. However, Jesus is not the Almighty from the time of the Holy Spirit leaving Him just before His death, until His anointing on Mount Zion immediately after His super-natural birth. During the interval of the church age, Jesus is God, but not the Almighty; because the fullness of Yahweh's Spirit, the Holy Spirit, doesn't indwell Him during this interval. Jesus spoke Revelation 1:8 during the interval of the church age, a point in time that He is the Lord God; and He is the First and the Last, the Almighty, who was and who is to come.

Revelation 1:8 (D. Israel) "I am the First and the Last," says the Lord God who is, "even who was and who is to come, the Almighty."

On the other hand, Revelation 11:17—18 is spoken from the point in time of the seventh trumpet, a point of time that is after the end of the church age and the resumption of the seventy weeks of years, and after the resurrection and rapture of the church. The church age ends at the resumption of the seventy weeks of years, when Jesus comes out of the midst of the church to indwell the spirit of the Branch. At this point in time, the church will cease to function as the body of Christ, even though it won't yet be raptured. The rapture will occur less than a year after the resumption of the seventy weeks of years and Jesus' super-natural birth.

Revelation 11:17—18 (D. Israel)

17 "We thank You, Lord God, the Almighty, who is and who was, because You have taken Your great power and begun to reign.

18 And the nations were enraged, and Your wrath came, and the time has come for the dead to be judged and to give reward to Your servants, to the prophets and to the saints and to those fearing Your name, the small and the great; and to destroy those who destroy the earth."

Jesus will once again become the Almighty at the resumption of the seventy weeks of years, at once again being anointed with the fullness of Yahweh's Spirit. After the resumption of the seventy weeks of years, and the after the rapture, Jesus is the Almighty who is and who was. He is not the Almighty who is and who was and who is to come, because He will have already come at the resurrection and rapture of the church.

The list of events of Revelation 11:17—18 are given at the point in time of the seventh trumpet, a point in time that is after Jesus has taken His great power and has begun to reign, and a point in time that is after the rapture; therefore, at a point in time that is after Jesus has changed from being the First and the Last, the Almighty who was and who is to come, to being the First and the Last, Almighty who is and who was. The taking of His great power will be at His anointing with Yahweh's Spirit, immediately after His super-natural birth on Mount Zion, about eight months before the mid-point of the seven year covenant. The rage of the nations will be their reaction to Jesus' anointing on Mount Zion at the resumption of the seventy weeks of years. God's wrath will come at the mid-point of the seven year covenant, immediately after the rapture of the church. The dead are not the physically dead, but the spiritually dead. At the sounding of the seventh trumpet, the end time testing of the nations by God will change to the judgment of God. For at the end of the sixth trumpet, it will be determined that none who have survived the plagues up to that point will have repented of their sins, of those needing repentance (Rev. 9:20—21). The reward of God's servants will probably be at the marriage of the Lamb in Heaven (Rev. 19:7—9). And the last event, the destroying of those who destroy the earth, will come during the hour of judgment and at the battle of Armageddon.

Jesus' super-natural birth will not be done in secret. All the nations will know of the Branch's declaration to the people of Israel, just before His rapture to the throne of God (Rev. 12:5). On that day, the day of the Branch's glorification, God will tell the Branch to go up upon the high mountain to Himself, and to declare to the people of Israel, "Behold your God!"

> Isaiah 40:9 (D. Israel) Go up upon the high mountain to Yourself, bearer of good news to Zion. Lift up your voice with strength, bearer of good news to Jerusalem. Lift up, do not fear, say to the cities of Judah, "Behold your God!"

At making his declaration the Branch will be glorified. He will be re-united with Jesus; thus, he will once again be Jesus. Immediately after the Branch becomes Jesus, Jesus will be anointed with the fullness of

Yahweh's Spirit, and raptured to the throne of God. So, He who was the Word who emptied Himself of God and became flesh, became Jesus' soul, who in the latter years becomes the Branch's soul, will once again become God at once again becoming Jesus' soul.

The reaction by the people of Israel to Jesus' super-natural birth, anointing, and rapture will be to run to Jesus. The Branch will be he who calls a nation he does not know, that nation being Israel, who will run to him at his glorification (Isaiah 55:5). At the time of Jesus' super-natural birth, when she who is in labor brings forth, the remainder of the sons of Israel will return to God (Micah 5:3). However, the reaction of the other nations, in particular the rulers, will be rage at this threat to their rule. It will be the anointing of Jesus on Mount Zion at the resumption of the seventy weeks of years, that will incite the rage of the nations. The rulers of the earth will muse vanity. They will plot together on how to overthrow God! Their plan will be to gather all their armies together and come to Jerusalem and do battle with God, knowing that Jesus' second advent will be at Jerusalem at the end of the seven year covenant.

PSALM SIXTEEN

A SECRET TREASURE OF DAVID.

1   Watch over me, God, for I seek refuge with You.

2   You will say to Yahweh, "You are my Lord. I was well not being together with You,

3   because of the saints who are in the earth; they are even the great ones, all my delight was in them."

4   Their sorrows will be multiplied who to another hasten. I have not poured out their drink offerings of blood, nor have I taken up their names on my lips.

5   Yahweh is the portion of my inheritance and my cup. You will uphold my lot.

6   The lines have fallen to me in pleasant places; yea, a beautiful inheritance is mine.

7   I will bless Yahweh who counsels me; my soul also instructs me in the nights.

8   I set Yahweh continually before me, when at my right hand I will not be shaken.

9   Therefore, my heart was glad, and my glory rejoiced;

10   moreover my flesh abided in hope, for You would not forsake my soul to Sheol, neither would You permit Your Holy One to see corruption.

11   You have made known to me the path of life. Fullness of joy will be in Your presence, pleasures at Your right hand forever.

The following is Matthew Poole's commentary of Psalm sixteen: "It is a great question among expositors, in whose name and person he speaketh this Psalm, whether his own or Christ's. It seems hard to exclude David's person, to whom almost the whole Psalm properly and literally belongs, and to whom parts of it do more conveniently belong than to Christ. And some parts of it peculiarly belong to Christ, of whom it is expounded by the two great apostles, Peter and Paul, Acts 2:25; 13:35. And yet it seems probable by the contexture of the Psalm, and the coherence of the several verses together, that the whole Psalm speaks of one and the same person."

Theologians are confused as to the speaker of Psalm sixteen, and don't recognize that David only penned the words that he received from God. Matthew Poole is correct in recognizing that the psalm speaks of one and the same person. With the exception of verses 2—3 the speaker of Psalm sixteen is the Branch. Although the speaker of the psalm switches from the Branch to the Word in verses 2—3, the coherence of the speaker remains intact, because the Word becomes the Branch's soul.

The Branch is the speaker of verse one, in which he prays for God to watch over him, stating that he seeks refuge with Him. The Branch will seek refuge with Yahweh at the time of his glorification and rapture. The speaker then switches to the Word in verses 2—3, in which the Word addresses the Branch. The Word describes what the Branch will say to Yahweh upon being raptured into His presence. Psalm sixteen is similar to Psalm ninety-one, in that both psalms begin with the Branch speaking, but both psalms switch to the Word speaking. In Psalm sixteen, the speaker of verse one is the Branch, the speaker of verses 2-3 is the Word, and the speaker of verses 4—11 is the Branch; whereas in Psalm ninety-one the speaker of verses 1-2 is the Branch, and the speaker of verses 3—13 is the Word.

We know that it is the Word who is addressing the Branch in Psalm 91:3—13, because of Psalm 91:9. In Psalm 91:9, the Word describes the fact that Yahweh is His refuge; thus, He states that the Branch will make Yahweh his habitation. The Branch will make Yahweh his habitation, given that the Word becomes the Branch's soul. In Psalm 16:2—3, the Word describes what the Branch will say to Yahweh at his rapture into Yahweh's presence, whereas in Psalm 91:2 it is the Branch who states what he will say to Yahweh at his rapture into Yahweh's presence.

Psalm 91:1—9 (D. Israel)

1   He who dwells in the covert of the Most High abides in the shadow of the Almighty.

2   I will say to Yahweh, "My refuge and fortress, my God." I trust in Him.

3   For He will snatch you from the trap of the trapper, from the plague of destructions.

4   With His pinions He will cover you; yea, under His wings you will take refuge; His faithfulness will be a buckler and a shield.

5   You will not fear from the terror of the night, from the arrow that will fly by day,

6   from the plague that will walk in the darkness, from the destruction that will devastate at noon.

7   A thousand may fall at your side, even a myriad because of your right hand.

8   It will not draw near you, only with your eyes will you look and see the retribution of the wicked.

9   Because You, Yahweh, are My refuge, you will have made the Most High your habitation.

In verse four, the Branch states that he has not honoured false gods by pouring out their drink offerings, nor lifted them up in prayer. Similarly in Psalm twenty-four, the Branch is described as not lifting up his soul to vanity. In Psalm twenty-four, it is the Branch who will stand up in Yahweh's holy place, at his glorification and anointing by Yahweh's Spirit on Mount Zion. It will be the Branch who will lift up the blessing that was originally given to Jacob, the blessing of becoming ruler of the nations.

Psalm 24:3—6 (D. Israel)

3   Who will go up upon the mountain of Yahweh, and who will stand up in His holy place?

4   One who will have clean hands and a pure heart, who will not have lifted up his soul to vanity, and will not have sworn to deceit.

5   He will lift up the blessing from Yahweh, and righteousness from the God of his salvation.

6   This one a generation will seek, those who will seek your face, Jacob.

In verse five, the Branch states that Yahweh is the portion of his inheritance and his cup. For at his glorification the Branch will first be reunited with Jesus, and then anointed with the fullness of Yahweh's Spirit. In Psalm twenty-three, Jesus' soul is the speaker, speaking from the point in time of being in Sheol after Jesus' death. Jesus' soul looked ahead to being taken out of Sheol to his rest in Heaven, then to his restoration to life as the soul of the Branch; and then to having his head made fat with the oil of joy, and his cup overflowing at his glorification and anointing by Yahweh's Spirit.

Psalm 23:1—5 (D. Israel)

1   Yahweh is my shepherd, I will not want.

2   He will make me lie down in pastures of grass; He will lead me to waters of rest;

3   He will restore my soul; He will lead me in paths of righteousness for His name's sake.

4   When I walk through the valley of the shadow of death, I will fear no evil, for You will be with me; Your rod and Your staff will comfort me.

5   You will prepare, before I arrive, a table in the presence of my enemy. You will make my head fat with oil, my cup will run over.

Standard translations have poorly translated verses 8-10.

(7737)pro   3068   3807a(5048)pro   8548   3588
  I set   Yahweh   before me   continually, when

4480(3225)pro   1077   pro(4131)
at my right hand   not I will be shaken.

3807a(3651)   8055   (3820)pro 2050a(1523)
Therefore,   was glad my heart, and rejoiced

(3519)pro
my glory;

  637   (1320)pro   7931 3807a(983) 3588 3808
moreover my flesh   abided   in hope,   for   not

   pro(5800)   (5315)pro 3807a(7585) 3808
You would forsake   my soul   to Sheol, neither

   pro(5414)   (2623)pro   3807a(7200)
would You permit Your Holy One   to see

  7845
corruption.

In verse 8a, the Branch reflects back to when he was Jesus' soul, and set Yahweh continually before him by stripping bare his soul to death. At Jesus' death Jesus' Spirit ascended to Heaven to Yahweh, whereas His soul descended to Sheol. So, at Jesus' death His soul set Yahweh continually before him, in that he gave up His Spirit to be continually with Yahweh. Similarly in Psalm seventy-three, the Branch describes being continually with Yahweh.

Psalm 73:21—22 (D. Israel)

21 Indeed, my heart, even my kidneys had been embittered.

22 I had been pierced, but I was brutish and did not understand. I
     was like the animals toward You, but I was continually with You.

Because the Branch is born having Jesus' soul, he was pierced at the
cross as Jesus. However, the Branch doesn't understand his identity until
he enters the sanctuaries of God. At realizing his identity, the Branch
understands that although he had been brutish and like the animals
toward God, not recognizing Yahweh's existence, he was continually at
the right hand of the Father. That is, Jesus, He who was the Branch's
Spirit, now sits continually at the right hand of Yahweh. Because the
Branch comes to understand his identity, he then understands that he
will be reunited with Jesus and raptured to the right hand of Yahweh in
Heaven. Therefore, he states in verse 8b, "when at my right hand I will
not be shaken."

In verse eight, translators have inappropriately translated the con-
junction, #3588, as "because," rather than as "when." The King James
has incorrectly translated verse eight as, "because he is at my right hand I
shall not be moved," whereas the correct translation is, "when at my right
hand I will not be shaken. Translators have incorrectly translated verse
eight to make Yahweh be at the right hand of the speaker, at the same
time that the speaker sets Yahweh continually before him. However, the
speaker of these verses is the Branch, who set He who was his Spirit at
the right hand of Yahweh at Jesus' death. The Branch still waits to be
at the right hand of Yahweh. Yahweh won't be at the right hand of the
Branch until the Branch's glorification and rapture.

In verse nine, the Branch states that his heart was glad and that his
glory rejoiced. His heart has glad after Jesus' death, because he as Jesus'
soul knew that he would eventually be reunited with his Spirit, and sit
at the right hand of Yahweh. Jesus' soul knew that he would be restored
to life as the Branch's soul; and he knew that he would be at the right
hand of Yahweh, after being glorified by being reunited with He who

was his Spirit. In addition, his heart was glad knowing that He who was his Spirit already sat at the right hand of Yahweh.

Most theologians incorrectly understand that his glory refers to his soul, whereas it refers to his Spirit. This can be determined from Psalm 73:24, Psalm 108:1, or Psalm 45:3. In Psalm 73:24, the Branch states that, "after the glory You will take me, the water for me in Heaven." The Branch will be taken by the Holy Spirit; he will be raptured, after being glorified by being reunited with Jesus, He who was his Spirit. In Psalm 108:1, the Branch states that he will praise God, so much the more with his glory. That is, he will praise God so much the more at being reunited with Jesus, He who was his Spirit, his glory. In Psalm 45:3, at the Branch's glorification, Yahweh directs the Branch to gird the sword of his Spirit on his thigh, his glory and majesty.

Psalm 45:3 (D. Israel) Gird your sword on your thigh, Mighty One, your glory and majesty.

It was the Word who became the soul of Jesus, and who then becomes the soul of the Branch. After the Branch's glorification, it will be the Word who once again becomes the soul of Jesus, wielding the sword of His Spirit at Jesus' second advent. At Jesus' second advent the nations of the world will gather to Jerusalem, attempting to defeat God in battle.

Revelation 19:13—15 (NAS)

13 And He is clothed with a robe dipped in blood; and His name is called the Word of God.

14 And the armies which are in heaven, clothed in fine linen, white and clean, were following Him on white horses.

15 And from His mouth comes a sharp sword, so that with it He may smite the nations; and He will rule them with a rod of iron; —

In Psalm 16:9, Jesus' Spirit, He who was the Branch's glory, rejoiced at being at the right hand of Yahweh after Jesus' death. Most translators have inappropriately placed a period after, "moreover my flesh abided in hope." They don't yet understand that flesh consists of both the body and the soul, given that they don't yet understand that the soul and the spirit are separate and distinct parts of humans' makeup. Jesus' flesh abided in hope, because Yahweh would not forsake His soul to Sheol, and because Yahweh would not allow Jesus' body to decay.

In verse eleven, after being given a long life (Psalm 91:16), the Branch looks ahead to his deliverance. He looks ahead to his refuge with God at his rapture, when he will be in Yahweh's presence forever. He looks ahead to when Yahweh will be continually before him, when Yahweh will be at his right hand, and he will never be shaken. Psalm twenty-one also describes the Branch's rapture into the presence of God, never again to be shaken.

Psalm 21:5—7 (D. Israel)
5   His glory will be great in Your deliverance, honor and majesty You will lay upon him.
6   For You will set upon him blessings forever; You will cause him to rejoice in the joy of Your presence
7   For the king will be secure with Yahweh, and in the mercy of the Most High he will not be shaken.

PSALM EIGHTEEN

For the chief musician by the servant of Yahweh, David, who spoke the words of this song in the day Yahweh delivered him from the hand of all his enemies and from the hand of Saul. And he said:

1 I love You, Yahweh, my strength.
2 Yahweh is my rock and my fortress and my deliverer, my God, my rock; I trust in Him, my shield and the horn of my salvation, my high tower to be praised.
3 I will call upon Yahweh, and I will be delivered from my enemy.
4 The cords of death encompassed me, the torrents of the wicked overwhelmed me;
5 the cords of Sheol encircled me; the snares of death confronted me.
6 In my distress I called out to Yahweh, and to my God I cried for help. He heard my voice from His temple, and my cry before Him entered His ears.
7 Then the earth shook and quaked; and the foundations of the mountains trembled and quaked, because it angered Him.
8 Smoke went up in His wrath, and fire from His mouth devoured coals kindled from it.
9 And He bowed the heavens and came down, and darkness was under His feet.
10 And He rode upon a cherub and flew; yea, He flew upon the wings of the wind.

11 He made darkness His covering, His pavilion around Him, darkness of water, dark clouds of the skies.

12 Out of the brightness before Him dark clouds passed through, hail and coals of fire.

13 And Yahweh thundered in the heavens, and the Most High uttered His voice, hail and coals of fire.

14 And he sent out His arrows and scattered them, even lightning shot out and confused them.

15 And the channels of water were seen, and the foundations of the world were bared at Your rebuke, Yahweh, at the blast of the breath of Your nostrils.

16 He sent from on high, He took me; He drew me out of many waters.

17 He delivered me from my strong enemy and from my haters, for they were stronger than I.

18 They confronted me in the day of my calamity, but Yahweh was my support.

19 And He brought me out to a broad place; He delivered me because He delighted in me.

20 Yahweh shall reward me according to my righteousness; He shall recompense me according to the cleanness of my hands.

21 For I have kept the ways of Yahweh, and have not been wicked apart from my God.

22 For all His judgments are before me, and I have not turned His statutes away from me.

23 And I have been upright with Him, and have kept myself from my iniquity.

24 Yea, Yahweh has rewarded Me according to My righteousness, according to the cleanness of My hands before His eyes.

25 With the faithful You have shown Yourself merciful; with the blameless person You have shown Yourself upright.

26 With the pure You have shown Yourself pure, but with the crooked You have shown Yourself perverse.

27 For You have saved a humble people, and haughty eyes You have made low.

28 Indeed, You have made My lamp shine; Yahweh My God has lit My darkness.

29 For by You I can run a troop; and by My God I can leap over a wall; the God who has made perfect His way; the word of Yahweh has been purified.

30 He is a shield to all who have taken refuge in Him.

31 For who is God from other than Yahweh? And who is a rock except our God,

32 the God who has girded Me with strength, and has made My way perfect?

33 He Made My feet like a deer; yea, He has made Me stand upon My high place;

34 teaching My hands to war, so My arm can brake a bronze bow.

35 Yea, You gave to me the shield of Your salvation, so Your right hand upheld Me. Yea, Your condescension has made Me great.

36 You enlarged My steps under Me, and My steps did not slip.

37 I pursued My enemies and overtook them, and I did not turn back until I had made an end of them.

38 I shattered them so that they were not able to rise; they fell under My feet.

39 Yea, You girded Me with strength for battle; You bowed under Me those rising up.

40 Yea, You gave to Me the neck of My enemy; and cut off those hating Me.

41 They cried but there was none to save, to Yahweh, but He did not answer them.

42 Yea, I crushed them like dust upon the face of the wind; I poured them out as mire of the streets.

43 You delivered Me from the strivings of the people; You have made Me head of the nations; people I do not know serve Me.

44 They listen to Me at hearing Me; the sons of the alien feign obedience to Me;

45 the sons of the alien lost heart and came trembling out of their strongholds.

46 Yahweh lives, and blessed be My rock; and be exalted the God of My salvation,

47 the God giving vengeance to Me, speaking the peoples under Me.

48 He delivered Me from My enemy; You also lifted Me up from those rising up against Me; You snatched Me from the man of violence.

49 Therefore, I will give thanks to You among the nations, Yahweh, and to Your name I will sing praises;

50 making great the deliverance of His King, and working mercy to His anointed, to David and His seed forever.

In verses 1—3 David is the speaker, expressing his love for Yahweh, and his trust in Him. The speaker of Psalm eighteen switches from David to the Branch in verse four. In verses 4—19, it is the Branch who is the speaker; he reflects back to when his soul was Jesus' soul, during the three days and nights he spent in Sheol after Jesus' death. This switch in speaker is similar to Isaiah thirty-eight, in which a key word or phrase triggers a prophetic utterance made through the speaker. In Isaiah 38:14, Hezekiah is the speaker, in which he prays that God be his surety. God responds by making a prophetic utterance through Hezekiah in Isaiah 38:15—20. This prophetic utterance is regarding Jesus, our surety for eternal life. In Isaiah 38:15—20, it is the Branch who is the speaker. The Branch reflects back to when he was Jesus' soul, and he states that what he said and did as Jesus was spoken to him and performed by Yahweh. Because of the bitterness of his soul, due to be separated from Jesus, all live who have He who was his Spirit in them; and they have the surety of eternal life.

Isaiah 38:15—20 (D. Israel)

15 What I spoke, even He had said to me, and Himself did. I have gone humbly all my years because of the bitterness of my soul.

16 Lord, because of them, they live; yea, for all have in them my life, my Spirit. Therefore, You have restored me, even causing me to live.

17 Behold, for peace was bitter to me, bitter; but You loved my soul from the pit of destruction. Assuredly You have cast behind Your back all my sins.

18 For Sheol cannot thank You, nor death praise You; those descending to the pit cannot hope for Your living truth.

19 The living is he who can thank You, as I do today, Father. To sons He reveals, God, Your truth.

20 Yahweh is for delivering me; yea, my songs we will sing to stringed instruments all the days of our lives in the house of Yahweh.

In Psalm 18:3, David declares that he will call upon Yahweh, and will be delivered from his enemy. God responds to David by making a prophetic utterance through David in Psalm 18:4—50. This prophetic utterance is regarding Jesus' soul who becomes the Branch's soul. After Jesus' death, Jesus' soul will call on Yahweh to deliver him from Sheol (Psalm 116:4). In addition, the Branch will call upon Yahweh, and will be delivered from his enemy at his glorification. In Psalm ninety-one, Yahweh describes the fact that the Branch will call upon Him, and He will deliver the Branch by setting him on high.

Psalm 91:14—16 (D. Israel)

14 "Because he will set his love on Me, even I will deliver him, I will set him on high. Because he will know My name, he will call on Me, and I will answer him.

15 I will be with him in distress; I will draw him out of it, and I will honor him.

16 I will have satisfied him with length of days, and I will have
caused him to see into My salvation."

In verses 4—19, the Word speaks as the Branch's soul, who reflects
back to the three days and nights after Jesus' death in which he was in
Sheol. In Psalm 116:3—6, the Word speaks as Jesus' soul who later becomes the Branch's soul, and describes his time in Sheol. Jesus' soul is
speaking from the point in time of being in Sheol.

Psalm 116:3—6 (D. Israel)
3   The cords of death encompassed me, the straits of Sheol
    found me;
4   trouble and sorrow I have found; therefore, on the name of
    Yahweh I call: "I pray, Yahweh, deliver my soul."
5   Yahweh is gracious and righteous, and our God is merciful;
    Yahweh watches over the simple.
6   I have been brought low, but because of me He saves.

Verses 7—15 describe Yahweh's response to the cry of Jesus' soul from
Sheol. Verses 16-19 describe God bringing Jesus' soul out of Sheol to
the broad place of Heaven, contrasted to the tight place of distress in
Sheol. In verses 20—23, the Word speaks from the point in time of
when He is the Branch's soul. In verses 24—50, the Word speaks from
the point in time of when He has once again become Jesus' soul, from
a point in time that is after the Branch has been reunited with the resurrected Jesus. This is a point in time that is after Jesus' second advent,
when He is head of the nations.

In verse forty-eight, Jesus describes that Yahweh delivered Him
from His enemy, the man of violence. Jesus is reflecting back to when
His soul was the Branch's soul, and Yahweh snatched Him from the man
of violence, the Antichrist, at the Branch's glorification and rapture. In
Psalm one hundred and forty, it is the Branch who prays that God preserve him from the Antichrist, the man of violence.

Psalm 140:1—4 (D. Israel)

1   Deliver me, Yahweh, from the evil man; preserve me from the man of violence,

2   who devise evil things in the heart; each day they stir up wars.

3   They sharpen their tongues like a snake; a viper's poison is under their lips. Selah.

4   Keep me, Yahweh, from the hands of the wicked; preserve me from the man of violence who plans to trip up my steps.

In verse fifty, Jesus refers to Himself as David. Jesus is describing the fact that He is the Davidic King. Jeremiah twenty-three describes the fact that the Branch will be raised up to become the Davidic King. The Branch will become the Davidic King at his glorification at being reunited with Jesus. At the Branch's glorification, the Branch's soul will once again become Jesus' soul. The Branch will be Jesus, the Davidic King.

Jeremiah 23:5—6 (D. Israel)

5   "Behold, days are coming," says Yahweh, "that I will raise up to David a righteous Branch; and a King will reign and prosper, and do justice and righteousness in the earth.

6   In His days Judah will be saved, and Israel will dwell safely; and this will be His name by which He will be called, Yahweh our righteousness."

Immediately after the Branch's glorification at being reunited with Jesus, he becomes Yahweh's anointed. The Branch will become Jesus at Jesus' super-natural birth, and then Yahweh will anoint Jesus with His Spirit.

In Psalm 2:6, Yahweh describes why the nations are enraged on the day of Jesus' super-natural birth. The nations are enraged, because Yahweh anoints Jesus with His Spirit on Mount Zion, immediately after

Jesus' super-natural birth. In Psalm 2:7—9, Jesus relates what Yahweh declares to Him on the day He is anointed on Mount Zion.

> Psalm 2:6—9 (D. Israel)
> 6   "Yea, I anointed My King on Zion, My holy mountain."
> 7   "I will declare concerning the statute of Yahweh: He said to Me, 'You are My Son, today I have begotten You.
> 8   Ask of me and I will give the nations as Your inheritance, even the ends of the earth as Your possession.
> 9   You will break them with a rod of iron; you will dash them as a potter's vessel.'"

Also in verse fifty, David's seed refers to the Branch's children. In Isaiah 53:10, Yahweh promises that when He makes Jesus' soul guilty, that his soul would see his seed. Jesus' soul is made guilty as the soul of the Branch. The Branch is born of normal parents; thus, the Branch is born a sinner.

> Isaiah 53:10 (D. Israel) But Yahweh will be pleased to crush Him, to make Him sick. When You make his soul guilty, he will see his seed, he will prolong his days, and the pleasure of Yahweh will prosper in his hands.

PSALM TWENTY-ONE
TO THE CHIEF MUSICIAN, A PSALM OF DAVID.

1 Yahweh, in Your strength the king will rejoice, and in Your deliverance how greatly he will rejoice.

2 You will give him the desire of his heart, and You will not withhold the request of his lips. Selah.

3 For You will meet him with the blessings of goodness; You will set a crown of fine gold on his head.

4 Life he has asked from You; You will give him length of days forever and ever.

5 His glory will be great in Your deliverance, honor and majesty You will lay upon him.

6 For You will set upon him blessings forever; You will cause him to rejoice in the joy of Your presence.

7 For the king will be secure with Yahweh, and in the mercy of the Most High he will not be shaken.

8 Your hand will find out all Your enemies. Your right hand will find out those hating You.

9 You will set them as a furnace of fire at the time of your presence. Yahweh will engulf them in His anger, and fire will consume them.

10 You will destroy their fruit from the earth, and their seed from the sons of man.

11 For they have stretched evil against You; they have planned a scheme, they will not prevail.

12 For You will set them back by Your string You will prepare against their faces.

13 Be exalted, Yahweh, in Your strength; we will sing and praise Your might.

Psalm twenty-one is spoken by the Word on behalf of a contemporary of the Branch. Verses 1—7 are spoken from a point in time that is before the Branch's glorification. These verses describe the deliverance that will be given the Branch at the time of his glorification. The Branch will become the King at being reunited with Jesus, and will rejoice in the strength of Yahweh at being anointed with Yahweh's Spirit.

Verses 8—13 are spoken from a point in time that is after the Branch's glorification at being reunited with Jesus; and after being anointed with Yahweh's Spirit, but before Jesus' second advent. Verse eleven describes a scheme planned against the Branch after he has become Jesus. This scheme is described in Psalm two. The nations will be enraged, because of Yahweh anointing Jesus on Mount Zion, immediately after Jesus' super-natural birth. So, they will plot to defeat God in battle at the battle of Armageddon at Jesus' second advent. The nations who gather to do battle with God will be commanded by the Antichrist, who will have become the beast, will have been possessed by the demon from the abyss (Rev. 13:3—8; 17:8; 19:19).

Psalm 2:1—9 (D. Israel)

1 Why do the nations rage, and the peoples ponder a vain thing?

2 The kings of the earth will take their stand; yea, the rulers take counsel against Yahweh and against His anointed.

3 "Let us tear apart their bands, and throw from us their cords."

4 He abiding in the heavens laughs; the Lord will mock at them.

5 Then He will speak to them in His anger; yea, in His wrath He will terrify them.

6 "Yea, I anointed My King on Zion, My holy mountain."

7   "I will declare concerning the statute of Yahweh: He said to Me,
    'You are My Son, today I have begotten You.

8   Ask of Me and I will give the nations as Your inheritance, even
    the ends of the earth as Your possession.

9   You will break them with a rod of iron; You will dash them as a
    potter's vessel.'"

Psalm twenty-one describes Jacob's blessing being given to the
Branch. Jacob's blessing will be realized by the Branch at the time of
his glorification and deliverance, his rapture to the throne of God (Rev.
12:5). At that time, he will receive Jacob's blessing of becoming ruler
of the nations. He will first be reunited with Jesus (Psalm 2:7), and
then be anointed with the fullness of the Father's Spirit, the Holy Spirit
(Psalm 2:6). Note that at the beginning of Psalm twenty-one, before
his glorification, the Branch is identified as "the king." At this point
in time, he is not God. However, in verse thirteen he is addressed as
"Yahweh." At this point in time, he is one with Yahweh, because of
being anointed with Yahweh's Spirit. Jeremiah twenty-three describes
the fact that the Branch will be raised up to David. The Branch will be
raised up to become the Davidic King at His glorification, at which time
he once again will be Jesus. He will be called Yahweh our righteousness,
because of being anointed with Yahweh's Spirit, and because Jesus is our
righteousness.

Jeremiah 23:5—6 (D. Israel)

5   "Behold, days are coming," says Yahweh, "that I will raise up to
    David a righteous Branch; and a King will reign and prosper,
    and will do justice and righteousness in the earth.

6   In His days Judah will be saved, and Israel will dwell safely; and
    this will be His name by which He will be called, Yahweh our
    righteousness."

PSALM TWENTY-TWO

TO THE CHIEF MUSICIAN, CONCERNING THE DEER OF THE DAWN, A PSALM OF DAVID.

1 My God, My God, why have You forsaken Me? Distant from My deliverance are the words of My roaring.

2 My God, I called out in the day time, but You did not answer; and in the night, and there was no silence to Me.

3 But You are holy, dwelling in the praises of Israel.

4 In You our fathers trusted; they trusted and You delivered them.

5 To You they cried out, and they were delivered; they trusted in You and were not ashamed.

6 But I am a worm, and not a man; a reproach of mankind, and despised by the people.

7 All who see Me mock at Me; they open lips, they shake heads, saying,

8 "Roll to Yahweh. Let him deliver Him. Let Him snatch Him away, since He delights in Him."

9 For You were My deliverer from the womb, causing Me to trust on My mother's breasts.

10 I was cast on You from the womb, from the belly of My mother You have been My God.

11 Do not be far from Me, for trouble is near; for there is none to help.

12 Many young bulls have circled Me; mighty bulls of Bashan have surrounded Me.

13 They open their mouths against Me, as a lion ripping and roaring.

14 I am being poured out like water, and all My bones are separated. My heart is like wax; it is melted in the midst of My inward parts.

15 My strength is dried up like a potsherd, and My tongue clings to My jaws.

16 Even to the dust of death You have appointed Me. Indeed, dogs have circled Me. A band of evildoers have enclosed Me at the piercing of My hands and feet.

17 I can count all My bones. They look, they stare at Me.

18 They divide My clothing among them, and make fall a lot for My garment.

19 But You, Yahweh, be not far off; My strength, hurry to My help.

20 Deliver My soul from the sword; My only, from the power of the dog.

21 Save Me from the mouth of the lion, and from the horns of the wild ox.

22 You answered me. I will declare Your name to my brothers; I will praise You in the midst of the assembly.

23 Those fearing Yahweh praise Him. All the seed of Jacob glorify Him, and all the seed of Israel be in awe of Him.

24 For He did not despise nor detest the affliction of the afflicted, nor did He hide His face from Him; but in His crying to Him, He heard.

25 From You is my praise in the great assembly. I will pay my vow before those fearing Him.

26 The meek will eat and be satiated; those seeking Yahweh will praise Him. Your heart will live forever.

27 All the ends of the earth will remember and return to Yahweh; and all the families of the nations will worship before You.

28 For the kingdom is Yahweh's, and He rules among the nations.

29 All the fat ones of the earth will have eaten and will worship.

30 All those going down to the dust will bow before Him, even His soul not being revived. A seed will serve Him, he will declare concerning the Lord to a generation.

31 They will come and declare his righteousness to the people that will be born, because he will have done this.

Most can recognize that verses 1—21 describe Jesus' death on the cross. In these verses, the Word speaks as the soul of Jesus. In verses 22—29, the Word speaks as the soul of the Branch. In verse twenty-two, the Branch states that God has answered him. The Branch is referring to the fact that God answered his prayer, when his soul was Jesus' soul. As Jesus was dying on the cross, He asked Yahweh to deliver His soul from those who were killing Him (Psalm 22:20—21). God answered Jesus' prayer, not by rescuing Him from the cross, but by restoring His only soul to life through the process of conception and birth into the tribe of Joseph. The vow that the Branch refers to in verse twenty-five has been incorrectly translated as vows in standard translations. The Branch describes his vow to God twice in Psalm one hundred and sixteen.

Psalm 116:12—14 (D. Israel)
12 What will I return to Yahweh for all His benefits to me?
13 The cup of salvation I will lift up, and in the name of Yahweh I will call out.
14 My vow to Yahweh I will complete in front, I pray, of all His people.

Psalm 116:17—19 (D. Israel)
17 To You I will offer the sacrifice of praise, and in the name of Yahweh I will call out.
18 My vow to Yahweh I will complete in front, I pray, of all His people;
19 in the courts of the house of Yahweh, in your midst, Jerusalem. Praise Yah!

With the Branch's effort (Isaiah 53:11) and with the help of Yahweh, the Branch will see into God's plan of salvation. Yahweh describes the fact that before He delivers the Branch from his enemies by setting him on high, He will cause the Branch to see into His salvation.

Psalm 91:14—16 (D. Israel)

14 "Because he will set his love on Me, even I will deliver him, I will set him on high. Because he will know My name, he will call on Me, and I will answer him.

15 I will be with him in distress; I will draw him our of it, and I will honor him.

16 I will have satisfied him with length of days, and I will have caused him to see into My salvation."

So, in Psalm one hundred and sixteen, the Branch vows to lift up the cup of salvation, lifting it up and offering it to the people of Israel. The Branch will explain to the people of Israel the truth of God's plan of salvation, calling out in the name of Yahweh. Indeed, the Branch will declare concerning the Lord to a generation (Psalm22:30).

Verses 25-29 provide very important information for this generation in the latter years. These verses indicate the catalyst that is required for the latter year pouring out of God's Spirit. We know from Isaiah 44:1-5 that it will be the Branch who will write with his hand for Yahweh and be named by the name of Israel, and who will help Israel regarding the pouring out of God's Spirit.

Isaiah 44:1—5 (D. Israel)

1 And now listen, Jacob My servant, even Israel: I have chosen him.

2 Thus says Yahweh, your maker and former from the womb, "He will help you. Do not fear, My servant Jacob, even Jeshurun, I have chosen him.

3 For I will pour our water upon the thirsty, and floods upon the dry ground; I will pour out My Spirit upon your seed, and My blessing upon your offspring.

4   And they will spring up in among grass, as willows by streams of water.

5   This one will say, 'I am for Yahweh'; and this one will call out in the name of Jacob; and this one will write with his hand for Yahweh, and be named by the name of Israel."

And we know that the Branch's vow is to lift up and offer the cup of salvation to the people of Israel, given that God has caused him to see into His plan of salvation. The Branch will have found God's words in Scripture regarding God's salvation, and will have eaten them (Jeremiah 15:16—19).

Jeremiah 15:16—19 is not Jeremiah's words, but is a prophetic utterance made through him in which the Branch is the speaker, he who has God's name called upon him. Jeremiah 15:16—19 is God's response to Jeremiah's complaint in Jeremiah 15:15, that he had endured reproach for God's sake. So, in Jeremiah 15:16—19, God responded with a prophetic utterance made through Jeremiah, in which the Branch is the speaker; the Branch being he who endured reproach for God's sake, when his soul was the soul of Jesus.

Jeremiah 15:16—19 (D. Israel)

16 Your words were found and I ate them, and your words were to me joy and gladness of heart; for Your name is called upon me, Yahweh God of hosts.

17 I did not sit in the circle of merrymakers, nor did I exalt. I sat alone because of the presence of Your hand; for You have filled me with indignation.

18 Why has my pain been continual and my wound incurable? It refuses to be healed. Surely You have become to me as deceitful water that is not faithful.

19 Therefore, thus says Yahweh, "If you restore, then I will restore you; you will stand before Me; yea, if you bring out the precious from the worthless, you will be as My mouth."

The Branch will see into God's plan of salvation, by eating God's words regarding God's plan of salvation as revealed in Scripture. The Branch will be afflicted by God in order that he learn God's statutes, and thus learn God's plan of salvation (Psalm 119:67—71). The Branch feels that an injustice has been done to him, because of the presence of God's hand upon him, that has resulted in him sitting alone. God's response to the Branch's complaints is that if he restores, if he brings out the precious from the worthless, then God will restore him. That is, if the Branch restores God's words that he has found, bringing out God's precious words which have been made worthless by poor translation and teaching, then God will restore him from the things caused by the presence of God's hand upon him. The Branch is not to keep to himself God's words that he has found, but he is to present them to the people of Israel and to the world.

Because of finding and eating God's words, the Branch will see and be satiated with his knowledge of God's salvation.

Isaiah 53:11 (D. Israel) From the work of his soul he will see; he will be satiated with his knowledge.

So, the Branch will teach the people of Israel this knowledge of God's salvation; thus, the meek will also eat God's words, and they also will be satiated with this knowledge. The meek are those who have humbled themselves by accepting Jesus as Lord. The heart of the meek, the inner being of the meek, will live forever due to Jesus' live righteous Spirit indwelling them. Those who accept Jesus as Lord will have eternal life. After gaining knowledge of the truth of God's salvation, the next step is to connect with God. As verse twenty-six states, those who seek Yahweh will praise Him; those who praise God with the truth of God's plan of salvation will receive the pouring out of God's Spirit. When God pours out His Spirit this will cause a great world wide revival. Members of all the families of the nations will return to Yahweh through belief in Jesus. The fat ones are those who have been made fat with the oil of joy of God's Spirit. They who are made fat with the oil of joy will have first eaten God's words, concerning the truth of His plan of salvation.

The Word is the speaker of verses 30—31. Standard translations have destroyed verse thirty, due to not recognizing the identity of the Branch.

3807a(6440)pro   3766   3605   (3381)pl
Before Him   will bow   all those going down to

    6083 2050a(5315)pro 3808   2421
(the) dust, even His soul   not   being revived.

     2233   (5647)pro   pro(5608)
(A) seed will serve Him, he will declare

     3807a(136)   3807a(1755)
concerning the Lord   to (a) generation.

Verse thirty reveals that Jesus' soul is not part of the resurrected Jesus. Jesus' soul was not revived at the time of Jesus' resurrection, but is restored to life into the tribe of Joseph as the soul of the Branch (Genesis 49:22—24; Isaiah 11:1); Jesus' soul will be reunited with the resurrected Jesus at the resumption of the seventy weeks of years. The resurrected Jesus consists of His glorified spiritual body and His Spirit, but not His soul. Jesus' soul restored to life as the soul of the Branch will declare concerning the Lord to a generation, before being glorified by being reunited with Jesus. Verse thirty-one describes the people of the generation who are taught by the Branch. They will declare the Branch's righteousness to the up coming generation, because of the Branch declaring to them concerning the Lord and His salvation.

PSALM TWENTY-THREE
A PSALM OF DAVID.

1 Yahweh is my shepherd, I will not want.
2 He will make me lie down in pastures of grass; He will lead me to waters of rest;
3 He will restore my soul; He will lead me in paths of righteousness for His name's sake.
4 When I walk through the valley of the shadow of death, I will fear no evil, for You will be with me; Your rod and Your staff will comfort me.
5 You will prepare, before I arrive, a table in the presence of my enemy. You will make my head fat with oil, my cup will run over.
6 Surely goodness and mercy will follow me all the days of my life, and I will dwell in the house of Yahweh for length of days.

Psalm twenty-three is probably the best known passage of Scripture of the Old Testament. It has been a source of encouragement, strength, and hope to believers down through the ages. While it is good that we as believers have received blessing from this psalm, we have failed to recognize the greater significance of it. Psalm twenty-three is a list of events, arranged in chronological order, that are spoken by and which occur to Jesus' soul who becomes the Branch's soul. In Psalm twenty-three, David is not the speaker, but has penned the words that he received from God. Psalm twenty-three is spoken from the point in time of the three days and nights that Jesus' soul spent in Sheol after His death. Jesus was the unblemished lamb who was slain to take away the sins of the world, and Yahweh is His shepherd. Yahweh making Jesus' soul lie down in pastures of grass, and leading him to waters of rest, refers to the taking of Jesus' soul from Sheol to his rest in Heaven. In Psalm 116:3—6, the Branch testifies to his soul being in Sheol, during the three days and nights after Jesus' death; then in Psalm 116:7, the resurrected Jesus tells he who was His soul to return to his rest, his rest in Heaven.

Psalm 116:3—7 (D. Israel)

3   The cords of death encompassed me, the straits of Sheol have found me;

4   trouble and sorrow I have found; therefore, on the name of Yahweh I call: "I pray, Yahweh, deliver my soul."

5   Yahweh is gracious and righteous, and our God is merciful; Yahweh watches over the simple.

6   I have been brought low, but because of me He saves.

7   Return, My soul, to your rest, for Yahweh will deal bountifully on account of you.

In verse three, Yahweh restoring Jesus' soul refers to the restoration of Jesus' soul to the land of the living as the soul of the Branch. In Isaiah 38:15—16, Hezekiah is not the speaker, but a prophetic utterance is made through him in which the Branch is the speaker. The Branch states that what he spoke as the soul of Jesus was said to him by Yahweh, and what he did as the soul of Jesus was performed by Yahweh. He states that because of the bitterness of his soul, from being separated from He who was his Spirit, all live who have in them his life, his Spirit. The Branch goes on to reveal that Yahweh has restored him, restored him from death by causing him to live.

Isaiah 38:15—16 (D. Israel)

15 What I spoke, even He had said to me, and Himself did. I have gone humbly all my years because of the bitterness of my soul.

16 Lord, because of them, they live; yea, for all have in them my
life, my Spirit. Therefore, You have restored me, even causing
me to live.

In verse three, Jesus' soul looks ahead to Yahweh leading him in
paths of righteousness, when he becomes the Branch's soul. Yahweh will
lead the Branch in paths of righteousness during his Christian walk.
Isaiah 53:12 reveals that Yahweh will divide righteousness to Jesus soul,
who becomes the Branch's soul. The Branch will be among the many
who are justified by Jesus' Spirit.

Isaiah 53:12 (D. Israel) My righteous servant will justify many,
but their iniquities he will bear. Therefore I will divide to him
with the many, —————

Yahweh will lead the Branch in paths of righteousness for His name's
sake, since He has promised to do so in Isaiah 53:12.

The Branch walking through the valley of the shadow of death describes the threat of death, at the time of him going to Mount Zion to
be glorified. At this time, the Antichrist, the man of violence, will set a
net for him (Psalm 140:4—5). Psalm 18:48 is spoken by the Branch,
from a point in time that is after his glorification at being reunited with
Jesus. The Branch who has become Jesus reflects back to when Yahweh
delivers him from the man of violence, at being snatched away at his
rapture, immediately after his glorification and anointing (Rev. 12:5).

Psalm 18:48 (D. Israel) He delivered Me from My enemy; You
also lifted Me up from those rising against Me; You snatched
Me from the man of violence.

Yahweh will prepare a table for the Branch before he arrives in
Heaven at his rapture. His enemy is Satan. Satan and his angels are not
cast out of access to Heaven, until after the Branch's glorification and

rapture (Rev. 12:5—9). "Before me" in verse five refers to time, not to position; this is similar to how it is interpreted in Genesis 30:30.

pro(6186)	3807a(6440)pro	7979
You will prepare	before me	(a) table

5048	(6887)pro	(1878)pro
in the presence (of) my enemy.	You will make fat

preb(8081)	(7218)pro	(3563)pro	7310
with oil	my head,	my cup	will run over.

Yahweh making the Branch's head fat with oil refers to Yahweh anointing him with the oil of joy of His Spirit, immediately after his re-unification with Jesus on Mount Zion (Psalm 2:6—7). At that time, his cup will run over with the fullness of Yahweh's Spirit, because Yahweh is the portion of his cup.

Psalm 16:5 (D. Israel) Yahweh is the portion of my inheritance and my cup. You will uphold my lot.

Verse six expresses the Branch's faith that goodness and mercy will follow him all his life, and at his rapture he will dwell in the house of Yahweh.

So, to sum up Psalm twenty-three, it lists the following events in chronological order, regarding Jesus' soul who becomes the Branch's soul.

1   the leading of Jesus' soul out of Sheol to his rest in Heaven
2   the restoration of Jesus' soul to the land of the living as the Branch's soul
3   the leading of the Branch in paths of righteousness, his Christian walk
4   the threat of death to the Branch at going to Mount Zion for his glorification, but the security he feels in God
5   the preparation in Heaven by God for the Branch's arrival upon his rapture

6   the Branch who will have become Jesus being anointed on Mount Zion with the fullness of Yahweh's Spirit, the portion of the Branch's cup

7   the Branch as Jesus dwelling in the house of Yahweh for length of days, after the Branch's glorification and rapture

PSALM TWENTY-FOUR
A PSALM OF DAVID.

1   The earth is Yahweh's and the fullness of it, the world and those dwelling in it.

2   For He founded it upon the seas, and established it upon the rivers.

3   Who will go up upon the mountain of Yahweh, and who will stand up in His holy place?

4   One who will have clean hands and a pure heart, who will not have lifted up his soul to vanity, and will not have sworn to deceit.

5   He will lift up the blessing from Yahweh, and righteousness from the God of his salvation.

6   This one a generation will seek, those who will seek your face, Jacob.

7   Lift up your heads, O gates, and be lifted up, O everlasting doors, and the King of glory will come in.

8   Who is the King of glory? Yahweh powerful and mighty, Yahweh mighty in battle.

9   Lift up your heads, O gates, and be lifted up, O everlasting doors, and the King of glory will come in.

10 Who is He, this King of glory? Yahweh of hosts, He is the king of glory. Selah.

Again in Psalm twenty-four, David is the penman, but the Word is the speaker. This psalm describes the Branch receiving the blessing of Jacob, and him becoming as Yahweh. However, this psalm has been poorly translated to make it appear that he who stands up in Yahweh's place refers to all who have repented and believe in God. It is asked, Who will ascend the mountain of Yahweh and stand up in His holy place? The Antichrist will attempt to stand up in Yahweh's holy place, by sitting in the yet to be built temple in Jerusalem.

II Thessalonians 2:3—4 (D. Israel)

3   Let no one by any means deceive you, since it will not come un-less the falling away comes first, and the man of sin is revealed, the son of destruction;

4   who opposes and exalts himself over all that is called God or object of worship, so that he sits in the temple of God as God.

But we know that any attempt to usurp the place of God will fail, in-cluding the Antichrist's attempt.

The one who will go up upon the mountain of Yahweh and stand up in His holy place must have the help and blessing of God to do so. To stand up in Yahweh's holy place will require that person to become as Yahweh. This will be achieved by the Branch by first being reunited with Jesus, and then he as Jesus being anointed with the fullness of Yahweh's Spirit. Psalm two describes this anointing on Mount Zion on the day of Jesus' super-natural birth, Jesus' super-natural birth being the reunification of the Branch with the resurrected Jesus. Psalm 2:6 is spoken by Yahweh, and Psalm 2:7 is spoken by Jesus on that same day, right after being reunited with the Branch and anointed with Yahweh's Spirit.

Psalm 2:6—7 (D. Israel)

6   "Yea, I anointed My King on Zion, my holy mountain."

7   "I will declare concerning the statute of Yahweh: He said to Me,
     'You are My Son, today I have begotten You.'"

Verse five describes the fact that the Branch will lift up the blessing
of standing up in Yahweh's holy place. This is the blessing of Jacob, the
blessing that was originally given to Jacob (Genesis 29:27). This blessing
gives entitlement to become ruler of the nations. Yahweh is the ruler of
the nations, so that person must become as Yahweh. This blessing was
passed on to both Judah and Joseph, because Jesus is from the tribe of
Judah, and the Branch is from the tribe of Joseph.

> Genesis 27:29 (D. Israel) "May the nations serve you, and the
> peoples bow to you; become the ruler of your brethren, and
> may your mother's sons bow to you; may those who curse you
> be cursed, and may those who bless you be blessed."

> Genesis 49:10 (NAS) "The scepter shall not depart from Judah,
> nor the ruler's staff from between his feet, until Shiloh comes,
> and to him shall be the obedience of the peoples."

> Genesis 49:26 (D. Israel) "The blessings of your father have pre-
> vailed over the blessings of my progenitors; as far as the summit
> of the everlasting hill they will be for the head of Joseph, and for
> the crown of the head of the prince of his brothers."

In Genesis 49:26 Jacob passes all his blessings on to Joseph. These blessings included the nations serving him and being under his rule, and as
indicated will be received at the summit of the everlasting hill of the
mountain of Yahweh.

Verse six has been incorrectly translated by standard translations. In
verse six, the Branch is addressed as Jacob, because the blessing to rule
the nations was originally given to Jacob.

2088   1755   1875   (1245)pl
This one (a) generation will seek, those who will seek

(6440)pro 3290   5542
your face, Jacob. Selah.

It will be the generation that hears the Branch' teaching regarding the
Lord, who will seek his face.

>   Psalm 22:30—31 (D. Israel)
>   30 —— A seed will serve Him, he will declare concerning the Lord
>   to a generation.
>   31 They will come and declare his righteousness to the people that
>   will be born, because he will have done this.

Verses 7—10 describe the rapture of the Branch who has become
the King of glory, who has become as Yahweh. Most incorrectly understand that the everlasting doors are the gates to the city of Jerusalem,
whereas they are the doors to Heaven. The everlasting doors are the
gates of righteousness, described by the Branch in Psalm 118:19-21. In
these verses, the Branch is seeking to be delivered from his enemies, by
being raptured through the gates of righteousness into Heaven.

>   Psalm 118:19—21 (D. Israel)
>   19 Open to me the gates of righteousness; I will enter into them, I
>   will thank Yah.
>   20 This is the gate to Yahweh, the righteous will enter into it.
>   21 I thank You, for You will answer me and be My deliverance.

In Psalm seventy-three, the Branch describes his glorification at being
reunited with Jesus; and then describes his rapture, being taken by the
water of God's Spirit, the portion of his cup (Psalm 16:5). He then will
be the King of glory and be beside Yahweh, the King of glory. He then
will be Jesus who will be one with Yahweh, due to being anointed with

the fullness of Yahweh's Spirit. Yahweh is one. Psalm 73:24—26 has been destroyed by standard translations.

Psalm 73:24—26 (D. Israel)

24 And after the glory You will take me, the water for me in Heaven.

25 And beside You, I will desire nothing on earth.

26 My flesh and my heart will be complete; God will be the rock of my heart and my portion forever.

PSALM FORTY

TO THE CHIEF MUSICIAN, A PSALM OF DAVID.

1 Waiting, I waited on Yahweh, and He stretched out toward me and heard my cry.

2 And He brought me up from the pit of roaring, from the clay, the mire; and He has lifted my feet upon a rock, establishing my steps.

3 And He has put in my mouth a new song of praise to our God; many will see and fear, and trust in Yahweh.

4 Blessed is the man who has set Yahweh as his trust, and does not turn to the proud, or those falling away to a lie.

5 Many things You have done, Yahweh my God. There is none to set in order for You, Your wondrous works and Your purposes towards us. I will declare and I will speak. They are more than have been declared.

6 Sacrifice and offering You did not delight in; my ears You opened for me; burnt offering and sin offering, You did not ask for.

7 At that time I said, "Behold I have come; in the roll of the book it is written concerning Me."

8 I delighted to do Your will, my God; yea, Your law was in my midst.

9 I have borne tidings of righteousness in the great assembly; behold, my lips have not restrained, Yahweh, You know.

10 I have not concealed Your righteousness in the midst of my heart. I have spoken of Your faithfulness and Your deliverance; I have not hidden Your mercy and Your truth from the great assembly.

11 May You, Yahweh, not withhold Your tender mercies from me; may Your mercy and Your faithfulness always watch over me.

12 For regarding me, evils have surrounded me until they are innumerable. My iniquities have overtaken me, and I am not able to see; they are more than the hairs of my head, and my heart forsakes me.

13 Be pleased, Yahweh, to snatch me away; Yahweh, hasten to my help.

14 They will be ashamed and humiliated together that seek my soul to sweep it away; they will be turned back and put to shame those delighting in my evil.

15 They will be desolate as a consequence of their shame, those saying to me, "Aha! aha!"

16 May all those who seek You rejoice and be glad in You; may those loving Your salvation always say, "Yahweh be magnified!"

17 But I am afflicted and needy; may the Lord take thought for me. You are my help and deliverer; my God, do not delay.

In Psalm forty, it is the Word who is the speaker, speaking as the Branch. David only penned the words he received from God. It is Jesus' soul who becomes the Branch's soul, who God brings up out of Sheol, the pit of roaring. This occurs the day after Jesus' resurrection (Matthew 12:40). It is Jesus' soul that God restores to life in the latter years, into the tribe of Joseph as the Branch. God will establish the Branch's steps upon the rock of Jesus, by dividing justification to him at him becoming a born again believer (Isaiah 53:12). God will put in the Branch's mouth a new song of praise, that will cause those who see this to fear and trust in Yahweh. In Psalm twenty-two, the Branch also describes his praise coming from Yahweh, and then states that he will pay his vow before those fearing Yahweh.

> Psalm 22:25 (D. Israel) From You is my praise in the great assembly. I will pay my vow before those fearing Him.

The Branch's vow to God is to lift up the cup of salvation, and offer it to the people of Israel (Psalm 116:12—14). So, the praise he offers up, given to him from God, is likely to be regarding God's plan of salvation. This will cause those seeing this act of God to fear and trust in Yahweh.

It will be the Branch who will set in order God's purposes towards us, in particular God's plan of salvation; God causing him to see into His salvation (Psalm 91:16), before he is set on high at his rapture.

> Psalm 91:14—16 (D. Israel)
> 14 "Because he will set his love on Me, even I will deliver him, I will set him on high. Because he will know My name, he will call on Me, and I will answer him
> 15 I will be with him in distress; I will draw him out of it, and I will honor him.
> 16 I will have satisfied him with length of days, and I will have caused him to see into My salvation."

In verses 6—8, the speaker is actually the Branch, not Jesus as traditionally believed from Hebrews 10:5—7. God did not cause the New Testament writers to see fully into His plan of salvation, as a consequence they did not properly understand the Old Testament scriptures that went beyond their understanding. In verses 6—8, the Branch is reflecting back to when he was Jesus, to when his soul was the soul of Jesus.

In verses 9—10, the Branch describes the fact he has borne tidings of righteousness in the great assembly, speaking of God's faithfulness and deliverance. This refers to the fulfilling of his vow to lift up the cup of salvation, and calling out in the name of Yahweh, as recorded in Psalm one hundred and sixteen.

> Psalm 116:12—14 (D. Israel)
> 12 What will I return to Yahweh for all His benefits to me?
> 13 The cup of salvation I will lift up, and in the name of Yahweh I will call out.
> 14 My vow to Yahweh I will complete in front, I pray, of all His people.

In Psalm one hundred and sixteen, salvation in Hebrew is plural, referring to the fact that the Branch will speak of the salvation resulting from God's faithfulness to make righteous whosoever believes in Jesus, as well as the salvation resulting from God's deliverance of the church at the resurrection and rapture. God has promised to give the Branch a long life (Psalm 91:16), but his iniquities will overtake him at him becoming old. Verse twelve describes his deterioration in old age, the result of being born a sinner. As indicated in verse fourteen, the Branch will have enemies that will attempt to destroy him; but he knows that God will keep him, snatching him away at his rapture (Rev. 12:5). In verse seventeen, the Branch concludes the psalm by asking that God not delay, not to delay to snatch him away. He is asking God that when he gets to Mount Zion to be glorified that God not delay, that God snatch him away by setting him on high (Psalm 91:14), that God open to him the everlasting doors of Heaven (Psalm 24:7).

PSALM FORTY-FIVE

TO THE CHIEF MUSICIAN, ON THE LILIES, FOR THE SONS OF KORAH; GIVING UNDERSTANDING, A SONG OF LOVE.

1 My heart is astir with a good matter. I speak my work for the King, my tongue being the stylus of a rapid writer.

2 You were the fairest of the sons of man; grace flowed through your lips. Therefore God will bless you forever.

3 Gird your sword on your thigh, Mighty One, your glory and your majesty.

4 And in Your majesty prosper; ride on the matter of truth and meekness and righteousness, and Your right hand will teach You fearful things.

5 Your arrows are sharp —— peoples fall under You —— in the heart of the enemies of the King.

6 Your throne, O God, is forever and ever; a scepter of uprightness is the septer of Your kingdom.

7 You have loved righteousness and hated wickedness; therefore God, Your God, has anointed You with the oil of gladness more than Your companions.

8 Myrrh and aloes and cassis are on all Your garments, out of palaces of ivory by which they have made You glad.

9 Daughters of kings are among Your precious ones; the queen strands at Your right hand in gold of Ophir.

10 Listen, daughter, and consider and incline your ear, and forget your people and your father's house;

11 even the king desires your beauty; indeed, he will be your Lord and you will bow down to him.

12 And the daughter of Tyre will come with a gift; the rich of the people will entreat your face.

13 All glorious within will be the daughter of the King; her clothing will be out of braided gold.

14 She will be led to the King in embroidered work, after her the virgins, her companions, will be brought to you.

15 They will be led with gladness and rejoicing; they will enter into the King's palace.

16 Your sons will be in place of your fathers; you will set them as rulers in all the earth.

17 I will cause your name to be remembered in all generations. Therefore the peoples will praise you forever and ever.

Confusion abounds among commentators regarding Psalm forty-five. Most agree that the first half refers to Jesus, but differ on whom the last half refers. Some see the queen, the King's daughter, the virgins, and the sons as all symbolic of the church, whereas others believe that they are the household of one of the kings of Israel. This confusion can be cleared up when we recognize the identity of the Branch. The Branch is the speaker of verse one. Part of the Branch's ministry will be to write for Yahweh the King. Since his ministry will be in the latter years, he will write with a modern day computer. The Hebrew word having Strong's number 4106 can mean rapid, ready, or skilled. All three meanings are apt descriptions of the modern day computer.

The Branch further describes his work for Yahweh the King, in Psalm one hundred and nineteen.

Psalm 119:126—128 (D. Israel)

126 It is time to work for Yahweh; they have made void Your law.

127 Therefore I love Your commandments more than gold, even more than fine gold.

128 Therefore, all the precepts, the totality, I will make straight;
every way of falsehood I hate.

God's precepts are like fine gold. Like fine gold, God's precepts are
precious; and like fine gold that is covered over with worthless material before being discovered, God's precepts are covered over with poor
translations. The Branch will hate every false way that God's precepts
have been mistranslated. Much of God's plan of salvation as set forth in
God's law, the Old Testament, has been made void by poor translation
and teaching. So, part of the Branch's work will be to set straight God's
precepts that deal with God's plan of salvation. God's plan of salvation
could be considered as the foundation of His Word. The Branch will set
straight the totality of God's Word, by setting straight the foundation
of His Word, by setting straight His plan of salvation. The Branch will
point out and explain the scriptures, that reveal the truth of how Jesus'
death achieves our salvation.

Verses 2—17 are spoken by Yahweh the Father. In Psalm 45:2,
Yahweh addresses the Branch, stating that he was the fairest of the sons
of man, and that grace flowed through his lips. Yahweh is referring to
the fact that the Branch was Jesus' soul during Jesus' first advent. It is
because the Branch is born having Jesus' soul, that God states that He
will bless the Branch forever. God will give the Branch the blessing of
Jacob, the blessing of becoming the ruler of the nations (Genesis 27:29).
God is able to give the Branch this blessing, because the Branch will become Jesus at being glorified at being reunited with Jesus, and become
as Yahweh at being anointed with the fullness of Yahweh's Spirit.

Psalm twenty-four describes the Branch being addressed as Jacob,
because he will stand up in Yahweh's holy place on Mount Zion, at
his reunification with Jesus and anointing by Yahweh's Spirit (Psalm
2:6). He will receive the blessing that was not only passed on to Judah
(Genesis 49:10), but also on to Joseph (Genesis 49:26); he will lift up

the blessing at standing up in Yahweh's holy place on Mount Zion. After being anointed with the fullness of Yahweh's Spirit, he will be raptured to the throne of God as the King of glory, through the everlasting doors of Heaven.

Psalm 24:3—10 (D .Israel)

3　Who will go up upon the mountain of Yahweh, and stand up in His holy place?

4　One who will have clean hands and a pure heart, who will not have lifted up his soul to vanity, and will not have sworn to deceit.

5　He will lift up the blessing from Yahweh, and righteousness from the God of his salvation.

6　This one a generation will seek, those who will seek your face, Jacob.

7　Lift up your heads, O gates, and be lifted up, O everlasting doors, and the King of glory will come in.

8　Who is the King of glory? Yahweh powerful and mighty, Yahweh mighty in battle.

9　Lift up your heads, O gates, and be lifted up, O everlasting doors, and the King of glory will come in.

10　Who is He, this King of glory? Yahweh of hosts, He is the King of glory.

In Psalm 45:3, God commands the Branch to gird on his sword, stating that it is the Branch' glory and majesty. God is commanding the Branch's reunification with Jesus, for Jesus' Spirit will become the Branch's sword (II Thess. 2:8). Jesus' Spirit is the Branch's glory and majesty. Standard translations have mistranslated this verse.

2296 (2719)pro　　5921　　　3409　　1368
Gird your sword　　　on (your) thigh, Mighty (One),

(1935)pro　　2050a(1926)pro
your glory and your majesty.

Revelation chapter nineteen describes Jesus' second advent, in which Jesus is called the Word of God, having the sword of His Spirit coming from His mouth to slay the armies gathered against Him. Jesus is called the Word of God in these verses, in order to show that Jesus' soul and Spirit have been reunited. The Branch's soul was the Word of God, from the days of eternity (John 1:1;1:14), whereas Jesus' Spirit was conceived at Jesus' conception (John 1:18), and is the sword that comes from Jesus' mouth. So, at Jesus' second advent we see the reunified Jesus, consisting of both His soul and Spirit. The soul of the Branch once again becomes Jesus' soul at the Branch's glorification, and we see Jesus' soul wielding the sword of His Spirit at His second advent.

Revelation 19:13—15 (NAS)
13 And He is clothed with a robe dipped in blood; and His name is called the Word of God.
14 And the armies which are in heaven, clothed in fine linen, white and clean, were following Him on white horses.
15 And from His mouth comes a sharp sword, so that with it He may smite the nations; and He will rule them with a rod of iron; and He treads the wine press of the fierce wrath of God, the Almighty.

Psalm 45:1—3 describes he who writes for Yahweh, and who is commanded to gird on his sword. Isaiah 44:5 describes he who writes for Yahweh, and who is named Israel. In addition, Isaiah 49:2—3 describes he whose mouth is made a sharp sword, and is called Israel. These verses are all describing the Branch. The girding on of the Branch's sword, and the making of the Branch's mouth a sharp sword are describing the same event. They are describing the Branch's reunification with Jesus' Spirit, He who was the Branch's Spirit at Jesus' first advent. In Isaiah 49:1—3, Jesus is addressing the peoples of the world, from a point in time that is after the reunification of His soul and Spirit, and after His second advent. In these verses, Jesus reflects back to when His soul was the

Branch's soul. Jesus describes the Branch's glorification at God making his mouth like a sharp sword, and his rapture at being hidden in the shadow of God's hand.

Isaiah 49:1—3 (D. Israel)

1 Listen to Me, coasts, and pay attention, peoples from afar. Since the womb Yahweh called Me; since the belly of My mother bringing to remembrance My name.

2 And He made My mouth like a sharp sword, in the shadow of His hand He hid Me. Even He made Me a choice arrow, in His quiver He hid Me.

3 And He said to Me, "You are My servant, Israel, You in whom I will be glorified."

Psalm 45:4—9 describe the Branch after becoming Jesus. Verses 4—5 describe Jesus' second advent. At Jesus' second advent, Jesus' soul will learn fearful things. He will learn the fearful power of His reacquired Spirit, as He defeats God's enemies in battle. Verse nine describes the queen standing at Jesus' right hand, during Jesus' millennial reign. The queen is she who is addressed in Psalm 45:10—17. She is the woman who marries the Branch before his glorification, and who bears his children.

In Psalm 45:10—17, Yahweh addresses the Branch's bride to be. In verses 10—11, Yahweh reveals to her the identity of the Branch, the fact that the Branch will become her Lord. The Branch will become her Lord and she will bow to him after his glorification. Yahweh instructs her to forget her people and her father's house. In other words, Yahweh indicates that she should accept to be the Branch's bride. Psalm 45:12—17 refers to the time of Jesus' millennial reign. The daughter of the King and her sons are the children of her marriage to the Branch. These children are the fulfillment of the promise given by Yahweh to Jesus' soul who becomes the Branch's soul.

In Isaiah, Yahweh promised that when Jesus' soul is made guilty, when he is made a sinner as the soul of the Branch, that he would see his seed. Yahweh crushed Jesus at His death, and makes his soul sick as the soul of the Branch. The Branch will have the sickness of being a sinner. However, Yahweh gives Jesus' soul the promise that when his soul is made guilty as the soul of the Branch, the Branch would see his offspring.

> Isaiah 53:10 (D. Israel) But Yahweh will be pleased to crush Him, to make Him sick. When You make his soul guilty, he will see his seed, he will prolong his days and the pleasure of Yahweh will prosper in his hands.

The fact that the Branch's daughter has companions that are virgins, indicates that she also will be of a young age at the start of the millennium. That being the case, she will be born late in the life of the Branch, given that the Branch will live a long life before his glorification and rapture (Isaiah 53:10; Psalm 91:16), combined with the fact that the kick off of the millennium will occur just over four years after the Branch's glorification and rapture.

The Branch who will have become Jesus at his glorification will be King throughout eternity. She who becomes the Branch's bride will be a queen throughout eternity, starting in the millennium. She will stand at Jesus' right hand. It is unclear how much authority she will have. What is clear is that she will have some authority and influence. She will have the authority to place her sons as rulers. She will have the ear of Jesus; thus, she will be entreated by even the rich. Yahweh Himself will give her recognition before the people of the world. Yahweh will cause her name to be remembered in all generations. Therefore, the peoples will praise her, give thanks to her, throughout eternity. She will be blessed.

PSALM FIFTY-SIX

TO THE CHIEF MUSICIAN; ON ACCOUNT OF THE SILENT DOVE OF THOSE FAR OFF; A SECRET TREASURE OF DAVID, IN THE PHILISTINES SEIZING HIM IN GATH.

1 Favor me, God, because man pants after me; all the day fighting, he oppresses me.
2 My enemies pant after me all the day, for many are proudly fighting against me.
3 The day I am afraid, I will trust in You.
4 In God I will praise His word; in God I trust, I will not fear. What can flesh do to me?
5 All the day they wrest my words; all their thoughts are against me for evil.
6 They stir up strife; they hide; they watch over my footprints, since they wait for my soul.
7 Is escape for them on account of iniquity? In anger cast down the peoples, O God.
8 My wandering You have counted; O put my tears in Your bottle, are they not in Your book?
9 That being so, my enemies will be turned back in the day I call; this I know for God is for me.
10 In God I will praise the word; in Yahweh I will praise the word.
11 In God I trust, I will not fear; what can man do to me? Upon me, O God, are Your vows.

12 I will render thanksgiving to You, for you will snatch my soul from death.

13 Were not my feet delivered from stumbling to walk before Yahweh in the light of the living?

Upon examination of Psalm fifty-six, it can be determined that once again it is the Branch who is the speaker. David only penned the words given him by God. The silent dove of those far off is Jesus' life giving Spirit. It is on account of Jesus, that the Branch walks before God in the light of the living. Jesus is of those far off, in that He didn't become available to indwell believers until after the cross, whereas this psalm was penned in about 1000 BC. The Branch will have enemies who desire to kill him. Similar to verse two, Psalm 57:3 describes one who pants after the Branch. In Psalm 57:1—3, the Branch seeks refuge from his enemy, the Antichrist, who pants after him.

Psalm 57:1—3 (D. Israel)

1 Be merciful to me, God, be merciful for my soul seeks refuge with You; even in the shadow of Your wings I seek refuge until the destruction passes.

2 I cry to God Most High, to God who will perfect through me.

3 He will send from Heaven and deliver me, reproaching the one who pants after me. Selah. God will send His mercy and His truth.

The Branch identifies himself in Psalm 57:2, by stating that God will perfect through him; given that he will become Jesus at being reunited with Him, and it will be through Jesus that God will perfect the church at the resurrection and rapture. The Branch seeks refuge from the one who pants after him, by being delivered by God at his rapture into His presence, into the shadow of His wings.

Psalm 56:5 reveals that those who fight against the Branch will wrest his words. However, not all who fight against the Branch will desire to kill him. Many will wrest his words only to discredit him. The Branch will write for Yahweh (Psalm 45:1; Isaiah 29:18; Isaiah 44:5), and also speak for Yahweh (Psalm 22:30; Psalm 116:13—14). Those who oppose the Branch will wrest, will twist his words in an attempt to discredit him. The Branch will be a descendant of Joseph, and in the blessing bestowed on Joseph it is foretold, that the masters of arrows will shoot at and hate him.

Genesis 49:22—24 (D. Israel)

22 "Joseph will be a fruitful branch, a fruitful branch on account of a spring;

23 his branches will go over the wall, and the masters of arrows will vex him, and shoot at and hate him;

24 but his bow will abide with strength, and the arms of his hands will be agile from the hands of the Mighty One of Jacob; from there will be the Shepherd, the Stone of Israel, ——"

Joseph's branches or daughters don't refer to the fruit of the womb, but are symbolic of the Branch's work for God. His work for God will cause him to bear fruit, the one who will be a descendant of an ancestor of Jesse (Isaiah 11:1); the one who will become the Shepherd, the Stone of Israel. The Branch's work for God will go over the wall, will be sent out into the world to accomplish God's purposes. However, many will oppose the Branch's work for God, wresting his words. The masters of arrows are not referring to archers, but to teachers. The Hebrew word #3384, that means to shoot arrows can also mean to teach. The masters of arrows are those who teach God's word. Many of the teacher's of God's word will shoot at the Branch's words with their teaching.

In verses four and ten, the Branch states that in God he praises His Word. The Branch is in God, because he has been born again by being indwelt by Jesus' life giving Spirit, and by Yahweh's Holy Spirit. Jesus is in him and the Father is in Jesus.

John 17:23 (NAS) "I in them, and Thou in Me, that they may be perfected in unity, that the world may know that Thou didst send Me, and didst love them, even as Thou didst love Me."

Conversely, since he who is born again is spirit, he not only has God indwelling him, but he is also in God.

John 17:21 (NAS) "—— that they all be one; even as Thou, Father, art in Me, and I in Thee, that they also may be in Us; that the world may believe that Thou didst send Me."

In verse eleven, the Branch states that God's vows are upon him. Yahweh God has vowed several things regarding the Branch. Yahweh has vowed that the Branch will see his seed, his biological children.

Isaiah 53:10 (D. Israel) But Yahweh will be pleased to crush Him, to make Him sick. When You make his soul guilty, he will see his seed, he will prolong his days, and the pleasure of Yahweh will prosper in his hands.

Yahweh's vow is upon the Branch that He will cause the Branch to have a long life before his glorification, and cause him to see into His salvation.

Psalm 91:14—16 (D. Israel)
14 "Because he will set his love on Me, even I will deliver him, I will set him on high. Because he will know My name, he will call on Me, and I will answer him.
15 I will be with him in distress; I will draw him out of it, and I will honor him.
16 I will have satisfied him with length of days, and I will have caused him to see into My salvation."

Unlike Jesus, the Father has vowed to keep the Branch (Psalm 91:11), and deliver him (Psalm 91:14), not allowing him to see death (Psalm 118:17—18).

> Psalm 118:17—18 (D. Israel)
> 17 I will not die; indeed, I will live and I will recount the works of Yah.
> 18 Chastening, Yah has chastened me, but He will not give me to death.

Yahweh has vowed that at the time of acceptance He will answer the Branch, and that He will keep the Branch, and give him for a covenant to the people to restore the earth. The time of acceptance is the time that the people of Israel officially accept Jesus as their Messiah and King. It is the time that the Branch is accepted as he who comes in the name of Yahweh (Psalm 118:26—27); and it is the day of his glorification by being reunited with Jesus, and then anointed with the fullness of Yahweh's Spirit. It is also the day of his deliverance at being rescued from his enemies, at his rapture into the shadow of God's wings in Heaven.

In Isaiah 49:7, the Branch is the despised soul, in that he was despised and hated when his soul was Jesus' soul.

> Isaiah 49:7—9 (D. Israel)
> 7 Thus says Yahweh, the redeemer of Israel, his Holy One, to the despised soul, to the one hated by the nation, to the servant of rulers, "Kings will see and stand up, leaders also will bow down on account of Yahweh who is faithful, the Holy One of Israel, even He has chosen you."
> 8 Thus says Yahweh, "At the time of acceptance I will answer you, and in the day of deliverance I will help you. For I will keep you and give you for a covenant to the people to restore the earth, to cause to inherit the desolated heritages;

9 to say to the prisoners, 'Go forth'; to those in darkness, 'Show yourselves.' —"

Indeed, Yahweh's vow is upon the Branch that he will lift up the blessing of Jacob, to stand up in Yahweh's holy place on the mountain of Yahweh.

Psalm 24:3—6 (D. Israel)

3 Who will go up upon the mountain of Yahweh, and who will stand up in His holy place?

4 One who will have clean hands and a pure heart, who will not have lifted up his soul to vanity, and will not have sworn to deceit.

5 He will lift up the blessing from Yahweh, and righteousness from the God of his salvation.

6 This one a generation will seek, those who will seek your face, Jacob.

In verse twelve, the Branch expresses his belief that Yahweh will snatch him from death. Most translations have put verse twelve in the past tense, but it is his future rapture to which he is referring. Verse thirteen tells why he expects Yahweh to snatch him from death. He asks the question, Were not my feet delivered from stumbling to walk before God in the light of the living? This is a reference to Psalm one hundred and sixteen, in which the Branch testifies to being is Sheol during the three days and nights after Jesus' death, and testifies to being told to return to his rest in Heaven, and testifies to having his soul delivered from death to walk before Yahweh in the lands of the living. The Branch knows that God will deliver him from death, because he knows that God's vows are upon him to do so. He believes that he is born with he who was Jesus' soul, who was brought up from Sheol to Heaven the day after Jesus' resurrection, to walk before Yahweh in the lands of the living in the latter years.

Psalm 116:3—9 (D. Israel)

3 The cords of death encompassed me, the straits of Sheol have found me;

4 trouble and sorrow I have found; therefore, on the name of Yahweh I call: "I pray, Yahweh, deliver my soul."

5 Yahweh is gracious and righteous, and our God is merciful; Yahweh watches over the simple.

6 I have been brought low, but because of me He saves.

7 Return, My soul, to your rest, for Yahweh will deal bountifully on account of you.

8 Because You delivered my soul from death, my eyes from tears, and my feet from stumbling,

9 I walk before Yahweh in the lands of the living.

It was the day after Jesus' resurrection that the resurrected Jesus told His soul to return to his rest in Heaven (Matthew 12:40). It will be in the latter years that his soul will be restored to the land of the living as a seed (Psalm 22:30). The Branch will be restored to life in time to be instrumental in the latter year pouring out of God's Spirit (Isaiah 44:1—5; Joel 2:15—29).

PSALM FIFTY-SEVEN

TO THE CHIEF MUSICIAN, DO NOT DESTROY; A SECRET TREASURE OF DAVID WHEN HE FLED IN THE CAVE FROM SAUL.

1 Be merciful to me, God, be merciful to me for my soul seeks refuge with You; even in the shadow of Your wings I will seek refuge until the destruction passes.

2 I cry to God Most High, to God who will perfect through me.

3 He will send from Heaven and deliver me, reproaching the one who pants after me. Selah. God will send His mercy and truth.

4 My soul was in the midst of lions; I lay among those on fire; the sons of men, their teeth were spears and arrows; their tongues were sharp swords.

5 Be exalted above the heavens, God, and may Your glory be over all the earth.

6 They have prepared a net for my steps; my soul is bowed down; they have dug a pit for me, they will fall into the midst of it. Selah.

7 My heart is fixed, God, my heart is fixed; I will sing and give praise.

8 Awaken, my glory; awaken, harp and lyre; I will awaken the dawn.

9 I will praise You among the peoples, Lord; I will sing to You among the nations.

10 For Your mercy will be great as far as the heavens, even Your truth as far as the clouds.

11 Be exalted above the heavens, God, and may Your glory be over all the earth.

Even though David penned this psalm, it is clear that the Branch is the speaker. It is the Branch who seeks refuge with Yahweh by being raptured into His presence. In Psalm ninety-one, the Word addresses the Branch through the written Word, and He describes the fact that the Branch will take refuge in Yahweh. The Branch will be raptured before the end time destruction, that starts at the opening of the first seal of the book of Revelation.

Psalm 91:3—4 (D. Israel)
3 For He will snatch you from the trap of the trapper, from the plague of destructions.
4 With His pinions He will cover you; yea, under his wings you will take refuge; His faithfulness will be a buckler and a shield.

Standard translations have destroyed verse two.

pro(7121)	3807a(430)	5945	3807a(430)
I cry	to God	Most High,	to God

1584	(5921)pro
who will perfect	through me.

It is the Branch through whom God will perfect the church at the resurrection and rapture, after the Branch's glorification and rapture. God will not forsake those who have put their trust in Him, for God will perfect and rapture the church through the Branch. At that time, God's mercy to the works of His hands will be everlasting, believers receiving eternal life.

Psalm 138:7—8 (D. Israel)
7 When I walk in the midst of distress, You will preserve me. On account of the wrath of my enemy, You will stretch out Your hand and deliver me.

8   Your right hand, Yahweh, will perfect through me; Your mercy
     will be everlasting. You will not forsake the works of Your hands.

God will reproach the Antichrist who becomes the beast, who pants
after the Branch; the Antichrist becoming the beast at being indwelt
by the demon from the abyss (Rev. 13:1—8; 17:8). After the Branch's
deliverance at his rapture, God will send Jesus, His mercy and truth
(Psalm 85:10—11) at the resurrection and rapture of believers. Psalm
eighty-five reveals the symbolism of mercy and truth. The Branch who
has sprung up from the earth is symbolized by truth and peace, whereas
Jesus who looks down from Heaven is symbolized by mercy and righteousness. So, when God sends His mercy and His truth it means that
He sends Jesus, after being reunited with the Branch.

Psalm 85:10—11 (D. Israel)
10   That glory may dwell in our land, mercy and truth must meet
     together, righteousness and peace must kiss.
11   Truth has sprung up from the earth, and righteousness looks
     down from Heaven.

Verse four refers to the fact that the Branch' soul was Jesus' soul,
who was in the midst of lions. Jesus' soul lay among those on fire in
Sheol, during the three days and nights after Jesus' death. In Psalm eighteen, the Branch reflects back to the three days and nights that his soul
spent in Sheol.

Psalm 18:4—5 (D. Israel)
4   The cords of death encompassed me, the torrents of the wicked
     overwhelmed me;
5   the cords of Sheol encircled me; the snares of death con-
     fronted me.

Verse five refers to the time of the resurrection and rapture. God
will be exalted above the sky, and His glory will be over all the earth

at the resurrection and rapture of believers (Mat.24:30). In verse six, the Antichrist will know that the Branch must make his way to Mount Zion at the time of his glorification. So, the Antichrist's confederates will prepare a net for his steps. In Psalm one hundred and forty, the Branch describes the man of violence, the Antichrist, who plans to trip up his steps.

Psalm 140:4—5 (D. Israel)

4 Keep me, Yahweh, from the hands of the wicked; preserve me from the man of violence who plans to trip up my steps.

5 The proud have hidden a trap for me, and cords; they have spread a net by the wayside; they have set snares for me. Selah.

Verses 7—9 describe that the Branch will sing praises to Yahweh, even after his glorification. In Psalm seventy-one, the Branch looks ahead to after his glorification, when he will sing praise to Yahweh.

Psalm 71:21—24 (D. Israel)

21 You will multiply my greatness, and turn to comfort me.

22 Indeed, I will praise You with an instrument of the harp; Your truth, my God, I will sing to You with the lyre.

23 Holy One of Israel, my lips will shout for joy when I sing to You, even my soul which You have redeemed.

24 My tongue will also utter Your righteousness all the day; for will be confounded, shammed those who seek my harm.

Psalm fifty-seven closes with the Branch describing the time of the resurrection and rapture. At the resurrection and rapture Jesus will descend as far as the clouds of the sky; God's mercy will descend as far as the sky, His truth as far as the clouds. God will be exalted above the sky, and His glory will be over all the earth.

PSALM SIXTY-NINE

TO THE CHIEF MUSICIAN, ON THE LILIES, OF DAVID.

1 Deliver Me, O God, for the waters have come as far as My soul.

2 I have sunk in the mire of the deep, and there is no foothold; I have come into the depths of he waters and the flood overflows Me.

3 I am weary with My crying, My throat is burnt, My eyes fail waiting for My God.

4 The ones hating without a cause are more than the hairs on My head; mighty are those destroying Me, My lying enemy.

5 At that time I restored what I did not take away. O God, You know about my foolishness, and my guiltiness is not hidden from You.

6 May those waiting on You not be ashamed in me, O Lord Yahweh of hosts; may those seeking You not be humiliated by me, O God of Israel.

7 Indeed, on account of You I bore reproach; shame covered my face.

8 I was a stranger to my brothers, even a foreigner to my mother's sons.

9 For zeal for Your house consumed me, and the reproaches of those reproaching You fell on me.

10 And my soul wept with fasting, and it was because of the reproaches to me.

11 And I made my clothing sackcloth, and to them I was a proverb.

12 Those who sat in the gate pondered on me, and I was the song of those drinking strong drink.

13 But as for me, my prayer is to You, Yahweh; at the time of acceptance, O God, in the greatness of Your mercy answer me by the truth of Your deliverance.

14 Snatch me away from the mire that I do not sink into it; may I be snatched away from those that hate me, and the depths of the waters.

15 Do not let the flood of waters overflow me, and do not let the depths swallow me, and do not let the pit shut its mouth on me.

16 Answer me, Yahweh, for Your mercy is good; according to the greatness of Your tender mercies turn to me.

17 And do not hide Your face from Your servant, for distress is mine; answer me quickly.

18 Draw near to my soul, redeem it; ransom me on account of my enemies.

19 You know of my reproach and my shame and my disgrace; my adversaries are before You.

20 Reproach broke my heart, and I was full of heaviness; and I looked for sympathy, but there was none; and for comforters, but I found none.

21 But they gave me gall as my food, and for my thirst they gave me vinegar to drink.

22 Let their table be a trap before them, even a snare to those at peace.

23 May You darken their eyes from seeing, and may their loins continually quake.

24 Pour upon them Your indignation, and may the burning of Your anger overtake them.

25 May their homes be desolate; may there not be an inhabitant in their dwellings.

26 For whom You smote they persecuted, and they gossip to the pain of Your wounded one.

27 Give iniquity upon their iniquity, and may they not enter into Your righteousness.

28 May they be blotted out from the book of life, and may they not be written down with the righteous.

29 But I am afflicted and in pain; your deliverance, O God, will set me on high.

30 I will praise the name of God in song, and I will magnify Him with thanksgiving.

31 And it will be more pleasing to Yahweh than a bullock, a young bull having horns, cleaving the hoofs.

32 The humble will see it and rejoice, those seeking God, and your heart will live.

33 Indeed, Yahweh hears the needy, and does not despise His prisoners.

34 Let the heavens and the earth praise Him, and the seas and everything moving in them.

35 For God will save Zion and He will build the cities of Judah, and they will dwell there and possess it.

36 And the seed of His servants will inherit it, and those who love His name will reside in it.

Psalm 69:1—4 is spoken by Jesus' soul from the point in time of Jesus' death. The mire of the deep and the waters that overflow Jesus' soul are what a soul descends through on its way to the pit of Sheol. In Psalm 40:1—2, it is the Branch who testifies to the fact that God has brought him up from the pit of roaring, the clay, and the mire, given that the Branch is born having Jesus' soul.

Psalm 40:1—2 (D. Israel)

1 Waiting, I waited on Yahweh, and He stretched out toward me and heard my cry.

2 And He brought me up from the pit of roaring, from the clay, the mire; and He lifted my feet upon a rock, establishing my steps.

In Psalm 69:14—15, it is the Branch again who prays for God not to allow him to suffer death, not to allow him to sink into the mire and the depths of the waters. The Branch is asking that his enemies not succeed in killing him.

Verses 5—18 are spoken by the Branch. In verse 5a and verses 7—12, the Branch reflects back to when his soul was Jesus' soul. At the time of Jesus' death, Jesus' soul restored what He did not take away. By stripping bare His soul of his life giving Spirit, Jesus' soul who has become the Branch's soul has provided the means for eternal life; for it is Jesus' life giving Spirit indwelling the believer's spirit that gives him eternal life.

In verse thirteen, the Branch prays for his deliverance from his enemies at the time of acceptance. The time of acceptance is the time that the nation of Israel officially accepts Jesus as her Messiah. It is the time when the Branch is accepted as he who comes in the name of Yahweh (Psalm 118:26). It is the day of the Branch's glorification and deliverance by being raptured.

Psalm 118:26—27 (D. Israel)
26 Blessed is he who comes in the name of Yahweh; we have blessed you from the house of Yahweh.
27 God is Yahweh, and He has given light to us. Bind the sacrificial feast with cords, even to the horns of the alter.

At that time, the people of Israel will call out to God to bind the sacrificial feast with cords to the horns of the alter. The sacrificial feast symbolizes Jesus' soul who has become the Branch's soul, whereas the blood smeared on the horns of the alter symbolizes Jesus' life giving Spirit. Just before Jesus' death, He stated that the people of Jerusalem would not see Him from then until they said, Blessed is he who comes in the name of the Lord (Mat. 23:39). Jesus was referring to the people of Jerusalem seeing Him on the day of the Branch's glorification. At Israel crying out to God for the unification of the Branch with the resurrected Jesus, the Branch will be glorified by being indwelt by the fullness of Jesus; thus, he will be Jesus once again. It is then that the people of Jerusalem will briefly see Jesus, before His rapture to the throne of God.

Immediately after the Branch's glorification, he will be anointed will the fullness of Yahweh's Spirit (Psalm 2:6—7), and raptured to the throne of God (Rev. 12:5).

Psalm 2:6—7 (D . Israel)
6   "Yea, I anointed My King on Zion, My holy mountain."
7   "I will declare concerning the statute of Yahweh: He said to me, 'You are My Son, today I have begotten You.'"

Psalm two describes Jesus' birth on the day of His anointing on Mount Zion. This is not Jesus' natural birth at Bethlehem to Mary, but His super-natural birth on Mount Zion to the nation of Israel. The reunification of the Branch with Jesus is depicted as Jesus' birth, because the same thing happens at His super-natural birth as happened at His natural birth. At Jesus' natural birth, the Word emptied Himself of God and became flesh, became Jesus' soul, and was united with Jesus' conceived body and Spirit; whereas at Jesus' super-natural birth Jesus' soul who has become the Branch's soul is reunited with the resurrected Jesus, He who was the Branch's body and Spirit at Jesus' first advent. Immediately after being anointed by Yahweh, the Branch who will have become Jesus will be delivered from his enemies by being raptured to the throne of God.

Revelation 12:5 (NAS) And she gave birth to a son, a male child, who is to rule all the nations with a rod of iron; and her child was caught up to God and to His throne.

Psalm 69:19—36 is spoken by Jesus' soul, from the point in time of being in Sheol during the three days and nights after Jesus' death. It is easy to see that verse twenty-one describes Jesus being given gall and vinegar while He was dying on the cross.

> Matthew 27:34 (King James) They gave him vinegar to drink mingled with gall: and when he had tasted thereof, he would not drink.

In verse twenty-nine, Jesus' soul expresses his faith that God will deliver him from Sheol, setting him on high. God set Jesus' soul on high the day after Jesus' resurrection (Mat. 12:40). In verses 30—32, Jesus' soul looks ahead to when he is restored to life in the latter years as the Branch's soul. The Branch will praise God in song, and the humble will see this and rejoice, because they will recognize the Branch's identity.

> Psalm 40:3 (D. Israel) And He has put in my mouth a new song of praise to our God; many will see and fear, and they will trust in Yahweh.

Those who humble themselves will live, they will receive eternal life through belief in Jesus.

In verse thirty-three, Jesus' soul states that Yahweh hears the needy, and doesn't despise His prisoners. God's prisoners were those who believed in God, but were in Sheol after their deaths. They were in Sheol because before Jesus' death the means to go to Heaven upon death was not yet provided. It was Jesus' death that provided the righteousness necessary for the believer to be taken out of Sheol to Heaven. In Zechariah, God describes the fact that Jesus' soul would also be one of Jesus' captives taken out of Sheol to Heaven. The day after Jesus' resurrection Jesus descended to Sheol and took God's captives out of the waterless pit of Sheol to the stronghold of Heaven.

Zechariah 9:11—12 (D, Israel)

11 Also You, by the blood of Your covenant I will send forth Your captives from the waterless pit.

12 Return to the stronghold, captives of the hope; ——

Psalm one hundred and sixteen also describes Jesus' soul being taken out of the waterless pit of Sheol the day after Jesus' resurrection. The resurrected Jesus tells His soul to return to his rest, his rest in Heaven (Psalm 116:7). All those who have believed and die after Jesus' death do not go to Sheol, but go directly to Heaven (II Corinthians 5:6—8). One of the thieves who died on a cross beside Jesus, is the first person recorded to have gone directly to Heaven upon his death. Because the thief believed in Jesus and died after Jesus died (John 19:31—33), he joined Jesus' Spirit in the Paradise of Heaven on the day of his death.

Luke 23:43 (NAS) And He said to him, "Truly I say to you, today you shall be with Me in Paradise."

In verses 35—36, Jesus' soul looks ahead to the end times when God will save Jerusalem. The cities of Israel that are destroyed during the end time will be built again after Jesus' second advent, and those who love God will reside there.

PSALM SEVENTY-ONE

1 With You, Yahweh, I seek refuge: I will eternally not be confounded.

2 With Your righteousness snatch me away, and cause me to escape. Incline Your ear to me and deliver me.

3 Be my rock of refuge to come to continually; You will command to deliver me, for You are my rock and fortress.

4 My God, deliver me from the hand of the wicked, from the hand of the perverse and cruel one.

5 For You are my hope, my Lord Yahweh, my trust from my youth.

6 On account of You I have been sustained from the womb; from the belly of my mother you took me. With You my praise will be continual.

7 I am a wonder to many, but You will be my refuge of strength.

8 My mouth will be filled with Your praise, Your glory all the day.

9 Do not cast me off at the time of old age; do not forsake me when my strength fails.

10 For my enemies speak against me, and those who watch for my soul take counsel together,

11 saying, "God has forsaken him; pursue and seize him, for there is none to deliver."

12 God, do not be far from me; my God, hasten to my help.

13 The adversaries of my soul will be ashamed, they will be consumed; those seeking my harm will be covered with reproach and dishonour.

14 And I will continually hope, and I will add to all Your praise.

15 My mouth will declare Your righteousness, all the day Your salvation; for I do not know the number.

16 I will come in the might of the Lord Yahweh; I will make remembered Your righteousness, Yours alone.

17 God, You have taught me from my youth, and I have declared your wonders until now.

18 And indeed, at being old and grey, God, do not forsake me until I have shown Your power to this generation, to all those coming Your might;

19 since Your righteousness, God, will be at the height, who will do great things.

20 God, who is like You, in that You showed me great troubles and evil things; but You restored, you made me live; even from the depths of the earth You restored, You brought me up.

21 You will multiply my greatness, and turn to comfort me.

22 Indeed, I will praise You with an instrument of the harp; Your truth, my God, I will sing to you with the lyre.

23 Holy One of Israel, my lips will shout for joy when I sing to You, even my soul which You have redeemed.

24 My tongue will also utter Your righteousness all the day; for will be confounded, for will be shammed those who seek my harm.

Once we recognize the identity of the Branch, it is easy to see that he is the speaker of Psalm seventy-one. It is the Branch who seeks refuge with Yahweh by means of being raptured into His presence at his glorification. In Psalm 91:1—2, the Branch speaks of what he will say to Yahweh at being raptured into His presence.

Psalm 91:1—2 (D. Israel)

1 He who dwells in the covert of the Most High abides in the shadow of the Almighty.

2 I will say to Yahweh, "My refuge and fortress, my God." I trust in Him.

Then in Psalm 91:3—4, the Word speaks to the Branch through the written Word, describing that Yahweh will snatch him from the trapper and from the plague of destructions. The trapper is the Antichrist, and the plague of destructions consists of the seals, trumpets, and bowls, as described in Revelation.

> Psalm 91:3—4 (D. Israel)
> 3 For He will snatch you from the trap of the trapper, from the plague of destructions.
> 4 With His pinions He will cover you; yea, under His wings you will take refuge. His faithfulness will be a buckler and a shield.

In verse sixteen, the Branch states that he will come in the might of the Lord Yahweh. The Branch will come in the might of the Lord Yahweh, after his glorification at being reunited with Jesus and his anointing with Yahweh's Spirit. The Branch will come in the might of the Lord Yahweh at the resurrection and rapture, and then at Jesus' second advent. As the Branch requests in verse eighteen, he will show God's power and might to that generation.

In verse seventeen, the Branch states that he has declared God's wonders until that time. It will be the Branch who will declare the wonderful works of Yahweh, both before (Psalm 40:5) and after (Psalm 73:28) his glorification and rapture.

> Psalm 40:5 (D. Israel) Many things You have done, Yahweh my God. There is none to set in order for You Your wondrous works and Your purposes towards us. I will declare and speak. They are more than have been declared.

> Psalm 73:24—28 (D. Israel)
> 24 And after the glory You will take me, the water for me in Heaven.
> 25 And beside You, I will desire nothing on earth.

26 My flesh and my heart will be complete; God will be the rock of
    my heart and my portion forever.

27 For behold, those departing from You will perish; You will cut
    off all who go a whoring from You.

28 But as for me, the drawing near of God to me will be good; I
    will set my refuge in the Lord Yahweh to declare all Your works.

Verse nineteen has been poorly translated by standard translations.
This verse is describing the great things God's Spirit will do at the height
of Mount Zion at the Branch's glorification.

2050a(6666)pro	430	5704
since Your righteousness, God, (will be)		at

4791 834	6213	(1419)pl
(the) height who	will do	great things.

When it is time for the Branch to be glorified by means of being reunited with Jesus, God directs him to go up upon Mount Zion and to
declare to the people, Behold Your God.

Isaiah 40:9 (D. Israel) Go up upon the high mountain to
Yourself, bearer of good news to Zion. Lift up your voice with
strength, bearer of good news to Jerusalem. Lift up, do not fear,
say to the cities of Judah, "Behold your God!"

At making this declaration, the Branch will be immediately reunited
with Himself, with Jesus, by means of Jesus coming out of the midst of
the church and indwelling the Branch's spirit. At being reunited with
Jesus, the Branch will once again be Jesus. And immediately after the
reunification, Jesus will be anointed will the full power and might of
Yahweh's Spirit, as described in Psalm 2:6.

Psalm 2:6—7 (D. Israel)

6　"Yea, I anointed My King on Zion, My holy mountain."

7　"I will declare concerning the statue of Yahweh: He said to Me, 'You are My Son, today I have begotten You.'"

The great troubles and evil things that the Branch speaks of in verse twenty, refer to what happened to him before being restored to life as the Branch. The troubles and evil things describe when the Branch's soul was Jesus' soul at the time of Jesus' crucifixion, and also the troubles and evil things he experienced during the three days and nights his soul spent in Sheol. Jesus spoke Psalm 22:11 at the time of His crucifixion, whereas Jesus' soul who later becomes the Branch's soul spoke Psalm 116:3—4 while being in Sheol.

Psalm 22:11 (D. Israel) Do not be far from Me, for trouble is near; for there is none to help.

Psalm 116:3—4 (D. Israel)

3　The cords of death encompassed me, the straits of Sheol found me;

4　trouble and sorrow I have found; therefore, on the name of Yahweh I call: "I pray, Yahweh, deliver my soul."

Psalm twenty-three and Isaiah thirty-eight describe the restoration of Jesus' soul to the land of the living as the Branch. Psalm 23:1-3 is spoken by Jesus' soul from the point in time of being in Sheol, in the depths of the earth. Jesus' soul first looks forward to being taken out of Sheol to Heaven, the pastures of grass and the waters of rest; then he speaks of his conviction that he will be restored to life, restored to the land of the living.

Psalm 23:1—3 (D. Israel)

1　Yahweh is my shepherd, I will not want.

2   He will make me lie down in pastures of grass; He will lead me
    to waters of rest.

3   He will restore my soul; He will lead me in paths of righteous
    for His name's sake.

In Isaiah 38:15—16, the Branch is the speaker, not Hezekiah. In these verses, the Branch reflects back to when he was Jesus. He relates that what Jesus spoke was spoken to Him by Yahweh, and the miracles that Jesus performed were performed by Yahweh. The Branch states that because of the years of the embitterment of his soul, as a result of being separated from his Spirit, all live who have He who was his Spirit in them. Then the Branch relates that because of laying down his life as Jesus, Yahweh has restored him to life.

Isaiah 38:15—16 (D. Israel)

15 What I spoke, even He had said to me, and Himself did. I
    have gone humbly all my years because of the bitterness of
    my soul

16 Lord, because of them, they live; yea, for all have in them my
    life, my Spirit. Therefore, You have restored me, even causing
    me to live.

In verse twenty-one, the Branch states that God will multiply his greatness, and turn to comfort him. God will multiply his greatness at his glorification, at Jesus' super-natural birth and anointing with Yahweh's Spirit. At that time, Yahweh will comfort him, answering his prayers that he be delivered from his enemies. Verses 22—24 describe the fact that even after his glorification, the Branch will sing praises to Yahweh throughout eternity. In Psalm 108:1—3, the Branch also declares that he will praise Yahweh, so much the more with his glory.

Psalm 108:1—3 (D. Israel)

1   My heart is fixed, God; I will give praise, so much the more with my glory.

2   Awake, harp and lyre; I will awaken the dawn;

3   I will praise You among the peoples, Yahweh. Yea, I will sing to You among the nations.

PSALM SEVENTY-THREE

A PSALM OF ASAPH.

1 Truly God is good to Israel, to those pure in heart;

2 but I almost turned my feet; at having nothing, my steps had slipped.

3 For I was jealous of the proud; I perceived the peace of the wicked.

4 For there are no pangs to their deaths, and their bellies are fat.

5 They are not in the toil of man, and they are not touched with the dealings of men.

6 Therefore they make pride their necklace; a garment of injustice covers them.

7 Their eyes bulge out from fat. They pass through the imaginations of the heart.

8 They mock and speak with evil oppression.

9 They speak from on high; they set their mouths against Heaven, and their tongues walk through the earth.

10 Therefore He will restore His people there, and the water of a full cup will be drained out on them.

11 And they say, How does God know, and is there knowledge in the Most High?

12 Behold, these are the wicked, even those always at ease; they increase wealth.

13 Surely in vain I have cleansed my heart; yea, I have washed my hands in innocence,

14 but I am stricken all the day, and my chastisement is toward mornings.

15 If I had spoken, been counted in this way; behold, a generation of Your sons I would have betrayed;

16 and I thought to understand this; it was troublesome in my eyes until I entered into the sanctuaries of God.

17 I discern their end.

18 Surely You will set them in slippery places; You will make them fall to ruins.

19 How they will come to desolation; in a moment finished, consumed from terrors, like a dream from awaking.

20 Lord, in being aroused You will despise their image.

21 Indeed, my heart, even my kidneys had been embittered.

22 I had been pierced, but I was brutish and did not understand. I was like the animals toward You, but I was continually with You.

23 You have taken in hand my right hand; in Your counsel You lead me.

24 And after the glory You will take me, the water for me in Heaven.

25 And beside You, I will desire nothing on earth.

26 My flesh and my heart will be complete; God will be the rock of my heart and my portion forever.

27 For behold, those departing from You will perish; You will cut off all who go a whoring from You.

28 But as for me, the drawing near of God to me will be good; I will set my refuge in the Lord Yahweh to declare all Your works.

It is the Branch who is the speaker of Psalm seventy-three, Asaph penning the words given him by God. This psalm probably gives us the best glimpse of the Branch's life and thinking before he is born again. In verse two, the Branch describes his youth, when he almost turned to follow a wrong path. He was jealous of the wealthy who had removed themselves from the toil of men. The Branch almost turned his feet to follow a path of seeking wealth, but comes to realize that this would not leave him with a pure heart. In verses 13—14, the Branch describes cleansing his heart and washing his hands in innocence. He is describing the repenting of his sins, and being cleansed by being born again. However, even after being born again he suffers from his chastisement placed upon him by God, in order that he learn God's statutes.

Psalm 119:67—71 (D. Israel)
67 Before I was afflicted I went astray, but now I keep Your word.
68 You are good and do good, teach me your statutes.
69 The proud have forged a lie against me; I with all my heart will keep Your precepts.
70 Insensitive like fat are their hearts; I take delight in Your law.
71 It was good for me that I was afflicted, so that I might learn Your statutes.

In verses 15—16, the Branch states that if he had spoken like the proud and wicked, he would have betrayed a generation of God's sons. This troubled his understanding until he entered God's sanctuaries. Verses 15—17 have been poorly translated by standard translations. What was troubling the Branch was not the fate of the proud and wicked, but why he would be betraying a generation of God's sons, if he spoke like the proud and wicked and was counted with them.

518	(559)pro	5608	3644	2009
If	I had spoken, been counted in this way, behold,			

1755	(1121)(pl)pro
(a) generation (of)	Your sons

(898)pro
I would have betrayed.

2050a(2803)	3807a(3045) 2063	5999
And I thought	to understand this; troublesome	

1931   preb(5869)pro 5704 pro(935)
it   (was)   in my eyes   until I entered (the)

(4720)pl   410   pro(995)   3897a(319)pro
sanctuaries (of) God.   I discern   ---- their end;

How can a person betray a generation of God's sons, especially a person that has not been following God? These verses are describing the Branch's struggle to understand his identity, to understand that he is the Branch. Normally a person would have to be in a position of great authority, in order for it to be possible to betray a generation of God's sons. However, since the Branch is born having Jesus' soul, if he did not repent of his sins and be born again, he would have betrayed a generation of God's sons; for the Branch is he who declares concerning the Lord to a generation.

> Psalm 22:30 (D. Israel) All those going down to the dust will bow before Him, even His soul not being revived. A seed will serve Him, he will declare concerning the Lord to a generation.

And it is the Branch whom a generation of God's sons will seek.

> Psalm 24:3—6 (D. Israel)
> 3   Who will go up upon the mountain of Yahweh, and who will stand up in His holy place?
> 4   One who will have clean hands and a pure heart, who will not have lifted up his soul to vanity, and will not have sworn to deceit.
> 5   He will lift up the blessing from Yahweh, and righteousness from the God of his salvation.
> 6   This one a generation will seek, those who will seek your face, Jacob.

After being born again and entering God's sanctuaries, the Branch will come to understand his identity. He will understand that his heart and kidneys, his soul, had been embittered; because of being separated from Jesus, He who was his Spirit. He will understand that he was brutish and was like the animals toward God, not recognizing God's existence. He will understand that despite this he was continually with God; in that Jesus, He who was his Spirit, is continually with Yahweh. In Isaiah 38:15—16, it is the Branch, not Hezekiah, who describes his soul being embittered due to the loss of his Spirit. The words that Jesus spoke during His ministry were given to Him by the Father, and it was the Father's Spirit in Jesus who performed the miracles. Because the Branch gave up He who was his Spirit at the cross, God has restored him to life in the latter years as the Branch's soul.

Isaiah 38:15—16 (D. Israel)

15 What I spoke, even He had said to me, and Himself did. I have gone humbly all my years because of the bitterness of my soul.

16 Lord, because of them, they live; yea, for all have in them my life, my Spirit. Therefore, You have restored me, even causing me to live.

Verses 24-28 describe the Branch's glorification and rapture to Heaven, but have been destroyed by standard translations.

2050a(310)	3519	pro(3947)pro	4325
And after (the) glory		You will take me,	(the) water

(3807a)pro preb(8064)	
for me	in Heaven.

2050a(5973)pro	3808	(2654)pro	preb(776)
And beside You,	nothing I will desire		on earth.

3615	(7607)pro 2050a(3824)pro
Will be complete my flesh	and my heart; (the)

6697   (3824)pro   2050a(2506)pro   430
rock (of) my heart   and my portion (will be) God

3807a(5769)
forever.

3588 2009   (7369)(pl)pro   6
For behold, those departing from You   will perish;

    (6789)pro   3605   2181   (4480)pro
You will cut off   all who go a whoring   from You.

2050a(589)   7132   430 (3807a)pro
But as for me, (the) drawing near (of) God   to me

          2896   (7896)pro   preb(136)   3068
(will be) good;   I will set   in the Lord   Yahweh

(4268)pro 3807a(5608) 3605 (4399)(pl)pro
my refuge   to declare   all   Your works.

In verse twenty-four, the Branch describes the glory that will be his at being reunited with Jesus, before being taken to Heaven by the water of God's Spirit. It is the Branch who will receive the blessing of Jacob of becoming the ruler of the nations. Because the Branch's soul was Jesus' soul, God will bless him with this blessing. The Branch will become Jesus at girding on the sword of his Spirit, at being re-united with the resurrected Jesus. Jesus is the Branch's glory and his majesty.

Psalm 45:2—4 (D. Israel)
2   You were the fairest of the sons of mankind; grace flowed through your lips. Therefore God will bless you forever.
3   Gird your sword on your thigh, Mighty One, your glory and your majesty.

4   And in Your majesty prosper; ride on the matter of truth and meekness and righteousness, and Your right hand will teach You fearful things.

After being raptured to Heaven, the Branch will desire nothing on earth. Yahweh will be the portion of his cup forever.

Psalm 16:5 (D. Israel) Yahweh is the portion of my inheritance and my cup. You will uphold my lot.

PSALM SEVENTY-FIVE

TO THE CHIEF MUSICIAN, DO NOT DESTROY; A PSALM OF ASAPH, A SONG.

1 We give thanks to you, God; we give thanks that Your name is near. Your wondrous works have been declared.

2 When I take away the appointed time, I will judge uprightly.

3 The earth will be melted, and all its inhabitants: I will make even its pillars. Selah.

4 I say to the boastful, "Do not boast," and to the wicked, "Do not lift up the horn.

5 Do not lift up your horn on high; do not speak with a stiff neck."

6 For exaltation will not be from the east, nor from the west, nor from the south.

7 For God is the judge: He will humble one, and He will exalt another.

8 Indeed, a cup is in the hand of Yahweh, and a full mixture of wine foams; He will pour out from this. Surely its dregs all the wicked of the earth must drain and drink.

9 And I will declare forever; I will sing praises to the God of Jacob.

10 And I will cut off all the horns of the wicked, but the horns of the righteous will be lifted up.

Psalm seventy-five is yet another portion of Scripture that is spoken by the Branch, Asaph being given these words by God. It is the Branch who declares God's works. In Psalm 40:5, the Branch describes declaring God's works before his glorification, and in Psalm 73:28 the Branch states that he will declare God's works after his glorification.

> Psalm 40:5 (D. Israel) Many things You have done, Yahweh my God. There is none to set in order for You, Your wondrous works and your purposes towards us. I will declare and speak. They are more than have been declared.

> Psalm 73:24—28 (D. Israel)
> 24 And after the glory You will take me, the water for me in Heaven.
> 25 And beside You, I will desire nothing on earth.
> 26 My flesh and my heart will be complete; God will be the rock of my heart and my portion forever.
> 27 For behold, those departing from You will perish; You will cut off all who go a whoring from You.
> 28 But as for me, the drawing near of God to me will be good; I will set my refuge in the Lord Yahweh to declare all Your works.

Verse two has been poorly translated by standard translations.

```
3588   pro(3947)           4150      589
When I take away (the) appointed time,   I

 4339      8199
uprightly   will judge.
```

The Branch will become Jesus at his glorification, and Jesus at His second advent will take away the appointed time that the Antichrist is given to act.

> Revelation 13:5 (NAS) And there was given him a mouth speaking arrogant words and blasphemies; and authority to act for forty-two months was given him.

In verse three, the melting of the earth probably refers to the flattening of the earth, by the monster earthquake at the seventh bowl of wrath (Rev. 16:17—21). In verse six, the Branch states that exaltation will not be from the east, nor from the west, nor from the south; for the Branch comes from the north, before he comes from the east as Jesus (Isaiah 41:25). Isaiah 41:25 is a two-legged double-step. Leg one describes the Branch before his glorification, who comes from the north, and who calls out in Yahweh's name; whereas leg two describes the Branch after his glorification at becoming Jesus, who will come from the east at the rapture (Mat. 24:27), and later come upon rulers at Jesus' second advent.

> Isaiah 41:25 (D. Israel)
> leg 1 step 1   "I have raised up one from the north,
> leg 2 step 1   and he will come from the rising of the sun.
> leg 1 step 2   He will call out in My name,
> leg 2 step 2   and He will come upon rulers as on mortar, even as a
>   potter tramples clay."

It will be the Branch who will call out to the nation of Israel in the name of Yahweh (Psalm 116:13), calling a nation he doesn't know, and who doesn't know him (Isaiah 55:5). The people of Israel will run to the Branch at his glorification.

> Psalm 116:13 (D. Israel) The cup of salvation I will lift up, and in the name of Yahweh I will call out.

> Isaiah 55:5 (D. Israel) "Behold, you will call a nation you do not know; and a nation that does not know you will run to you because of Yahweh your God, even because of the Holy One of Israel, for He will glorify you."

As verse nine states, the Branch will declare concerning God's works forever, forever after his glorification. Even with his glory the Branch will sing praises to Yahweh.

Psalm 108:1—3 (D. Israel)

1   My heart is fixed God; I will sing and give praise, so much the more with my glory.

2   Awake, harp and lyre. I will awaken the dawn;

3   I will praise You among the peoples, Yahweh. Yea, I will sing to You among the nations.

In verse ten, the Branch states that he will cut off the horns of the wicked, given that after his glorification he will come as Jesus at Jesus' second advent. At Jesus' second advent, the wicked will be consumed out of the earth, but the righteous will be exalted. As Psalm one hundred and four states, Let sinners be consumed out of the earth, and let the wicked be no more. Those who have humbled themselves and accepted Jesus as Lord, and thus have received God's righteousness indwelling them, will be exalted at Jesus' second advent. They will be given authority, sitting down with Jesus on His throne.

Revelation 3:21 (NAS) He who overcomes I will grant to him to sit down with me on My throne, as I also overcame and sat down with My Father on His throne.

PSALM EIGHTY-FIVE

TO THE CHIEF MUSICIAN, A PSALM FOR THE SONS OF KORAH.

1   Yahweh, You have favored Your land; You have turned back the captivity of Jacob.
2   May You lift up the iniquity of Your people; may You cover all their sins. Selah.
3   May You remove all Your wrath; may You turn back from the heat of Your anger.
4   Restore us, God of our salvation, and break up Your anger against us.
5   Will You be angry with us forever? Will You draw out Your anger generation after generation?
6   Will You not turn? Revive us that Your people may rejoice in You.
7   Cause us to see Your mercy, Yahweh, and give to us Your salvation.
8   I hear what Yahweh God speaks, for He speaks peace to His people and to His faithful, but let them not turn back to folly.
9   Indeed, His deliverance is near to those who fear Him.
10 That glory may dwell in our land, mercy and truth must meet together, righteousness and peace must kiss.
11 Truth has sprung up out of the earth, and righteousness looks down from Heaven.
12 Indeed, Yahweh will give good things, and our land will give its produce.

13 Righteousness will go before Him, and prepare the way of His
     footsteps.

The Branch is the speaker of Psalm eighty-five. In verse one, the Branch
refers to God favoring Israel, turning back her captivity. The Branch is
referring to God favoring the land of Israel, by turning back her captivity at the latter year invasion by Gog and her allies (Ezekiel chapters 38—39)). Ezekiel 39:21 describes God's judgment on the armies
of Gog and her allies, who invade Israel in the latter years. In Ezekiel
39:25, God describes the turning back of Israel's captivity from Gog and
her allies. In Ezekiel 39:26, God describes the fact that the people of
Israel will bear their shame on account of trespassing against Him. It reveals that this time will be during the time Israel is dwelling securely. In
Ezekiel 39:8, 39:11, and 39:14 God reveals that Israel will be dwelling
securely at the time of the invasion by Gog and her allies. So, this is an
indication that Israel will have made peace with the Palestinians before
the invasion by Gog and her allies. This does not mean that the seven
year covenant will be in effect at this time. The seven year covenant has
nothing to do with the Palestinians, but will occur almost a generation
later, and will be an agreement between the Antichrist and Israel.

Ezekiel 39:21—29 (D. Israel)
21 "Then I will set My glory on the nations, and all the nations will
     see My judgment which I will execute, and My hand that I will
     lay upon them.
22 So, the house of Israel will know that I am Yahweh their God
     from that day onward.
23 And the nations will know that for their iniquity the house of
     Israel was exiled, because they acted unfaithfully against Me; so
     I have hidden My face from them, and have given them into the
     hand of their adversaries; and they have fallen by the sword all
     of them.

24 According to their uncleanness and according to their transgressions I have done to them, and have hidden My face from
them."

25 Therefore thus says Yahweh, "Now I will turn back the captivity
of Jacob, and I will be jealous for My holy name;

26 since they will have borne their shame and all their treachery
which they will have trespassed against Me, when they dwell
securely on their land with none causing them to fear.

27 When I bring them back from the peoples and have gathered
them from the lands of their enemies, and I am sanctified in
them in the eyes of many nations;

28 then they will know that I am Yahweh their God, because I
caused them to be led into captivity among the nations, but I
have gathered them to their land; and will leave none of them
there any longer.

29 And I will not hide My face any more from them, for I will pour
out My Spirit on the house of Israel," says the Lord Yahweh.

In Ezekiel 14:13, God reveals that when the land of Israel grevously
trespasses against Him, then He will stretch out His hand and send
famine upon it.

Ezekiel 14:13 (King James) Son of man, when the land sinneth
against me by trespassing grievously, then will I stretch out my
hand upon it, and I will break the staff of the bread thereof, and
will send famine upon it, and will cut off man and beast from it:

So, the nation of Israel will suffer from famine, because of trespassing against God; and this will occur after establishing peace with the
Palestinians. Israel will bear her shame at this time; the shame of being
afflicted by drought and famine, and the shame of being over run by the
armies led by Gog. The book of Joel records the fact that the Branch will
be in Israel at this time of crisis for Israel. Joel describes that at this time

Israel will not only be suffering from a severe drought and famine, but will also be invaded by the northern armies of Gog and her allies. The Branch is the teacher of righteousness of Joel 2:23, whose ministry is to teach Israel God's plan of salvation, and why Jesus is the righteousness of whosoever believes in Him.

Joel 2:15—23 (D. Israel)

15 Blow a trumpet in Zion, consecrate a fast, call an assembly,

16 gather the people, sanctify the congregation, assemble the elders, gather the children and those sucking the breasts. Let the bridegroom come out of his room, and the bride from her chamber.

17 Let the priests weep at the porch and toward the alter, ministers of Yahweh; and let them say, "Have pity, Yahweh, on Your people, and do not give Your inheritance to reproach, that the nations should rule over them. Why should they say among the peoples, 'Where is their God?'"

18 Then Yahweh will be jealous for His land, and will have pity on His people.

19 And Yahweh will answer and say to His people, "Behold, I will send grain to you, and new wine and fresh oil, and you will be satisfied with it; and I will not any longer make you a reproach among the nations,

20 but I will remove the one from the north far from upon you, and I will drive him into a land of drought and desolation, with his face toward the eastern sea, and his rear toward the western sea. And his stench will come up, and his foul odour will ascend, for he will have grown great to perform."

21 Do not fear, land; rejoice and be glad, for Yahweh will be magnified at doing it.

22 Do not fear, beasts of the field, for the pastures of the wilderness will grow green; for the tree will bear its fruit, and the fig tree and the vine will give their strength.

23 So, sons of Zion, rejoice and be glad in Yahweh your God; for He has given you the teacher of righteousness; and the rain will come down to you; the early rain, but at first the latter rain.

In Psalm 85:2—7, the Branch prays for the forgiveness and salvation of the people of Israel. Those who humble themselves, repent of their sins, and accept Jesus as Lord, will have their iniquity lifted up and their sins covered. Those who believe in Jesus will have the sickness of sin lifted up from them, and their sickness of sin will be healed for them. They will be made complete, and will be at peace with God. In Isaiah 53:5, completeness can also be translated as peace. He who believes in Jesus is at peace with God.

Isaiah 53:5 (D. Israel) Nevertheless our sickness He has lifted up, and our sorrows He has carried, though we regarded Him stricken by God and afflicted; but He was wounded on account of our transgressions, crushed on account of our iniquities, chastening for our completeness was upon Him, and with His wound it is healed for us.

He who believes in Jesus will be justified by having his spirit indwelt and made righteous by Jesus.

Isaiah 53:12 (D. Israel) My righteous servant will justify many, ——

Jesus will reach the mark of being without sin for those who believe in Him.

Isaiah 53:12 (D. Israel) —— even the sin of many He will lift up, and for transgressors He will reach the mark.

Jesus indwelling the believer's spirit will lift up and remove the sin of his spirit, reaching the mark of being without sin for his spirit, and covering the sins of his soul.

In verse eight, the Branch states that he hears what Yahweh speaks, and that He speaks peace to His people, and to His faithful. Those who are faithful to Yahweh will believe in Jesus, given that Jesus was sent by Yahweh, and the words that Jesus spoke were given by Yahweh. Those who reject Jesus and do not believe in Him have God's wrath upon them.

John 3:36 (King James) He that believeth on the Son hath everlasting life: and he who believeth not the Son shall not see life; but the wrath of God adideth on him.

In verse nine, the Branch states that God's deliverance is near to those who fear Him. The Branch will start his ministry to the people of Israel about a generation before the rapture. The Branch is referring to the nearness of the deliverance of the rapture. Those who are raptured will be delivered from the day of Yahweh, the day of the wrath of God. The day of Yahweh is the period of time that stretches from immediately after the rapture until Jesus' second advent.

Joel 2:30—32 (D. Israel)
30 "And I will give signs in the heavens and on earth, blood, fire, and columns of smoke.
31 The sun will be turned into darkness, and the moon into blood, before the great and awesome day of Yahweh comes."
32 And it will be that all who have called on the name of Yahweh will be delivered, when on Mount Zion and in Jerusalem there will be an escape, as Yahweh has said, even among those who are left whom Yahweh will call.

Those who call on the name of Yahweh must call on Him in the name of Jesus, the name of Jesus being Yahweh's name that He called upon Jesus.

Just as the Branch has Yahweh's name called upon him (Jer. 15:16), so too does Jesus have Yahweh's name called upon Him (Luke 1:31). The splitting of the Mount of Olives provides the escape for those in Jerusalem, who are left behind at the rapture.

Standard translations have destroyed verses 10—11.

3807a(7931) 3519   preb(776)pro   2617
That may dwell glory   in our land,   mercy

2050a(571)   6298   6664
and truth   must meet together, righteousness

2050a(7965)   5401
and peace   must kiss.

571   4480(776)   6779
Truth out of the earth   has sprung up,

2050a(6664)   4480(8064)   8259
and righteousness from Heaven   looks down.

In verses 10—11, the Branch describes the necessity of his reunification with Jesus. The Branch who has sprung up from the earth is symbolized by truth and peace, whereas Jesus who looks down from Heaven is symbolized by mercy and righteousness. In order that glory, that God, dwell in the land of Israel, the Branch must first be reunited with Jesus.

In verse twelve, the Branch states that Yahweh will give good things and that the land of Israel will give its produce. The Branch is referring to the land giving its produce, on account of Yahweh sending rain to end the serve drought. Hosea describes Israel's harvest at that time, which is also the time of the turning back of Israel's captivity.

Hosea 6:11 (D. Israel) Also, Judah, a harvest is set for you when I turn back the captivity of My people.

One good thing that Yahweh will give will be the pouring out of His Spirit, as described in Joel. After God sends rain to end the severe drought, He will pour out His Spirit upon those who worship Him with the truth of His salvation.

Joel 2:28—29 (D. Israel)

28 "And it will be afterward that I will pour out My Spirit on all flesh; and your sons and your daughters will prophesy, and your elders will dream dreams, and your youth will see visions.

29 And even on the servants and the handmaids I will pour out My Spirit in those days."

In verse thirteen, the Branch states that righteousness will go before Yahweh, to prepare the way of His footsteps in the land of Israel. There are two stages of righteousness that will prepare the way for God dwelling in the land of Israel. The first stage is the righteousness that is given to the believer through belief in Jesus. The believer has the righteousness of God indwelling him, because Jesus indwells and makes righteous the believer's spirit. The second stage is the righteousness of Yahweh's Spirit at the latter year pouring out of His Spirit. Isaiah describes the righteousness that will result from the latter day pouring out of God's Spirit. Israel has been a spiritual wilderness from the time of the Babylonian captivity, but the spiritual wilderness will be turned into a fruitful field at the latter year pouring out of God's Spirit.

Isaiah 32:13—16 (D. Israel)

13 The thorn and the brier will come up on the ground of My people, even on all the joyful houses of the jubilant city.

14 For the palace will be abandoned, the crowd of the city deserted; hill and watchtower will be for dens for a long duration, a joy of wild donkeys, the pasturage of flocks;

15 until the Spirit is poured out upon us from on high, and the wilderness becomes a fruitful field, and the fruitful field is reckoned as a forest.

16 And justice will dwell in the wilderness, and righteousness will abide in the fruitful field.

PSALM NINETY-ONE

1 He who dwells in the covert of the Most High abides in the shadow of the Almighty.

2 I will say to Yahweh, "My refuge and fortress, my God." I trust in Him.

3 For He will snatch you from the trap of the trapper, from the plague of destructions.

4 With His pinions He will cover you; yea, under His wings you will take refuge; His faithfulness will be a buckler and a shield.

5 You will not fear from the terror of the night, from the arrow that will fly by day,

6 from the plague that will walk in the darkness, from the destruction that will devastate at noon.

7 A thousand may fall at your side, even a myriad because of your right hand.

8 It will not draw near you, only with your eyes will you look and see the retribution of the wicked.

9 Because You, Yahweh, are My refuge, you will have made the Most High your habitation.

10 Evil will not befall you, and the plague will not draw near to your tent,

11 for His angels He will command concerning you, to keep you in all your ways.

12 Upon their hands they will bear you up, lest you dash your foot on a stone.

13 You will tread on the lion and the adder; you will trample the young lion and the snake.

14 "Because he will set his love on Me, even I will deliver him, I will set him on high. Because he will know My name, he will call on Me, and I will answer him.

15 I will be with him in distress; I will draw him out of it, and I will honor him.

16 I will have satisfied him with length of days, and I will have caused him to see into My salvation."

Once we recognize the identity of the Branch, it is easy to see that he is the speaker of verses 1—2. It is the Branch who seeks refuge with Yahweh, by means of being raptured into His presence. The opening of Psalm fifty-seven is similar to the opening of Psalm ninety-one. In Psalm fifty-seven, the Branch prays for his deliverance, seeking refuge with Yahweh until the destruction passes. The Branch states that through him God will perfect, since at his deliverance he will be glorified by being reunited with Jesus; thus, he will become Jesus, and it is through Jesus that God perfects believers at the resurrection and rapture. At the Branch's rapture, he will escape the trapper, the Antichrist, and the plague of destructions of the end time.

Psalm 57:1—3 (D. Israel)

1 Be merciful to me, God, be merciful for my soul seeks refuge with You; even in the shadow of Your wings I seek refuge until the destruction passes.

2 I cry to God Most High, to God who will perfect through me.

3 He will send from Heaven and deliver me, reproaching the one who pants after me. Selah. ——

Verse nine reveals the speaker of verses 3—13. The faithful translation of verse nine doesn't make sense, unless we recognize who the speaker is, and whom he is addressing. Translators have had difficulty with this verse, since the speaker making Yahweh his refuge doesn't necessarily mean that he whom he is addressing will make Yahweh his habitation. However, since it is the Word who is the speaker who is addressing the Branch through Scripture, it does mean that he who is being addressed will make Yahweh his habitation; for it is the Word who becomes Jesus' soul, who in the latter years becomes the Branch's soul. Standard translations have destroyed verse nine.

3588	859	3068	(4268)pro
Because You,	Yahweh,	(are) my refuge,	(the)

5945	(7760)pro	(4583)pro
Most High	you will have made	your habitation.

Because Yahweh is the Word's refuge, the Branch will make Yahweh, the Most High, his habitation at his glorification and rapture to the throne of God (Rev. 12:5).

Verses 7—8 describe Jesus' second advent, when the Branch will learn the fearful power of the sword of his reacquired Spirit. Psalm 45:3 describes the Branch's glorification, at being commanded by God to gird on the sword of his Spirit, his glory and his majesty.

Psalm 45:3—4 (D. Israel)
3 Gird your sword on your thigh, Mighty One, your glory and your majesty.
4 And in Your majesty prosper; ride on the matter of truth and meekness and righteousness, and Your right hand will teach You fearful things.

During Jesus' temptation, the devil quoted Psalm 91:11—12 to Jesus. However, these verses aren't referring to Jesus, but to the Branch. God has vowed to keep the Branch, not allowing him to see death; whereas Jesus came to die so that we might have eternal life. In Isaiah

49:7—9, Yahweh addresses the Branch, and again states that He will keep the Branch. The Branch is the despised soul in that he is born having Jesus' soul, Jesus being despised and hated by Israel as a false Messiah.

> Isaiah 49:7—9 (D. Israel)
>
> 7 Thus says Yahweh the Redeemer of Israel, his Holy One, to the despised soul, to the one hated by the nation, to the servant of rulers, "Kings will see and stand up, leaders also will bow down on account of Yahweh who is faithful, the Holy One of Israel, even He has chosen you."
>
> 8 Thus says Yahweh, "At the time of acceptance I will answer you, and in the day of deliverance I will help you. For I will keep you and give you for a covenant of the people to restore the earth, to cause to inherit the desolated heritages;
>
> 9 to say to the prisoners, 'Go forth'; to those in darkness, 'Show yourselves.' ----

The time of acceptance is the time that the nation of Israel officially accepts Jesus as her Messiah and King. On that day, Yahweh will answer the Branch's prayer for deliverance, delivering him by setting him on high at his glorification and rapture.

Verse thirteen refers to Jesus' second advent, when the Branch has become Jesus, and tramples God's enemies who come against him at the battle of Armageddon. This verse is similar to Isaiah 41:25, which is a two-legged double-step. Leg one refers to he Branch before his glorification, whereas leg two refers to the Branch after his glorification when he has become Jesus. The Branch will come from the north, whereas Jesus will come from the east at the rapture. The Branch will call out to the nation of Israel in Yahweh's name (Psalm 116:13); whereas Jesus will trample on those aligned with the Antichrist at the battle of Armageddon, from those of low rank to rulers.

Isaiah 41:25 (D. Israel)

leg 1 step 1   "I have raised up one from the north,

leg 2 step 1   and he will come from the rising of the sun.

leg 1 step 2   He will call out in My name,

leg 2 step 2   and he will come upon rulers as on mortar, even as a
                potter tramples clay."

Psalm 91:14—16 is spoken by Yahweh, who declares His faithfulness regarding the Branch. Verses 14—15 are similar to Isaiah 49:8, in which Yahweh speaks of answering and delivering the Branch. Yahweh will answer and deliver the Branch, by setting him on high at his glorification and rapture. Verse sixteen has been destroyed by standard translations.

753	(3117)pl	pro(7646)pro
(With) length (of)	days	I will have satisfied him,

2050a(pro)(7200)pro	preb(3444)pro
and I will have cause him to see	into My salvation.

Standard translations have changed the meaning of verse sixteen by deleting the prefix "into" before My salvation. God will not only give the Branch a long life, but more importantly He will cause the Branch to see into His plan of salvation. The Branch will see how Jesus' death enabled Him to give eternal life to whosoever believes in Him. Similarly, Isaiah describes the Branch having a long life, and being satiated with the knowledge he sees, the knowledge he gains of God's plan of salvation.

Isaiah 53:10—11 (D. Israel)

10 But Yahweh will be pleased to crush Him, to make Him sick. When You make his soul guilty, he will see his seed, he will prolong his days, and the pleasure of Yahweh will prosper in his hands.

11 From the work of his soul he will see; he will be satiated with his knowledge.

PSALM ONE HUNDRED AND EIGHT
A SONG, A PSALM OF DAVID.

1 My heart is fixed, God; I will sing and give praise, so much the more with my glory.

2 Awake, harp and lyre; I will awaken the dawn;

3 I will praise You among the peoples, Yahweh. Yea, I will sing to You among the nations.

4 For Your mercy will be great from above the heavens, and Your truth as far as the clouds.

5 Be exalted above the heavens, God, and may Your glory be above all the earth.

6 So that Your beloved ones may be delivered, deliver me by Your right hand, even answer me.

7 God has spoken in His holiness: I will rejoice, I will portion out Shechem, and measure out Succoth;

8 Gilead will be mine, Manasseh will be mine, with Ephraim the strength of my head, Judah my scepter.

9 Moab will be my wash pot; over Edom I will cast my shoe; over Philista I will shout in triumph.

10 Who will bring me to the strong city? Who will lead me as far as Edom?

11 Will not God? You have cast us off, God, and have not gone out with our armies.

12 Give to us help from distress, since vain is deliverance by man.

13 With God we will do valiantly, and He will tread down our
adversaries.

The first part of Psalm one hundred and eight is similar to Psalm fifty-seven. In verse one, the Branch states that he will praise God, so
much the more with his glory. That is, he will praise God even more
after his glorification. Similar to Psalm fifty-seven, verses 4-5 describe
the time of the rapture. God's mercy and truth will descend as far as the
clouds at the rapture. As indicated in Psalm eighty-five, mercy symbolizes Jesus' Spirit, and truth symbolizes the Branch's soul, he who was
Jesus' soul. In Psalm eighty-five, the Branch who has sprung up from the
earth is symbolized by truth and peace, whereas Jesus who looks down
from Heaven is symbolized by mercy and righteousness.

Psalm 85:10-11 (D. Israel)
10 That glory may dwell in our land, mercy and truth must meet
together, righteousness and peace must kiss.
11 Truth has sprung up from the earth, and righteousness looks
down from Heaven.

God will be exalted above the sky at the rapture of the church. In verse
six, the Branch asks God to answer him, to deliver him. He points out
that he must be delivered before God's beloved ones can be delivered;
for it will be through him after his glorification, that God will perfect
the church at its deliverance and rapture. In verses 7—9, the Branch
describes some of the territories that will be his after his glorification.

In verse ten, the Branch speaks of going to a strong city in Edom,
and that God has not gone out with Israel's armies. Isaiah 16:1—5 clarifies the fact that the Branch will seek refuge in Edom, before being
sent to Mount Zion for his glorification and rapture. The Branch is
the Lamb who as the soul of Jesus shed his blood, his life giving Spirit,
to give eternal life to whosoever believes in Jesus. The Branch will seek
refuge in Edom, probably at the Antichrist's first incursion into Israel,

about the start of the seven year covenant. At the time of the resumption of the seventy weeks of years, the Branch will be sent to Mount Zion for his glorification and rapture. Less than a year later the daughter of Zion, the people of Jerusalem, will flee to Moab. They will flee Jerusalem at its capture by the Antichrist, at the mid-point of the seven year covenant. God commands Moab to hide his outcasts who flee out of Jerusalem. Moab and Edom were within modern day Jordan. After Jesus' second advent, the Branch as Jesus will sit on his throne, judging and hastening righteousness.

Isaiah 16:1—5 (D. Israel)

1   Send the Lamb who will rule the earth, from Sela of the wilderness to the mountain of the daughter of Zion.

2   And it will come to pass that she will flee like a bird; the nest forsaken, the daughters of Moab will be at the fords of the Arnon.

3   Take counsel, do judgment; make your shadow as the night in the middle of the day; hide the outcasts, do not uncover the fugitive.

4   Let My outcasts sojourn with you, Moab. Be a hiding place for them from the face of the destroyer. For the extortioner will cease; the destruction will be finished; the oppressor will be consumed out of the land.

5   And a throne will be established with mercy; and he will sit upon it in faithfulness in the tabernacle of David, judging and seeking justice, and hastening righteousness.

PSALM ONE HUNDRED AND SIXTEEN

1 I love that Yahweh hears My voice, My supplication;

2 for He has inclined His ear to Me, and in My days I have called on Him.

3 The cords of death encompassed me, the straits of Sheol have found me;

4 trouble and sorrow I have found; therefore, on the name of Yahweh I call: "I pray, Yahweh, deliver my soul."

5 Yahweh is gracious and righteous, and our God is merciful; Yahweh watches over the simple.

6 I have been brought low, but because of me He saves.

7 Return, My soul, to your rest, for Yahweh will deal bountifully on account of you.

8 Because You delivered my soul from death, my eyes from tears, and my feet from stumbling,

9 I walk before Yahweh in the lands of the living.

10 I believed; yea, I spoke; I was greatly afflicted.

11 I said in my haste, "all men are untrue."

12 What will I return to Yahweh for all His benefits to me?

13 The cup of salvation I will lift up, and in the name of Yahweh I will call out.

14 My vow to Yahweh I will complete in front, I pray, of all His people.

15 Precious in the eyes of Yahweh is the death of His saints.

16 O Yahweh, truly I am Your servant; I am Your servant, the son of Your handmaid; You have loosened my bond.

17 To you I will offer the sacrifice of praise, and in the name of
Yahweh I will call out.

18 My vow to Yahweh I will complete in front, I pray, of all His
people;

19 in the courts of the house of Yahweh, in your midst, Jerusalem.
Praise Yah!

In Verses 1—2, the Word speaks as Jesus during His first advent. He
states that He loves that Yahweh hears Him, and that during His days
He has called out to Yahweh. Standard translations have changed the
meaning of these verses, having the speaker loving Yahweh, rather than
loving the fact that Yahweh hears Him.

```
(157)pro 3588 8085    3068    853    (6963)pro
I love        that hears Yahweh ---        My voice,


    (8469)pro        3588   5186        (241)pro
My supplication;    for (He) has inclined    His ear

(3807a)pro 2050a(preb)(3117)(pl)pro    pro(7121)
  to Me        and in My days    I have called on
```

(Him).

Verses 3—6 are spoken by Jesus' soul in Sheol, during the three days
and nights after Jesus' death. Jesus was crucified on a Friday, and was
resurrected on Sunday morning, the third day (Mat. 16:21). However,
His soul spent three days and nights in Sheol, the heart of the earth, and
he was taken out of Sheol on Monday afternoon by the resurrected Jesus
(Mat. 12:40).

Matthew 12:40 (NAS) for just as Jonah was three days and
three nights in the belly of the sea monster, so shall the Son of
Man be three days and nights in the heart of the earth.

In verse six, Jesus' soul states that because of him God saves. Standard translations of verse six are very different, but technically acceptable.

(1809)pro   2050a(3807a)pro
I have been brought low, but because of me

pro(3467)
He saves.

God saves because of Jesus' soul, in that Jesus stripped bare His soul to death, stripped bare His soul of his live righteous Spirit at Jesus' death; and in so doing, freed His Spirit to make atonement for the believer by indwelling and making righteous his spirit.

Isaiah 53:12 is a two-legged double-step. Leg one describes the destiny of Jesus' Spirit after Jesus' death, whereas leg two describes the destiny of Jesus' soul after Jesus' death. Jesus' soul stripped bare his Spirit at Jesus' death, and as the soul of the Branch was counted with transgressors of God, until being born again through belief in Jesus. Because the Branch is a transgressor of God, God divides to him justification, like all the many who believe in Jesus.

Isaiah 53:12 (D. Israel)
leg 1 step 1   My righteous servant will justify many,
leg 2 step 1   but their iniquities he will bear.
leg 2 step 2   Therefore, I will divide to him with the many, and he will divide the spoil with the strong; because he will have stripped bare his soul to death, and will be counted with transgressors;
leg 1 step 2   even the sin of many He will lift up, and for transgressors He will reach the mark.

The resurrected Jesus consists of Jesus' glorified spiritual body and His Spirit; which is the seed of God, those parts of Jesus that were conceived at Jesus' conception. It was Jesus' soul who existed before Jesus' conception as the Word; who became flesh, who became Jesus' soul. It is the seed of God who indwells the spirit of the believer, and justifies him, making his spirit righteous and unable to sin. It is the believer's soul that is still capable of sin.

> I John 3:9 (J. P. Green) Everyone who has been begotten of God does not sin, because His seed abides in him, and he is not able to sin, because he has been born of God.

Verse seven is spoken by the resurrected Jesus, who descended into Sheol Monday afternoon, and told His soul to return to his rest. Jesus is telling His soul to return to his rest in Heaven. Jesus' soul was taken out of Sheol to Heaven along with the rest of God's captives that were taken from Sheol to Heaven (Zech. 9:11—12). It was the freeing of Jesus' Spirit at His death, that enabled Him to give live to the spirits of believers of God in Sheol; thus, enabled Him to take them out of Sheol to the stronghold of Heaven. The captives of the hope were those in captivity in Sheol, who had the hope of the resurrection and eternal life.

Zechariah 9:11—12 (D. Israel)
11 Also You, by the blood of Your covenant I will send forth Your captives from the waterless pit.
12 Return to the stronghold, captives of the hope. ——

Verses 8—19 are spoken by the Branch, Jesus' soul being restored to life as the soul of the Branch. Standard translations have poorly translated verses 8-9.

3588   (2502)pro   (5315)pro 4480-(4194) 853
Because You delivered   my soul   from death, ---

(5869)pro 4480-1832) 853 (7272)pro   4480(1762)
my eyes   from tears, ---   my feet from stumbling,

pro(1980) 3807a(6440) 3068   preb(776)pl
  I walk   before   Yahweh in (the) lands (of)

def(2416)pl
the living.

The Branch states that it was because Jesus delivered his soul from death and Sheol, that he walks before Yahweh in the lands of the living. Similarly in Psalm fifty-six, the Branch asks, Were my feet not delivered from stumbling to walk before God in the light of the living? In Psalm fifty-six, the Branch expresses his confidence that God will snatch him from death, given that he believes that he is the Branch; thus, God's vows are upon him to do so. The Branch believes that he is born having Jesus' soul; thus, he believes that his soul was delivered from death and Sheol the day after Jesus' resurrection.

> Psalm 56:11—13 (D. Israel)
> 11 In God, I trust, I will not fear, what can man do to me? Upon me, God, are Your vows.
> 12 I will render thanksgiving to You, for You will snatch my soul from death.
> 13 Were not my feet delivered from stumbling to walk before God in the light of the living?

In verses 10—11, the Branch describes his realization of his identity. He understands and believes that he has indeed been born with Jesus' soul. He believes that his soul spent three days and nights in Sheol, that his soul was taken out of Sheol to Heaven the day after Jesus' resurrection, and that he has been restored to life as the soul of the Branch in the latter years. Because he believes that he is the Branch, he speaks of it, but he is afflicted by the negative response he receives. In Psalm twenty-three, it is Jesus' soul who speaks from Sheol, and looks ahead to being restored to life, after being taken out of Sheol to the pastures of grass and waters of rest of Heaven.

Psalm 23:1—3 (D. Israel)

1   Yahweh is my shepherd, I will not want.

2   He will make me lie down in pastures of grass; He will lead me to waters of rest;

3   He will restore my soul; He will lead me in paths of righteousness for His name's sake.

In verses fourteen and eighteen, the Branch speaks of his vow to Yahweh. Translators have incorrectly made vow plural. The Branch's vow is to lift up the cup of salvation and offer it to the people of Israel, calling out in the name of Yahweh. Standard translations have poorly translated verse thirteen.

    3563   (3444)pl   pro(5375)
(The) cup (of) salvation I will lift up,

2050a(preb)(8034)   3068   pro(7121)
and in (the) name (of) Yahweh   I will call out.

The Branch asks, What will I return to Yahweh for all His benefits to me? The Branch's response is his vow to lift up the cup of salvation and offer it to the people of Israel. Since God has caused him to see into God's salvation (Psalm 91:16), he vows to explain to the people of Israel his insight into God's plan of salvation; for with his effort and with God's help, he will see, he will see into God's plan of salvation.

Isaiah 53:10—11 (D. Israel)

10   But Yahweh will be pleased to crush Him, to make Him sick. When You make his soul guilty, he will see his seed, he will prolong his days, and the pleasure of Yahweh will prosper in his hands.

11   From the work of his soul he will see; he will be satiated with his knowledge.

Psalm 91:14—16 (D. Israel)

14 "Because he will set his love on Me, even I will deliver him, I will set him on high. Because he will know My name, he will call on Me, and I will answer him.

15 I will be with him in distress; I will draw him out of it, and I will honor him.

16 I will have satisfied him with length of days, and I will have caused him to see into My salvation."

PSALM ONE HUNDRED AND EIGHTEEN

1 Give thanks to Yahweh for He is good, for His mercy is everlasting.

2 Let Israel now say that His mercy is everlasting.

3 Let the house of Aaron now say that His mercy is everlasting.

4 Let those who fear Yahweh now say that His mercy is everlasting.

5 Out of distress I will call Yah, He will answer me with the broad place of Yah.

6 Yahweh is for me, I will not fear; what can man do to me?

7 Yahweh is for me among those helping me, and I will look upon those hating me.

8 It is better to seek refuge in Yahweh than trust in man.

9 It is better to seek refuge in Yahweh than trust in princes.

10 All the nations will surround me; in the name of Yahweh, surely I will cut them off.

11 They will surround me, indeed they will surround me; in the name of Yahweh, surely I will cut them off.

12 They will surround me like bees; they will be extinguished like a fire of thorns. In the name of Yahweh, surely I will cut them off.

13 Pushing, you will push me to fall. But Yahweh will help me.

14 My strength and my song is Yah, and He will be my deliverance.

15 The voice of joyful shouting and deliverance is in the tents of the righteous.

16 The right hand of Yahweh will work in strength; the right hand of Yahweh will be exalted; the right hand of Yahweh will work in strength.

17 I will not die; indeed, I will live and I will recount the works of Yah.

18 Chastening, Yah has chastened me, but He will not give me to death.

19 Open to me the gates of righteousness; I will enter into them, I will thank Yah.

20 This is the gate to Yahweh; the righteous will enter into it.

21 I thank You, for You will answer me and be my deliverance.

22 The stone the builders rejected became the head of the corner;

23 this was from Yahweh, it is marvellous in our eyes.

24 Such was the day Yahweh made; we will rejoice and be glad in it.

25 I pray now, Yahweh, deliver; I pray now, Yahweh, make us prosper, please.

26 Blessed is he who comes in the name of Yahweh; we have blessed you from the house of Yahweh.

27 God is Yahweh, and He has given light to us. Bind the sacrificial feast with cords, even to the horns of the alter.

28 You are my God and I thank You; my God, I exalt You.

29 Give thanks to Yahweh for He is good, for His mercy will be everlasting.

Psalm one hundred and eighteen opens similar to Psalm one hundred and sixteen. In Psalm 116:1—2, Jesus speaks from the point in time of His first advent; then in verse three the speaker switches to Jesus' soul, who is in distress in Sheol. In Psalm 118:1—4, Jesus speaks from a point in time that is after His second advent, addressing the people of Israel; then in verse five the speaker switches to the Branch, who is in distress just before his glorification and rapture. Yahweh's mercy that is everlasting refers to His mercy of giving eternal life at the resurrection and rapture. Similarly, In Psalm one hundred and thirty-eight, the Branch describes God's everlasting mercy, when God perfects the church through him at the resurrection and rapture.

Psalm 138:8 (D. Israel) Your right hand, Yahweh, will perfect through me; Yahweh, Your mercy will be everlasting. You will not forsake the works of Your hands.

God will perfect the church through the Branch, given that the Branch will become Jesus at his glorification.

The Branch is the speaker of verses 5—21. In verse five, the Branch states that out of distress he will call on Yah, and that Yah will answer him with the broad place of Yah. At the time of his glorification, his enemies led by the Antichrist will try to kill him. However, the Branch is confident that God will deliver him from his enemies, at his rapture to Heaven, the broad place of Yah. In Psalm 138:7, the Branch again speaks of his confidence that God will deliver him from his enemy.

Psalm 138:7 (D. Israel) When I walk in the midst of distress, You will preserve me. On account of the wrath of my enemy, You will stretch out Your hand and deliver me.

In verses 10—12, the Branch states that all the nations will surround him, but that he will cut them off in the name of Yahweh. The Branch is referring to the battle of Armageddon, when he will have become Jesus. The Word became flesh, became Jesus' soul, who becomes the Branch's soul in the latter years. So, after the Branch's reunification with Jesus his soul is once again Jesus' soul, and in the book of Revelation we see the Word wielding the sword of His Spirit at Jesus' second advent.

Revelation 19:11—15 (NAS)

11 And I saw heaven opened; and behold, a white horse, and He who sat upon it is called Faithful and True; and in righteousness He judges and wages war.

12 And His eyes are a flame of fire, and upon His head are many diadems; and He has a name written upon Him which no one knows except Himself.

13 And He is clothed with a robe dipped in blood; and His name is called the Word of God.

14 And the armies which are in heaven, clothed in fine linen, white and clean, were following Him on white horses.

15 And from His mouth comes a sharp sword, so that with it He may smite the nations; and He will rule them with a rod of iron; and He treads the wine press of the fierce wrath of God, the Almighty.

In verse thirteen, the Branch describes someone who pushes at him to cause him to fall. The Branch is referring to the Antichrist, the trapper of Psalm 91:3, the man of violence of Psalm 140:4. The verb that is translated as "pushing" in verse thirteen is the same verb that is translated as "trip up" in Psalm 140:4.

Psalm 140:4—5 (D. Israel)

4 Keep me, Yahweh, from the hands of the wicked; preserve me from the man of violence who plans to trip up my steps.

5 The proud have hidden a trap for me, and cords; they have spread a net by the wayside; they have set snares for me. Selah.

The Antichrist will know that the Branch must make his way to Mount Zion at the time of his glorification. So, the Antichrist's confederates will set ambushes for him along the way.

In verses 15—16, the voice of joyful shouting and deliverance will be in the dwellings of the righteous, after the Branch's deliverance at his glorification and rapture. At that point in time, the righteous will know that it will be less than a year, until their deliverance at the rapture of the church. The right hand of Yahweh will work in strength and be exalted at the rapture of the church. Following the rapture, the right hand of Yahweh will work in strength at the battle of Armageddon. In Psalm one hundred and eight, the Branch prays for his deliverance so that God's beloved ones, the church, can be delivered at the rapture. He prays that

God be exalted above the heavens, and His glory be above all the earth at the rapture of the church.

> Psalm 108:5—6 (D. Israel)
> 5 Be exalted above the heavens, God, and may Your glory be above all the earth.
> 6 So that Your beloved ones may be delivered, deliver me with Your right hand, even answer me.

In verses 17—18, the Branch states that he will not die, that God will not give him to death. The Branch knows this because God's vows are upon him. The Branch believes that he is indeed the Branch, he whose soul was Jesus' soul who was delivered from death and Sheol, to walk before Yahweh in the lands of the living. (Psalm 116:8—9)

> Psalm 116:8—9 (D. Israel)
> 8 Because You delivered my soul from death, my eyes from tears, my feet from stumbling,
> 9 I walk before Yahweh in the lands of the living.

Therefore, he knows that God's vows are upon him to snatch him from death at his glorification and rapture.

> Psalm 56:11—13 (D. Israel)
> 11 In God I trust, I will not fear; what can man do to me? Upon me, God, are Your vows.
> 12 I will render thanksgiving to You, for You will snatch my soul from death.
> 13 Were not me feet delivered from stumbling to walk before God in the light of the living?

In verse eighteen, chastening will have been put upon the Branch by God, in order that he learn God's word.

Psalm 119:67—71 (D. Israel)

67 Before I was afflicted I went astray, but now I keep Your word.

68 You are good and do good; teach me Your statutes.

69 The proud have forged a lie against me; I with all my heart will keep Your precepts.

70 Insensitive like fat are their hearts; I delight in Your law.

71 It was good for me that I was afflicted, so that I might learn Your statutes.

Chastening will also be upon the Branch, because he is born with Jesus' soul. Chastening was upon Jesus so that humankind's sickness of sin could be healed.

Isaiah 53:5 (D. Israel)

Nevertheless our sickness He has lifted up, and our sorrows He has carried, though we regarded Him stricken by God and afflicted; but He was wounded on account of our transgressions, crushed on account of our iniquities, chastening for our completeness was upon Him, and with His wound it is healed for us.

Jesus' death enabled His Spirit to indwell the believer and make atonement for him, making the believer's spirit righteous. However, Jesus' death resulted in Jesus' soul becoming a transgressor of God as the soul of the Branch, until he is born again through belief in Jesus; thus, he obtains peace with God. He who knew no sin, God gave sin as the soul of the Branch, so that we might become the righteousness of God in Jesus' Spirit (II Cor. 5:21). The chastening of the cross carried over to the Branch's soul, in that he is born a sinner.

In verses 19—20, the Branch asks that the gates of righteousness, the gate to Yahweh be opened to him. He is asking that the gates of Heaven be opened to him at his glorification and rapture. Less than a year after the Branch's rapture, the righteous will enter the gate to Yahweh at the resurrection and rapture of the church. Psalm twenty-four describes the Branch and his glorification and rapture. The Branch is he who will receive the blessing of Jacob to stand up in Yahweh's holy place, and become ruler of the nations. The Branch will first be reunited with Jesus; thus, he will become Jesus; and then Jesus will be anointed with the fullness of Yahweh's Spirit on Mount Zion (Palm 2:6—7); thus, He will become as Yahweh. In Psalm twenty-four, the gates of righteousness are described as the everlasting doors.

Psalm 24:3—10 (D. Israel)

3   Who will go up upon the mountain of Yahweh, and who will stand up in His holy place?

4   One who will have clean hands and a pure heart, who will not have lifted up his soul to vanity, and will not have sworn to deceit.

5   He will lift up the blessing from Yahweh, and righteousness from the God of his salvation.

6   This one a generation will seek, those who will seek your face, Jacob.

7   Lift up your heads, O gates, and be lifted up, O everlasting doors, and the King of glory will come in.

8   Who is the King of glory? Yahweh powerful and mighty, Yahweh mighty in battle.

9   Lift up your heads, O gates, and be lifted up, O everlasting doors, and the King of glory will come in.

10 Who is He, this King of glory? Yahweh of hosts, He is the King of glory.

Verses 22—27 are spoken be an anonymous contemporary of the Branch, who has gained understanding from the Branch's teaching. The Branch's contemporary will understand that when the Branch became a born again Christian, the stone rejected by the builders became the head of the corner. Standard translations have destroyed Psalm 118:22.

68	3988 def(1129)pl	1961
(The) stone rejected the builders		became

3807a(7218)	6438
---- (the) head (of) (the) corner;	

Jesus was rejected by the builders, the Jewish priests, as the Son of God. The Son of God, the seed of God, are those parts of Jesus that were conceived at Jesus' conception. The resurrected Jesus is the Son of God, consisting of His glorified spiritual body and His Spirit. It was the Word who was the corner who existed before Jesus' conception, who emptied Himself of God at Jesus' conception and became flesh, became Jesus' soul. So, when the Branch becomes a born again Christian, the stone rejected by the builders became the head of the corner, just as Jesus becomes the head of all the members of His church when they are born again (Ephesians 1:22—23).

In verse twenty-five, the Branch's contemporary prays for Yahweh to deliver, and to make the people of Israel prosper. At this point in time, that is just before the Branch's deliverance at his rapture, the nation of Israel will not be at war. Israel will have entered into a seven year covenant with the Antichrist. However, the Branch's contemporary will understand that the Antichrist will break the covenant with them, and will capture Jerusalem at the mid-point of the seven year covenant. The Branch's contemporary will understand that the Branch must first be delivered at his glorification and rapture, before the righteous can be delivered at the resurrection and rapture of the church. So, he is praying first for the Branch's deliverance, then for the church's deliverance, and then for prosperity for Israel after Jesus' second advent.

In verse twenty-six, the Branch's contemporary states, Blessed is he who comes in the name of Yahweh. He is referring to the Branch coming to Mount Zion for his glorification and rapture. Jesus stated just before His death, that the people of Jerusalem wouldn't see Him again until they say, Blessed is he who comes in the name of the Lord (Mat. 23:39). The people of Jerusalem will see Jesus again, immediately upon the Branch's glorification, at which time the Branch will become Jesus.

In verse twenty-seven, the Branch's contemporary states that Yahweh has given them light, has given them understanding. Those in Israel who have listened to the Branch's teaching will understand that the Branch must be reunited with Jesus. They will understand that mercy and truth must meet together, that righteousness and peace must kiss. They will understand that truth and peace symbolize the Branch, who has sprung up from the earth; whereas mercy and righteousness symbolize Jesus, who looks down from Heaven.

Psalm 85:10-11 (D. Israel)

10   That glory may dwell in our land, mercy and truth must meet together, righteousness and peace must kiss.

11   Truth has sprung up out of the earth, and righteousness looks down from Heaven.

Because of their understanding, the people at the temple will cry out to God, Bind the sacrificial feast with cords, even to the horns of the alter. This will be their cry for the reunification of the Branch with Jesus. The sacrificial feast symbolizes Jesus' soul, who has become the Branch's soul; whereas the blood smeared on the horns of the alter symbolizes Jesus' life giving Spirit. On the day of atonement, the goat for the sin offering symbolizes Jesus who died to make atonement for whosoever believes in Him (Leviticus 16:9). The sacrificial feast of the sin offering is described in Leviticus 4:1—10, and consists of the fat that covers the inwards of the slain goat (Leviticus 4:8—9). The blood of the slain goat for the sin offering was smeared on the horns of the alter of sweet incense before Yahweh (Leviticus 4:7), whereas the sacrificial feast was burnt on the alter of burnt offering (Leviticus 4:10). At Jesus' rejection by the Jewish priests, the people cried out to Pilate for Jesus' death by crucifixion. The result of Jesus' death was the separation of Jesus' soul and Spirit; thus, Jesus' death interrupted the Jewish dispensation, and begun the age of grace or church age. At the acceptance of Jesus as Israel's Messiah and King, the people will cry out to God for Jesus' super-natural birth. The result of Jesus' super-natural birth will be the end of the church age, and the resumption of the seventy weeks of years of the Jewish dispensation.

The speaker of verses 28—29 is the Branch, who speaks these verses just as he is about to be glorified and raptured. The Branch thanks Yahweh for what He is about to do at his glorification and rapture. The Branch then exhorts the people to give thanks to Yahweh, for He is good. The Branch states that God's mercy will be everlasting. Like verses 1—4, God's mercy that is everlasting refers to God's mercy to the church, at giving believers eternal life at the resurrection and rapture. The resurrection and rapture of the church will occur less than a year after the Branch's glorification and rapture.

PSALM ONE HUNDRED AND NINETEEN

126 It is time to work for Yahweh; they have made void Your law.
127 Therefore I love Your commandments more than gold, even
more than fine gold.
128 Therefore, all the precepts, the totality, I will make straight;
every way of falsehood I hate.

Psalm one hundred and nineteen is spoken by the Branch. It is written
in an alphabetical arrangement. Sets of eight verses each begin with the
same letter of the Hebrew alphabet. Because of this arrangement, there
isn't much flow of thought to the psalm. The main theme of the psalm is
the Branch's love for God's Word. In verses 126—128, the Branch states
that it is time to work for Yahweh, because they have made void His law.
Standard translations have destroyed verses 126—128.

     6256   3807a(6213) 3807a(3068)
(It is) time   to work   for Yahweh;

    (6565)pro   (8451)pro
they have made void Your law.

5921-3651 (157)pro   (4687)pro
Therefore   I love   Your commandments

4480(2091)   2050a(4480)(6337)
more than gold, even more than fine gold,

5921-3651 3605   (6490)pl   3605
Therefore,   all (the) precepts, (the) totality,

(3474)pro   3605 734   8267 (8130)pro
I will make straight; every way (of) falsehood I hate.

One of several errors that standard translations have made in these verses is to flip flop the order of two prepositional phrases. By so doing, they have made it time for Yahweh to work, rather than time for the speaker to work. These very verses are an example of what the Branch is referring to in Psalm 119:126—128. Theologians have made void important parts of God's law, God's Word, by poor translation and teaching. Like gold that is covered over by worthless material, God's precepts have been covered over with incorrect translations and false teaching. Much of God's plan of salvation as set forth in God's law of the Old Testament has been made void by incorrect translations. So, part of the Branch's work will be to set straight God's precepts, that deal with His plan of salvation. God's plan of salvation could be considered the foundation of God's Word. However, incorrect translation has knocked the foundation out of level; thus, the totality of God's Word has been knocked out of level. The Branch's work is to set straight the totality of God's precepts by setting straight its foundation. In Palm forty-five, the Branch also describes his work for Yahweh. He speaks his work for Yahweh the King with the stylus of a rapid writer, a modern day computer.

Psalm 45:1 (D. Israel) My heart is astir with a good matter. I speak my work for the King, my tongue being the stylus of a rapid writer.

PSALM ONE HUNDRED AND THIRTY-EIGHT

A PSALM OF DAVID.

1   I will thank You with my whole heart; I will sing to You before the gods.

2   I will bow down toward Your holy temple, and give thanks to Your name on account of Your mercy and Your faithfulness; for You will magnify Your word according to all Your name.

3   In the day I call even You will answer me; You will make me bold with strength in my soul.

4   All the kings of the earth will thank You, Yahweh, for they will hear the words of Your mouth.

5   And they will sing in the ways of Yahweh, for the glory of Yahweh will be great.

6   Yea, Yahweh will be exalted, yet the humble He will see; but the proud He will know from afar.

7   When I walk in the miss of distress, You will preserve me. On account of the wrath of my enemy, You will stretch out Your hand and deliver me.

8   Your right hand, Yahweh, will perfect through me; Yahweh, Your mercy will be everlasting. You will not forsake the works of Your hands.

Psalm one hundred and thirty-eight is spoken by the Branch. In verses 1—2, the Branch looks ahead to Jesus' millennial reign. At that time, the Branch will have become Jesus, and God's mercy will have been given to the church at the resurrection and rapture. God will have magnified His Word by fulfilling His promises in His Word, to those who humbled themselves and accepted Jesus as their Lord. In verse three, the Branch will call on Yahweh on the day of acceptance, the day that Israel officially accepts Jesus as her Messiah and King. This is the day of the Branch's deliverance, by being glorified and then raptured to Heaven. In Isaiah forty-nine, Yahweh states that He will answer the Branch at the time of acceptance. Yahweh will answer the Branch by glorifying him, then snatching him away at his rapture. In Isaiah 49:7, the Branch is referred to as the despised soul, because he is born with Jesus' soul, Jesus being despised by Israel as a false Messiah.

Isaiah 49:7—8 (D. Israel)

7   Thus says Yahweh, the Redeemer of Israel, his Holy One, to the despised soul, to the one hated by the nation, to the servant of rules, "Kings will see and stand up, leaders also will bow down on account of Yahweh who is faithful, the Holy One of Israel, even He has chosen you."

8   Thus says Yahweh, "At the time of acceptance I will answer you, and in the day of deliverance I will help you. For I will keep you and give you for a covenant of the people to restore the earth, to cause to inherit the desolated heritages";

In Psalm one hundred and eighteen, the Branch also speaks of Yahweh answering him and being his deliverance, at his rapture through the gates of righteousness of Heaven.

Psalm 118:19—21 (D. Israel)

19 Open to me the gates of righteousness; I will enter into them, I will thank Yah.

20 This is the gate to Yahweh; the righteous will enter into it.

21 I thank You, for You will answer me and be my deliverance.

Verses 4—6 describe the millennium, when Yahweh's great glory will be evident to all on earth. In verse seven, the Branch expresses his confidence that Yahweh will preserve him, and snatch him from the wrath of his enemy. His enemy is the Antichrist, the man of violence. Standard translation have incorrectly made enemy plural. In Psalm one hundred and forty, the Branch prays that God deliver him from the Antichrist, the man of violence.

Psalm 140:4—5 (D. Israel)

4 Keep me, Yahweh, from the hands of the wicked; preserve me from the man of violence who plans to trip up my steps.

5 The proud have hidden a trap for me, and cords; they have spread a net by the wayside; they have set snares for me. Selah.

The Branch is confident that Yahweh will deliver him from his enemy, because he believes that he indeed is the Branch who has God's vows upon him.

Psalm 56:11—13 (D. Israel)

11 In God I trust, I will not fear, what can man do to me? Upon me, God, are Your vows.

12 I will render thanksgiving to You, for You will snatch my soul from death.

13 Were not my feet delivered from stumbling to walk before God in the light of the living?

He believes that he is born having Jesus' soul, who was delivered from death and Sheol after Jesus' death, to walk before Yahweh as the soul of the Branch in the latter years. Therefore, he believes that Yahweh's vows are upon him to keep him and deliver him. In Psalm one hundred and sixteen, the Branch speaks of being delivered from death and Sheol, and walking in the lands of the living. He will walk in the lands of the living in the latter years, after being in Sheol during the three days and nights after Jesus' death (Psalm 116:3—6), and after the resurrected Jesus takes his soul out of Sheol to Heaven (Psalm 116:7).

Psalm 116:8—9 (D. Israel)

8   Because You delivered my soul from death, my eyes from tears, and my feet from stumbling,

9   I walk before Yahweh in the lands of the living.

Verse eight has been destroyed by standard translations. In verse eight the Branch states that Yahweh will perfect through him; given that he will become Jesus at his glorification, and it will be through Jesus that Yahweh will perfect the church at the resurrection and rapture.

(3225)pro   3068   1584   (1157)pro
Your right hand, Yahweh, will perfect through me;

3068   (2617)pro   3807a(5769)
Yahweh, Your mercy (will be) everlasting. (The)

(4639)pl   (3027)(pl)pro 3808   pro(7503)
works (of)   Your hands not   You will forsake.

Again in Psalm fifty-seven, the Branch states that Yahweh will perfect through him, after he is delivered from the Antichrist, the one who pants after him.

Psalm 57:1—3 (D. Israel)

1   Be merciful to me, God, be merciful for my soul seeks refuge with You; even in the shadow of Your wings I seek refuge until the destruction passes.

2   I cry to God Most High, to God who will perfect through me.

3   He will send from Heaven and deliver me, reproaching the one who pants after me.——

At the perfection of the church at its resurrection and rapture, God's mercy to the righteous will be everlasting. God will not forsake the righteous, the works of His hands.

PSALM ONE HUNDRED AND FORTY

TO THE CHIEF MUSICIAN, A PSALM OF DAVID.

1 Deliver me, Yahweh, from the evil man; preserve me from the man of violence,

2 who devise evil things in the heart; each day they stir up wars.

3 They sharpen their tongues like a snake; a viper's poison is under their lips. Selah.

4 Keep me, Yahweh, from the hands of the wicked; preserve me from the man of violence who plans to trip up my steps.

5 The proud have hidden a trap for me, and cords; they have spread a net by the wayside; they have set snares for me. Selah.

6 I will say to Yahweh, "You are my God." Hear, Yahweh, the voice of my prayer.

7 Yahweh the Lord will be the power of my deliverance; You will overshadow my head in the day of battle.

8 Do not grant, Yahweh, the desires of the wicked; do not let his evil plan succeed, and they be exalted.

9 As for the head of those who will surround me, the mischief of their lips will cover them.

10 Coals will fall on them; He will cast them into the fire, into deep pits from which they will not rise.

11 The man of the tongue will not be established in the earth; evil will hunt the man of violence to overthrow him.

12 I know that Yahweh will execute the cause of the afflicted, and the right of the poor.

13 Surely the righteous will give thanks to Your name; the righteous will dwell in Your presence.

In Psalm one hundred and forty, the Branch is the speaker. He speaks this psalm when he is preparing to go from Sela in Edom, in modern day Jordan, to Mount Zion for his glorification and rapture. Psalm one hundred and eight describes the fact that the Branch will have sought refuge in Edom, before he is sent to Mount Zion for his glorification and rapture.

Psalm 108:10—11 (D. Israel)
10 Who will bring me to the strong city? Who will lead me as far as Edom?
11 Will not God? You have cast us off, God, and have not gone out with out armies.

Isaiah sixteen describes the Lamb who is the Branch, who is sent from Sela in Edom to Mount Zion for his glorification and rapture.

Isaiah 16:1 (D. Israel) Send the Lamb who will rule the earth, from Sela in the wilderness to the mountain of the daughter of Zion.

In verse one, the Branch describes an evil man and a man of violence, from whom he seeks deliverance. There are lots of evil men and lots of violent men, but few of either are in a position to stir up wars. These men will be in positions of power. According to the Branch, the fate of these men is to be cast into the fire (Verse 10). So, the evil man would be the false prophet of Revelation 13:11—18, and the man of violence would be the Antichrist who is indwelt by the beast from the abyss (Rev. 13:1—8; 17:8). These are the two who will be cast into the fire (Rev. 19:20).

In verses 4—5, the Branch asks God to preserve him from the man of violence. The Branch states that the man of violence plans to trip up his steps, and has set traps by the wayside. The Antichrist will know that the Branch must make his way from Sela to Mount Zion for his glorification. So, the Antichrist will have his confederates set a net to trap the Branch along his journey. Similarly, in Psalm 57:6, the Branch testifies that a net has been prepared for his steps. The net is set by the confederates of the Antichrist, the one who pants after him. In Psalm 57:2—4, the Branch first identifies himself by stating that God will perfect through him. God will perfect through him at the resurrection and rapture, after he has become Jesus. The Branch further identifies himself by testifying that he lay among those on fire. Since the Branch is born having Jesus' soul, he lay among those on fire in Sheol, for the three days and three nights after Jesus' death.

Psalm 57:2—6 (D. Israel)

2   I cry to God Most High, to God who will perfect through me.

3   He will send from Heaven and deliver me, reproaching the one who pants after me, Selah. God will send His mercy and His truth.

4   My soul was in the midst of lions; I lay among those on fire; the sons of men, their teeth were spears and arrows; their tongues were sharp swords.

5   Be exalted above the heavens, God, and may Your glory be over all the earth.

6   They have prepared a net for my steps; my soul is bowed down; they have dug a pit for me, they will fall into the midst of it. Selah.

ISAIAH 9:1–7

1 —— He will have degraded the land of Zebulun and the land of Naphtali, but later He will glorify the way of the sea beyond Jordan, Galilee of the nations.

2 The people who walk in darkness will see a great light; those dwelling in the land of the shadow of death, light will shine upon them.

3 You will multiply the nation, but the joy will not increase. They will rejoice before You like the rejoicing at harvest, when they rejoice at their dividing of the spoil.

4 For the yoke of his burden and the staff on his shoulder, the rod of the oppressor, will be broken as the day of Midian.

5 For every boot of the one trampling will be with trembling, but his garment will be rolled in blood; even it will be for burning, fuel for the fire.

6 For a child will be born to us, a son will be given to us; and the government will be on His shoulders; and His name will be called Wonderful Counselor, Mighty God, Everlasting Father, Prince of Peace;

7 to the greatness of the government and to peace there will be no end, being on the throne of David and over his kingdom, to establish it and to sustain it with justice and with righteousness from then even to forever. The zeal of Yahweh of hosts will accomplish this.

Isaiah 9:1 describes Jesus' ministry in Galilee (Mat. 4:12—16). Verse three skips ahead in time, and describes when God multiplies the nation of Israel as a result of the 1967 war. However, even though Israel's territories were multiplied at that time, it doesn't bring her joy. The last part of verse three has been poorly translated by standard translations.

(8055)pro	3807a(6440)pro	prek(8057
They will rejoice	before You	like (the) rejoicing

preb(7105) prek(834)	(1523)pro	preb(2505)pro
at harvest, when	they rejoice	at their dividing

```
        7998
(of) (the) spoil.
```

Verse three skips ahead in time again, and describes joy that will come to Israel. This describes the joy of dividing the spoil taken from the nations of the last oppressor of Israel. The Antichrist is the last oppressor of Israel, who will first pass through Israel to conquer Egypt, but then return to lay siege and capture Jerusalem.

> Zechariah 9:8 (D. Israel) And I will encamp about My house, because of an army from he who will have passed through, even from he who will have returned; and an oppressor will not pass over them again, for then I will see with My eyes.

It will be the nations under the Antichrist that trample Jerusalem under foot, for the last half of the seven year covenant (Rev. 11:2). After the battle of Armageddon, the people of Israel who join the battle will divide the spoil, the spoil taken from the nations who come against them at Jesus' second advent.

> Zechariah 14:14 (NAS) And Judah will also fight at Jerusalem; and the wealth of the surrounding nations will be gathered, gold and silver and garments in great abundance.

Verses 4—5 describe the event that allows the people of Israel to divide the spoil, that event being the defeat of the armies of the Antichrist. Verse six describes who is responsible for the defeat of the Antichrist's armies. He who defeats the Antichrist is the child who is born to the nation of Israel, and immediately has the government on his shoulders. Verse six is describing Jesus' super-natural birth on Mount Zion to the nation of Israel, not His natural birth at Bethlehem to Mary. Isaiah 9:6 parallels Revelation 12:5. In both verses, the responsibility of ruling the nations as God is immediately placed upon Him at His birth. In Isaiah 9:6, the government is immediately upon His shoulders, whereas in Revelation 12:5 He is immediately caught up to the throne of God.

Revelation 12:1—5 (NAS)

1   And a great sign appeared in heaven: a woman clothed with the sun, and the moon under her feet, and on her head a crown of twelve stars;

2   and she was with child; and she cried out, being in labor and in pain to give birth.

3   And another sign appeared in heaven: and behold, a great red dragon having seven heads and ten horns, and on his heads were seven diadems.

4   And his tail swept away a third of the stars of heaven, and threw them to the earth. And the dragon stood before the woman who was about to give birth, so that when she gave birth he might devour her child.

5   And she gave birth to a son, a male child, who is to rule all the nations with a rod of iron; and her child was caught up to God and to His throne.

Verse six gives the names that Jesus will be called at His super-natural birth. To understand the names given to Jesus, we must first recognize that this birth is Jesus' super-natural birth to the nation of Israel, the reunification of His soul and Spirit, not His natural birth to Mary. Once we recognize that this is Jesus' super-natural birth, we can recognize that the last three names actually are descriptions of three events that relate to the soul of Jesus, who is born into the tribe of Joseph as the Branch. And we can recognize that these events are listed in chronological order. Mighty God describes what happens to the Branch's soul at the birth, at his reunification with Jesus at Jesus' super-natural birth. The Branch is then Jesus; thus, he is Mighty God. Everlasting Father describes the fact that immediately after the reunification of Jesus' soul and Spirit, Jesus is indwelt with the fullness of the Father's Spirit; thus, He is Everlasting Father. Prince of Peace describes the fact that Jesus establishes world wide peace, after defeating the Antichrist at His second advent; thus, He is Prince of Peace. So, since the last three names are listed in chronological order, and Jesus' soul once again becomes Mighty God at Jesus' super-natural birth, we can deduce that Wonderful Counselor must be a name that relates to the Branch's soul at a point in time that is before Jesus' super-natural birth.

Wonderful Counselor describes the Branch, who counsels the people of Israel regarding God's plan of salvation, and counsels them in regard to the wonder of the latter year pouring out of God's Spirit. So, the Branch is Wonderful Counselor. So indeed, the son that is born to the nation of Israel in the last days will be appropriately called Wonderful Counselor, Mighty God, Everlasting Father, Prince of Peace.

As verse seven states, the child that is born to the nation of Israel will be on the throne from then to forever. He will establish and sustain His throne with justice and righteousness.

ISAIAH 11:1-4

1   And a shoot will come forth from the stem of Jesse, and a branch
    from his roots will bear fruit.
2   And the Spirit of Yahweh will rest upon Him, the spirit of wis-
    dom and understanding, the spirit of counsel and might, the
    spirit of knowledge and the fear of Yahweh.
3   And He will delight in the fear of Yahweh, and He will not
    judge by the sight of His eyes, nor will He decide by the hearing
    of His ears.
4   But He will judge the poor with righteousness, and decide with
    equity for the humble of the earth; and He will strike the earth
    with the rod of His mouth, even with the Spirit of His lips He
    will slay the wicked.

Isaiah 11:1—4 describe the coming Messiah. Verse one describes
the fact that the Messiah will be a descendant of Jesse, and also a descendant of a branch from an ancestor of Jesse. Jesus was the descendant
of Jesse, being from the tribe of Judah. The Branch is the descendant of
the branch of an ancestor of Jesse, being from the tribe of Joseph. The
Branch is a descendant of Jesse's ancestor Jacob, through Jacob's son
Joseph. Similar to Isaiah 11:1, Genesis 49:22 describes that the Branch
will be fruitful. Genesis 49:26 describes that he will receive the blessing
of Jacob, the blessing of becoming the ruler of the nations. The blessing to rule the nations was originally given to Jacob (Genesis 27:29),
but was passed on to both Judah (Genesis 49:10) and Joseph (Genesis
49:26).

Genesis 49:22—26 (D. Israel)

22 "Joseph will be a fruitful branch, a fruitful branch on account of a spring;

23 his branches will go over the wall, and the masters of arrows will vex him, and shoot at and hate him;

24 but his bow will abide with strength, and the arms of his hands will be agile from the hands of the Mighty One of Jacob; from there will be the Shepherd, the Stone of Israel,

25 from the God of your father; and he will help you; then together with the Almighty, even He will bless you with the blessings of the heavens above, the blessings of the deep lying below, and the blessings of the breasts and the womb.

26 The blessings of your father have prevailed over the blessings of my progenitors; as far as the summit of the everlasting hill they will be for the head of Joseph, and for the crown of the head of the prince of his brothers."

Jeremiah describes the one from the tribe of Joseph who will be raised up to David. The Branch will be born a sinner, then will become a born again Christian, and then will be reunited with Jesus and will become Jesus, the Davidic King. He will be called Yahweh our righteousness, because immediately after he becomes Jesus he is anointed with the fullness of Yahweh's Spirit, and because Jesus is our righteousness.

Jeremiah 23:5—6 (D. Israel)

5 "Behold, days are coming," says Yahweh, "that I will raise up to David a righteous Branch; and a King will reign and prosper, and do justice and righteousness in the earth.

6 In His days Judah will be saved, and Israel will dwell safely; and this will be His name by which He will be called, Yahweh our righteousness."

In Zechariah 3:1—9, Joshua symbolizes the Branch (verse 8).

Zechariah 3:1—9 (D. Israel)

1   And he showed me Joshua the high priest standing before the angel of Yahweh, and Satan standing at his right hand to oppose him.

2   And Yahweh said to Satan, "Yahweh rebukes you, Satan; yea, Yahweh who has chosen Jerusalem rebukes you. Is this not a brand snatched from the fire?"

3   And Joshua was clothed with filthy garments, and stood before the angel.

4   And he spoke and said to those standing before him, saying, "Remove the filthy garments from him." And he said to him, "See, I have removed your iniquity, and will clothe you with stately robes";

5   and said that they should put a clean turban on his head. So they put the clean turban on his head, and clothed him with clothes. And the angel of Yahweh stood by.

6   And the angel of Yahweh admonished Joshua, saying,

7   "Thus says Yahweh of hosts, 'If you walk in My way, and if you keep My charge, then you will also govern My house and keep My court; and I will give you access among these who stand by.

8   Hear now, Joshua the high priest, you and your fellows who sit before you, for they are the men in the sign; for behold, I will bring forth My servant the Branch.

9   For behold, the stone that I have set before Joshua, on one stone are seven eyes. Behold, I have engraved its engravings,' says Yahweh of hosts, 'and I will remove the iniquity of the land in one day.'"

Just like Joshua, the Branch will be born a sinner, and will need God to remove his iniquity (Zech. 3:3—4). Joshua was admonished to walk in Yahweh's way, and to keep Yahweh's charge. If he did so, Joshua would govern God's house, and keep God's court (Zech. 3:6—7). So too, if the Branch walks in Yahweh's way and keeps His charge, he will govern

God's house and keep God's courts after his glorification. The stone set before Joshua symbolizes Jesus, and the seven eyes symbolize the seven spirits of Yahweh. The stone set before Joshua indicates what awaits the Branch at his glorification. At the Branch's glorification, he will be reunited with Jesus; thus, he will become Jesus, who is then anointed with the fullness of Yahweh's Spirit on Mount Zion (Psalm 2:6—7). In addition, the Branch who will have become Jesus will have all seven of the spirits of Yahweh (Rev. 5:6).

Again in Zechariah 6:11—13, Joshua symbolizes the Branch. It will be the Branch who will lift up the glory at his glorification, to sit on his throne as priest and King.

Zechariah 6:11—13 (D. Israel)

11 "And take silver and gold, and make crowns and set them on the head of Joshua the son of Jehozadak.

12 And speak to him, saying, 'Thus says Yahweh of hosts, saying, "Behold a man, the Branch is his name; and from his place he will spring up; and he will build the temple of Yahweh;

13 Even he will build the temple of Yahweh; and he will lift up the glory, and he will sit and rule on his throne; and he will be a priest on his throne, and the counsel of peace will between the two offices.""

Isaiah 11:2 describes that Yahweh's Spirit will rest upon the Messiah. Yahweh's Spirit rested upon Jesus from His baptism with God's Holy Spirit until His death; and will rest upon Jesus again, immediately after the Branch's glorification at being reunited with Jesus. Verse two also describes six of the seven spirits of Yahweh, that will rest upon the Messiah. The seventh spirit of Yahweh is not listed here, because Jesus had no need of it at His first advent; thus, He was not yet given it. The seventh spirit of Yahweh is the spirit of judgment, and is described two times in Scripture. The spirit of judgment will be needed by Jesus, for example, at His second advent. The spirit of judgment will be needed when He sits over the judgment of the wicked. Jesus did not come to judge at His first advent (John 8:15), but judgment was given Him to execute at His second advent. (John 5:22—27).

John 5:22—27 (NAS)

22 "For not even the Father judges anyone, but He has given all judgment to the Son,

23 in order that all may honor the Son, even as they honor the Farther. He who does not honor the Son does not honor the Father who sent Him.

24 "Truly, truly, I say to you, he who hears My word, and believes Him who sent Me, has eternal life, and does not come into judgment, but has passed out of death into life.

25 "Truly, truly, I say to you an hour is coming and now is, when the dead shall hear the voice of the Son of God; and those who hear shall live.

26 "For just as the Father has life in Himself, even so He gave to the Son also to have life in Himself;

27 and He gave Him authority to execute judgment, because He is the Son of Man."

In John 5:25, the dead refer to the spiritually dead, those of the spiritually dead who hear and believe Jesus' words have eternal life. Jesus was not given the spirit of judgment for His first advent, but will have the spirit of judgment for His second advent. The spirit of judgment is described twice in Isaiah.

Isaiah 4:3—4 (D. Israel)

3 And it will come to pass that the one who remains in Zion, and who is left in Jerusalem, holy will be said of him, everyone who is written among the living in Jerusalem.

4   When the Lord will have washed away the filth of the daughters
    of Zion, and will have purged the blood of Jerusalem from its
    midst by the spirit of judgment, even the spirit of burning.

Isaiah 28:5—6 (D. Israel)

5   In that day Yahweh of hosts will become a crown of glory, and
    a diadem of beauty to the remnant of His people;

6   and the spirit of judgment for He who sits over the judgment,
    and might for those turning back the battle to the gate.

So, the seven spirits of Yahweh are: the spirit of wisdom, the spirit
of understanding, the spirit of counsel, the spirit of might, the spirit
of knowledge, the spirit of the fear of Yahweh, and the spirit of
judgment.

Jesus will strike the earth with the rod of His mouth, with the Spirit
of His lips, at His second advent. The rod of Jesus' mouth is the sword
of His mouth (Isaiah 49:2), which is His Spirit. In Isaiah 49:1—3, Jesus
is the speaker, speaking from a point in time that is after His second
advent. He is reflecting back to when His soul became the Branch's soul;
and He describes the fact that the Branch's soul was reunited with Jesus,
at the making of his mouth like a sharp sword.

Isaiah 49:1—3 (D. Israel)

1   Listen to Me, coasts, and pay attention, peoples from afar. Since
    the womb Yahweh called Me; since the belly of My mother
    bringing to remembrance My name.

2   And He made My mouth like a sharp sword, in the shadow of
    His hand He hid Me. Even He made Me a choice arrow, in His
    quiver He hid Me.

3   And He said to Me, "You are My servant, Israel, You in whom I
    will be glorified."

It was the Word who became Jesus' soul, who then becomes the Branch's soul; who once again becomes Jesus' soul at the Branch's glorification, who wields the sword of His Spirit at Jesus' second advent.

Revelation 19:11—15 (NAS)

11 And I saw heaven opened; and behold, a white horse, and He who sat upon it is called Faithful and True; and in righteousness He judges and wages war.

12 And His eyes are a flame of fire, and upon His head are many diadems; and He has a name written upon Him which no one knows except Himself.

13 And He is clothed with a robe dipped in blood; and His name is called the Word of God.

14 And the armies which are in heaven, clothed in fine linen, white and clean, were following Him on white horses.

15 And from His mouth comes a sharp sword, so that with it He may smite the nations; and He will rule them with a rod of iron; and He treads the wine press of the fierce wrath of God, the Almighty.

Jesus will come out of he midst of the church at His reunification with the Branch; and at Jesus' second advent the Branch who will have become Jesus' soul will consume the Antichrist with his reacquired Spirit, the Spirit of His mouth.

II Thessalonians 2:7—8 (D. Israel)

7 For the mystery of lawlessness already works; only He is restraining him now until He comes out of the midst.

8 And then the lawless one will be revealed, whom the Lord will consume with the Spirit of His mouth, and will destroy by the appearance of His coming;

At the time of the Branch's glorification, he is commanded to gird on the sword of his Spirit, his glory and his majesty.

Psalm 45:3—5 (D. Israel)

3   Gird your sword on your thigh, Mighty One, your glory and
    your majesty.

4   And in Your majesty prosper; ride on the matter of truth and
    meekness and righteousness, and Your right hand will teach You
    fearful things.

5   Your arrows are sharp — people fall under you — in the heart
    of the enemies of the King.

It appears that Jesus Himself has both the authority and the power
to execute judgment, consuming the Antichrist and smiting the nations
that come against Him with His Spirit. The spirit of judgment from
Yahweh that is given Jesus, must be the desire and the passion to execute
judgment, as indicated in Zephaniah.

Zephaniah 3:8—9 (D. Israel)

8   "Therefore, wait for Me," declares Yahweh, "for the day that I
    rise up to the prey. For My judgment is to gather the nations,
    for Me to assemble the kingdoms, to pour out on them My
    indignation, all the fury of My anger; for with the fire of My
    jealousy will be consumed all the earth.

9   For then I will return to the peoples a purified language, in
    order for all of them to call on the name of Yahweh, to serve
    Him with one accord."

All those that do wickedness will be consumed and turned to ashes at
Jesus' second advent.

Malachi 4:1—3 (King James)

1   For, behold, the day cometh, that shall burn as an oven; and all
    the proud, yea, and all that do wickedly, shall be stubble: and
    the day that cometh shall burn them up, saith the Lord of hosts,
    that it shall leave them neither root nor branch.

2   But unto you that fear my name shall the Sun of righteousness
     arise with healing in his wings; and ye shall go forth, and grow
     up as calves of the stall.

3   And ye shall tread down the wicked; for they shall be ashes
     under the soles of your feet in the day I shall do this, saith the
     Lord of hosts.

ISAIAH 16:1-5

1   Send the Lamb who will rule the earth, from Sela of the wilderness to the mountain of the daughter of Zion.

2   And it will come to pass that she will flee like a bird; the nest forsaken, the daughters of Moab will be at the fords of the Arnon.

3   Take counsel, do judgment; make your shadow as the night in the middle of the day; hide the outcasts, do not uncover the fugitive.

4   Let My outcasts sojourn with you, Moab. Be a hiding place for them from the face of the destroyer. For the extortioner will cease; the destruction will be finished; the oppressor will be consumed out of the land.

5   And a throne will be established with mercy; and he will sit upon it in faithfulness in the tabernacle of David, judging and seeking justice, and hastening righteousness.

Most theologians correctly recognize that Isaiah 16:5 refers to Jesus reigning as King, starting at His second advent. However, theologians have made Isaiah 16:1—4 void and worthless. Because theologians have rejected so many key scriptures, they have left themselves with no hope of recognizing the significance of Isaiah 16:1—4. Again and again throughout Scripture, God talks about events occurring or about to occur at the time of the scripture being given, but then He switches to end time events. Theologians don't yet recognize the identity of the Branch; thus, they have failed to recognize that the events regarding

Moab, as described in Isaiah chapters fifteen and sixteen, switch to end time events; they switch not just in Isaiah 16:5, but in Isaiah 16:1—5. Standard translations have destroyed Isaiah 16:1—4.

7971   3733   4910   776
Send (the) Lamb who will rule (the) earth,

4480(5554)   4057 413   2022
from Sela (of) (the) wilderness to (the) mountain (of)

  1323   6726
(the) daughter (of) Zion.

  2050a(1961)   prek(5775)
And it will come to pass like (a) bird (she)

 5074 7064 7971 1961   (1323)pl
will flee:(the) nest forsaken, will be (the) daughters

  4124   (4569)pl 3897a(769)
(of) Moab (at) (the) fords of (the) Arnon.

935 6098 6213 6415 7896 prek(3915)
Take counsel, do judgment, make as (the) night

(6738)pro   preb(8432) (6672)pl 5641
your shadow in (the) midst (of) midday; hide

  (5080)pl   5074 408   1540
(the) outcasts, (the) fugitive not do uncover.

 1481 (preb)pro (5080)pl 4124 1933
Let sojourn with you My outcasts, Moab. Be (a)

 5643 (3807a)pro 4480(6440)
hiding place for them from (the) face (of) (the)

7703   3588   656   def(4160)
destroyer. For will cease the extortioner;

3615   7701   8552
will be finished (the) destruction; will be consumed

7429   4480   def(776)
(the) oppressor out of   the land.

In verse one, the Lamb is the Branch who will be in Sela (Petra), because of seeking refuge in Edom, in modern day Jordan (Psalm 108:10—11). The Branch will probably seek refuge at Sela as a result of the Antichrist's first incursion into Israel, about the start of the seven year covenant (Dan. 11:41). The Lamb is not being sent to the ruler, but the Lamb is the future ruler, who is being sent to the mountain of the daughter of Zion. Translators have adulterated verse one by inserting "to" before the verb, #4910, which is in the participle form. In the particle form #4910 can be translated as a verb or as a noun. God will command that the Lamb be sent to Jerusalem for his glorification, to be reunited with Jesus and then anointed with the fullness of Yahweh's Spirit, at the resumption of the seventy weeks of years. In John 1:29, John 1:36, Acts 8:32, and I Peter 1:19 Jesus is depicted as the Lamb whose blood would take away the sin of the world. Then in Revelation, Jesus is depicted as the Lamb as if slain, who is King of kings and Lord of lords. But note in Revelation, Jesus is not referred to as the Lamb until after His reunification with His soul at the resumption of the seventy weeks of years, not until the time of the opening of the first seal.

Revelation 5:5—6 (NAS)
5 "—— behold, the Lion that is from the tribe of Judah, the Root of David, has overcome so as to open the book and its seven seals."
6 And I saw between the throne (with the four living creatures) and the elders a Lamb standing, as if slain, having seven horns

and seven eyes, which are the seven Spirits of God, sent out into all the earth.

Jesus is not depicted as the Lamb during the time of being separated from His soul, because it is more appropriate to call the Branch the Lamb. And the reason for this is that the Lamb's shed blood symbolizes Jesus' life giving Spirit. At the time of Jesus' death, Jesus' soul was stripped bare to death (Isaiah 53:12), stripped bare of His life giving Spirit. The Lamb shed His blood, His life giving Spirit, to take away the sin of the world.

In verse two, it is the daughter of Zion who will flee like a bird. Translators have incorrectly made the daughters of Moab to be like a fleeing bird. Jerusalem is depicted to be like a bird who flees the nest, because the people of Israel are given the wings of an eagle to flee Satan and the Antichrist, at the mid-point of the seven year covenant.

Revelation 12:13—14 (King James)

13 And when the dragon saw he was cast unto the earth, he persecuted the woman which brought forth the man child.

14 And to the woman were given two wings of a great eagle, that she might fly into the wilderness, into her place, where she is nourished for a time, and times, and a half a time, from the face of the serpent.

Half of Jerusalem will go into exile at Jerusalem's capture by the Antichrist's forces, at the mid-point of the seven year covenant (Zech 14:2; Rev. 11:2). Because of Isaiah 16:1—4, the people fleeing Jerusalem will know that their destination is the fords of the Arnon river in Moab, in modern day Jordan. After forsaking the nest of Jerusalem, the people fleeing will look ahead to encountering the people of Moab at the Arnon, hoping and trusting that the people of Moab will hide them from the destroyer, the Antichrist. The people of Jerusalem will know that Moab has been commanded by God to hide His outcasts fleeing out of Jerusalem.

In verse four, God assures the people of Moab that the oppressor, the Antichrist and his forces, will be consumed out of the land (Is.13:6—9; Mal. 4:1—3). And in fact, a righteous King, the Lamb, will replace the Antichrist as ruler of the land. In verse five, "he" refers to the Lamb who will have become Jesus, who will sit on his throne seeking justice and hastening righteousness.

When we believe the key scriptures that open the door to understanding God's plan of salvation, we can recognize that Isaiah 16:1—5 is a list of the following end time events in chronological order.

1   the Lamb being sent from Sela to Jerusalem to be reunited with his Spirit at the resumption of the seventy weeks of years, about eight months before the mid-point of the seven year covenant
2   the people of Jerusalem fleeing to Moab at the mid-point of the seven year covenant
3   Moab hiding the outcasts of Jerusalem during the last half of the seven year covenant, from the destroyer, the Antichrist
4   the destroyer, the oppressor and his forces, being consumed out of the land at the end of the seven year covenant
5   the Lamb sitting on his throne and ruling in Jerusalem after his reunification with his Jesus, and after the completion of the seven year covenant

ISAIAH 28:9–19

9   Whom will He teach knowledge, and whom will He cause to understand the message? Those weaned from milk, those taken from the breasts?

10 For precept will be with reference to precept, precept with reference to precept; line with reference to line, line with reference to line; a little here, a little there.

11 For through stammering lips and with another tongue He will speak to this people,

12 He who will have said to them, "This is the rest, and give rest to the weary, and this one is the rest."

13 But they would not hear, so the word of Yahweh will be to them precept with reference to precept, precept with reference to precept; line with reference to line, line with reference to line; a little here, a little there, to the end that they will go, and they will fall backward, and they will be broken, and they will be snared, and they will be taken.

14 Therefore, hear the word of Yahweh, scornful men, rulers of this people who will be in Jerusalem:

15 because you will say, "We have made a covenant with death, and with Sheol we have made an agreement; when the overflowing scourge passes through it will not come to us, for we have made a lie our refuge, and in falsehood we are hidden."

16 Therefore, thus says the Lord Yahweh, "Behold, I will lay in Zion a stone, a tried stone, a precious cornerstone. The foundation will be founded. He who has believed will not make haste.

17 And I will make justice for a line, and righteousness for a plumb line; and hail will sweep away the refuge of the lie, and water will overflow the hiding place.

18 And your covenant with death will be cancelled, and your agreement with Sheol will not stand. When the overflowing scourge passes through, even you will be a trampling place to it.

19 As often as it passes through it will take you. For morning by morning it will pass through, in the day and in the night; and it will only be a terror to understand the report."

In the latter years, Yahweh will speak to the people of Israel through the Branch, who will be God's messenger. The Branch will give the people of Israel understanding of God's Word by giving them truth with reference to truth, and line with reference to line from His Word. In Isaiah 42:19—21, the Branch is described as God's messenger, who will magnify the law and make it honorable. Isaiah 42:19—21 is a two-legged double-step in which leg one refers to the nation of Israel, whereas leg two refers to the Branch.

Isaiah 42:19—21 (D. Israel)
leg 1 step 1   Who is blind, yet My servant;
leg 2 step 1   or deaf as My messenger I send?
leg 1 step 2   Who is blind as he who is at peace, even blind as the servant of Yahweh? You have seen many things, but have not taken heed.
leg 2 step 2   His ears are open, but he can not hear; Yahweh is pleased for the sake of his righteousness; he magnifies the law and makes it honorable.

At the beginning of the Branch's ministry to the nation of Israel, the Branch will be deaf to God's voice. However, with the Branch's effort (Isaiah 53:10-11), and with God's help (Psalm 91:16), the Branch will see into God's salvation.

Isaiah 53:10—11 (D. Israel)

10 But Yahweh will be pleased to crush Him, to make Him sick. When You make his soul guilty, he will see his seed, he will prolong his days, and the pleasure of Yahweh will prosper in his hands.

11 From the work of his soul he will see; he will be satiated with his knowledge.

Psalm 91:16 (D. Israel) I will have satisfied him with length of days, and I will have caused him to see into My salvation.

Because of his insight, the Branch will be able to magnify the law and make it honorable. The Branch will magnify the law by giving precept with reference to precept, and by giving line with reference to line from God's Word. In Isaiah 28:9, it is asked, who will Yahweh teach knowledge, and whom will He cause to understand the message? Those weaned from milk, those taken from the breasts? For it is easier to teach a baby a subject, that to teach someone who believes that he already knows the subject.

In Isaiah 42:19—21, the nation of Israel is described as seeing many things, but not taking heed. Isaiah 28:11—12 points out some of the important things that they have not heeded. They did not heed the sign given after Jesus' resurrection, the sign of the pouring out of Yahweh's Spirit. At that time, believers in Jesus spoke in tongues, with stammering lips; and believers spoke to the hearer in his own language, in a tongue which the believers did not know (Acts 2:1—8). In addition, it is pointed out that the people of Israel have not heeded the methods of obtaining rest; those methods being the observance of the Sabbath day of rest, giving rest to the weary each Jubilee year, and most importantly the rest received through belief in Jesus. In Matthew Jesus called out to the weary to come to Him, that He might give them rest.

Matthew 11:28—30 (NAS)

28 "Come to Me, all who are weary and heavy-laden, and I will
    give you rest.
29 Take My yoke upon you, and learn from Me, for I am gentle
    and humble in heart; and you shall find rest for your souls.
30 For My yoke is easy, and My load is light."

Because the nation of Israel has not heeded that Jesus is their rest,
Yahweh will send to them the Branch in the latter years. The Branch will
teach the people of Israel knowledge of God's way, knowledge of God's
plan of salvation. However, the proud will not listen to God's message
delivered through the Branch. They will refuse to humble themselves,
and accept God's way. They will reject God's message of how to obtain
salvation. Many of those who reject God's message will be snared by the
Antichrist at the capture of Jerusalem, and many will be taken in death
by the great army of the sixth trumpet.

In verses 14—19, Yahweh addresses the end time rulers in Jerusalem.
These rulers will react with scorn to God's message delivered by the
Branch. They will turn further away from God by making a covenant
with the Antichrist, part of which will be the forging of a lie to discredit
the Branch. In Psalm 119:69, the Branch relates that a lie has been
forged against him by the proud, the proud being those who refuse
to humble themselves and accept God's way. In particular, it will be
the proud rulers in Jerusalem that will forge this lie against the Branch
(verse 15).

Psalm 119:69 (D. Israel) The proud have forged a lie against
me; I with all my heart will keep Your precepts.

The covenant agreed to by the rulers in Jerusalem is described as being
with death and Sheol. This describes the Antichrist, the little horn of
Daniel 7:8; in that he will be indwelt by the beast from the abyss, from
death and Sheol.

Revelation 17:8 (NAS) The beast that you saw was and is not, and is about to come up from the abyss and to go to destruction. And those who dwell on the earth will wonder, whose name has not been written in the book of life from the foundation of the world, when they see the beast, that he was and is not and will come.

So, how will it come about that Israel will find it advantageous to make a covenant with the Antichrist? From Zechariah 9:13—14, it can be deduced that the antichrist will be from Greece. The last conqueror to oppress Israel will be the Antichrist. Zechariah 9:8 describes that the last oppressor will first pass through Israel, but then he will return. The Antichrist will first pass through Israel, the beautiful land, to conquer Egypt (Dan.11:40—43), and then he will return to lay siege and conquer Jerusalem at the mid-point of the seven year covenant (Zech. 14:2; Rev. 11:2). It is recognized that in Daniel 11:40—43 the king of the north refers to the Antichrist, and the king of the south refers to the ruler of Egypt.

Daniel 11:40—43 (NAS)

40 "And at the end time the king of the South will collide with him, and the king of the North will storm against him with chariots, with horsemen, and with many ships; and he will enter countries, overflow them, and pass through.

41 "He will also enter the Beautiful Land, and many countries will fall; but these will be rescued out of his hand, Edom, Moab and the foremost of the sons of Ammon.

42 "Then he will stretch out his hand against other countries, and the land of Egypt will not escape.

43 "But he will gain control over the hidden treasures of gold and silver, and over all the precious things of Egypt; and Libyans and Ethiopians will follow at his heels."

We know that the Antichrist will conquer three nations before going on to control the entire world (Daniel 7:8).

> Daniel 7:8 (NAS) "While I was contemplating the horns, behold, another horn, a little one, came up among them, and three of the first horns were pulled up by the roots before it; and behold, this horn possessed eyes like a man, and a mouth uttering great boasts."

And Daniel 8:9 describes the Antichrist growing exceedingly great toward the south, toward the east, and toward Israel, the beautiful land.

> Daniel 8:9 (NAS) And out of one of them came forth a rather small horn which grew exceedingly great toward the south, toward the east, and toward the Beautiful Land.

Daniel 11:40—43 tells us that the Antichrist wages war against Egypt with land forces and ships, that he overflows countries and passes through them, that one of the countries he enters is Israel, and that the end result is that he captures Egypt. So, we can see a sequence of actions by the Antichrist, that would line up with him uprooting the three rulers described in Daniel 7:8. The Antichrist will first grow exceedingly great toward the south, going to war with Egypt with ships, Egypt being directly south of Greece; then he will grow exceedingly great toward the east, conquering Turkey which is directly east of Greece; then he will grow exceedingly great toward the Beautiful Land, conquering Syria which is directly toward Israel from Turkey; then he will enter and pass through Israel and conquer Egypt with land forces. Thus, the three nations that the Antichrist conquers to start his world dominion may well be Turkey, Syria, and Egypt. By conquering Syria, he more fully becomes the king of the north, who then passes through Israel and conquers Egypt, the king of the south. In order to pass through Israel, it appears that he will attempt to conquer her, but gets bogged down and makes a covenant with the rulers in Jerusalem. The fact that the Antichrist initially attempts to conquer Israel is indicated by the Branch. The Branch describes that God has not gone out with Israel's armies, at the time that the Branch seeks refuge in Edom.

Psalm 108:10—11 (D. Israel)

10 Who will bring me to the strong city? Who will lead me as far as Edom?

11 Will not God? You have cast us off, God, and have not gone out with our armies.

It appears that in order to speed up his advance on Egypt, the Antichrist agrees to cease his attempt to conquer Israel. In return the rulers in Jerusalem agree to allow the Antichrist's armies passage through Israel to Egypt, and agree to issue a lie against the Branch, the Antichrist's enemy. As stated in Isaiah 28:15, the lie is the condition for the overflowing scourge of the Antichrist's armies not coming to conquer Jerusalem.

In Isaiah 28:16, Yahweh responds to the latter year rulers in Jerusalem, and their lie against the Branch. Yahweh declares that He will lay the cornerstone in Jerusalem, and that the foundation will be founded. The Branch is the cornerstone, being the cornerstone from the days of eternity before Jesus' conception when his soul was the Word. So, despite the ruler's lie issued against the Branch, and despite the Antichrist's attempt to kill him, the Branch will be established as ruler in Jerusalem. This will occur after the Branch's glorification at his reunification with Jesus, and after Jesus' second advent. He who believes God's message as delivered by the Branch will not make haste, at the capture of Jerusalem by the Antichrist. Those who believe will be raptured just as the Antichrist is capturing Jerusalem at the mid-point of the seven year covenant.

In Isaiah 28:17, it can be deduced that the lie of verse fifteen will be issued by the latter year rulers in Jerusalem from a war time defensive bunker. This lie against the Branch will be issued, when the Antichrist has finished capturing Turkey and Syria, and starts an offensive into Israel. The defensive bunker is the refuge of the lie. This bunker's refuge and hiding place will be swept away by melting hail, probably the hail of the seventh bowl of wrath.

> Revelation 16:21 (King James) And there fell upon men a great hail out of heaven, every stone about the weight of a talent: and men blasphemed God because of the plague of hail; for the plague thereof was exceedingly great.

In verse eighteen, the covenant between the rulers in Jerusalem and the Antichrist will be cancelled by the Antichrist. He will first pass through Israel to capture Egypt, as agreed to in the covenant; but he then cancels the covenant when he again passes through Israel on his return from Egypt, and it is then that he captures Jerusalem.

> Zechariah 9:8 (D. Israel) And I will encamp about My house, because of an army from he who will have passed through, even from he who will have returned; and an oppressor will not pass over them again, for then I will see with My eyes.

Jerusalem will then be the trampling place for the overflowing scourge, for the armies of the Antichrist.

> Revelation 11:1—2 (NAS)
> 1   And there was given to me a measuring rod like a staff; and someone said, "Rise and measure the temple of God, and the alter, and those who worship in it.
> 2   And leave out the court which is outside the temple, and do not measure it, for it is given to the nations; and they will tread under foot the holy city for forty-two months."

Regarding verse nineteen, the rulers in Jerusalem will know about the overflowing scourge of the armies of the Antichrist, but there will be another overflowing scourge from death and Sheol that they won't believe exists. This overflowing scourge will be a great army led by the four fallen angels of the sixth trumpet, and it will take one third of mankind in death.

Revelation 9:13—19 (NAS)

13 And the sixth angel sounded, and I heard a voice from the four horns of the golden alter which is before God,

14 one saying to the sixth angel who sounded the trumpet, "Release the four angels who are bound at the great river Euphrates."

15 And the four angels, who had been prepared for the hour and the day and the month and year, were released, so that they might kill a third of mankind.

16 And the number of the horsemen was two hundred million; I heard the number of them.

17 And this is how I saw in the vision the horses and those who sat on them: the riders had breastplates the color of fire and of hyacinth and of brimstone; and the heads of the horses are like the heads of lions; and out of their mouths proceed fire and smoke and brimstone.

18 A third of mankind was killed by these three plagues, by the fire and the smoke and the brimstone, which proceeded out of their mouths.

19 For the power of the horses is in their mouths and in their tails; for their tails are like serpents and have heads; and with them they do harm.

Many theologians incorrectly believe that the army of two hundred million is that of the Chinese. However, this army matches the description of the army in the book of Joel, and this army is Yahweh's army.

Joel 2:1—11 (D. Israel)

1 Blow a trumpet in Zion, and sound an alarm on My holy mountain! Let all the inhabitants of the land tremble, for the day of Yahweh is coming; for it is near;

2   a day of darkness and gloominess, a day of clouds and thick darkness. As the dawn spread out over the mountains, a great and mighty people the like of it will not have been from the past, nor will be after it until many generations.

3   A fire devours before it, and a flame burns behind it. The land is the garden of Eden before it, but a wilderness of desolation behind it; and indeed, there is no escape from it.

4   Its appearance is as horses, and like war horses, so they run.

5   Like the sound of chariots, they skip on the tops of the mountains; like the sound of a flame of fire devouring chaff; as a mighty people set in order for battle.

6   The peoples are in anguish before it; all faces are flushed.

7   They will run as mighty ones; they climb up the wall as men of battle; and each walks in his ways, and they do not change their paths.

8   And each does not press his brother; each warrior walks in his path. And if they fall upon the sword they are not cut off.

9   They rush on the city, they run on the wall, they climb on the houses, they enter through the window like a thief.

10   The earth quakes before it, the heavens shake, the sun and moon are darkened, and the stars gather in their brightness.

11   And Yahweh utters His voice before His army; yea, exceedingly great is His camp, for mighty is he who executes His word. Indeed, great is the day of Yahweh, and exceedingly fearful, and who can endure it?

The great army in Joel is described as being greater than any seen in the past, as will the two hundred million army of the sixth trumpet. The great army of Joel will not die if struck by a weapon, neither will the army of the sixth trumpet that will be from death and Sheol. This army is Yahweh's, even though it is led by four fallen angels, and is from death and Sheol. It is Yahweh's army, because He prepares it to accomplish His purposes (Rev. 9:13—14). The army of the sixth trumpet is the final test by God, to see if any more of humankind will repent of their sins. Revelation 9:20—21 reveals that none of the survivors of the sixth trumpet repent, of those of who are in need of repentance. Therefore, the next phase of God's wrath is ready to begin. In Revelation 11:18, during the seventh trumpet, it is declared that the time has come to judge the dead; the dead being the spiritually dead, not the physically dead. At this point in time, God's wrath changes from testing to judgment. God's judgment will be poured out in the bowls of wrath.

ISAIAH 29:17-24

17 Is it not a little while and Lebanon will be turned into a fruitful field, and the fruitful field will be reckoned as a forest?

18 And in that day the deaf will hear the words of a book, and the eyes of the blind will see out of gloom and out of darkness.

19 And the humble in Yahweh will increase joy; and the poor of mankind will rejoice in the Holy One of Israel;

20 for the terrible one will have been brought to naught, and the scorner will cease; and all watching for evil will be cut off,

21 those making an offender of a man by a word, and they who ensnare him that reproves in the gate, and they who turn aside the righteous by a thing of naught.

22 Therefore, thus says Yahweh, who redeemed Abraham, to the house of Jacob, "Jacob will not be ashamed at this time, nor will his face turn pale at this time;

23 for when his children see the work of My hand in his midst, they will sanctify My name; yea, they will sanctify the Holy One of Jacob, and they will be in awe of the God of Israel.

24 And those who wandered in spirit will know discernment, and those who murmured will learn insight."

In Isaiah 29:17—24, Yahweh spoke concerning the time of the latter year pouring out of His Spirit. In verse seventeen, Lebanon refers to Israel. Lebanon is sometimes used to describe that which is great and glorious, like the lofty cedars of Lebanon. Israel will become glorious in the latter years, because of the pouring out of God's Spirit. Isaiah 32:15

reveals that it will be the latter year pouring out of God's Spirit, that will cause Israel to become a fruitful field. Israel will be a spiritual wilderness from the time of the Babylonian captivity, until God pours out His Spirit on the people of Israel.

Isaiah 32:13—15 (D. Israel)

13 The thorn and the brier will come up on the ground of My people, even on all the joyful houses of the jubilant city.

14 For the palace will be abandoned, the crowd of the city deserted; hill and watchtower will be for dens for a long duration, a joy of wild donkeys, the pasturage of flocks;

15 until the Spirit is poured out on us from on high, and the wilderness becomes a fruitful field, and the fruitful field is reckoned as a forest.

If we don't have Jesus abiding in us, we can bear no fruit. Those who have God's Spirit poured out upon them will be born again Christians.

John 15:5 (NAS) "I am the vine, you are the branches; he who abides in Me, and I in him, he bears much fruit, for apart from Me you can do nothing.

God will pour out His Spirit in response to our worship of him with the truth of His plan of salvation. The fact that the worship of God with the truth of his salvation will result in the pouring out of His Spirit, will in turn draw many more to salvation through belief in Jesus.

Verse eighteen states that the deaf will hear the words of a book, and that the blind will see. This verse is describing the fact that those who were deaf to God's words will hear the words of the Branch's book, which explains God's words; and those who were blind to God's salvation will see, on account of the Branch's book. Isaiah 44:1—5 reveals that the Branch will write for Yahweh, and that he will be instrumental in the latter year pouring out of God's Spirit.

Isaiah 44:1—5 (D. Israel)

1 And now listen, Jacob My servant, even Israel: I have chosen him.

2 Thus says Yahweh, your maker and former from the womb, "He
   will help you. Do not fear, My servant Jacob, even Jeshurun, I
   have chosen him.

3 For I will pour out water upon the thirsty, and floods on dry
   ground; I will pour out My Spirit upon your seed, and My
   blessing upon your offspring.

4 And they will spring up in among grass, as willows by streams
   of water.

5 This one will say, 'I am for Yahweh'; and this one will call out
   in the name of Jacob; and this one will write with his hand for
   Yahweh, and be named by the name of Israel."

As Isaiah 44:1—2 reveals, God has chosen the Branch to help Israel,
help in particular with understanding God's plan of salvation, and the
worship of God that will result in the pouring out of His Spirit. As
Genesis 49:22 indicates, the Branch will bear fruit on account of the
spring of God's Spirit; Joseph will be a fruitful branch, a fruitful branch
on account of a spring. Isaiah 44:5 describes the First and the last ones;
Jesus being the First during His first advent, and the resurrected Jesus
and the Branch being the last ones. It will be the Branch who will write
for Yahweh, being named by the name of Israel.

Verse nineteen describes the result of God pouring out His Spirit.
Those who have humbled themselves and accepted Jesus as Lord, and
who worship God with the truth of His plan of salvation will receive the
oil of joy of God's Spirit. Those who are poor in spirit (Matthew 5:3)
will rejoice in the Holy One of Israel.

In verse twenty, the terrible one being brought to naught refers to
the destruction of the army of Gog, that invades Israel shortly before

the latter year pouring out of God's Spirit. God will deal wondrously with Israel in the latter years through a series of events (Joel 2:26). He will destroy the terrible one, the invading army of Gog; He will give Israel the teacher of righteousness, and send rain to end a severe drought (Joel 2:23); and He will pour out His Spirit on the house of Israel (Joel 2:28—29). Through these events it will be evident even to the scorner, that God has done these things, as His Word has recorded these events before they occur. The cutting off of those watching for evil could be referring to them being cut of from God's Spirit, or it could mean that they will be cut off by death, similar to Ananias and Sapphira (Acts 5:1—10).

In verse twenty-two, Yahweh states that Jacob will not be ashamed at that time, the time of the pouring out of His Spirit. Shortly before the pouring out of God's Spirit, Israel will become a reproach, on account of under going a severe drought, and because of being over run by the northern army of Gog. Joel describes this reproach that comes upon Israel (Joel 2:17). However, Joel also describes that God will remove Israel's reproach by sending rain, and by removing the northern army from Israel (Joel 2:19—20). At this time, God will give to Israel the Branch, the teacher of righteousness (Joel 2:23). Yahweh states that after He gives Israel the teacher of righteousness, sends rain to give produce, and removes the northern armies, then Israel will not be ashamed (Joel 2:26—27). Yahweh then states that He will pour out His Spirit on all flesh (Joel 2:28—29). Joel is in agreement with Isaiah 44:3, which indicates that the pouring out of God's Spirit will be after God sends rain to end a severe drought.

Joel 2:15—29 (D. Israel)

15 Blow a trumpet in Zion, consecrate a fast, call an assembly,

16 gather the people, sanctify the congregation, assemble the elders, gather the children and those sucking the breasts. Let

the bridegroom come out of his room, and the bride from her chamber.

17 Let the priests weep at the porch and toward the alter, ministers of Yahweh; and let them say, "Have pity, Yahweh, on Your people, and do not give Your inheritance to reproach, that the nations should rule over them. Why should they say among the peoples, 'Where is their God?'"

18 Then Yahweh will be jealous for His land, and will have pity on His people.

19 And Yahweh will answer and say to His people, "Behold, I will send grain to you, and new wine and fresh oil, and you will be satisfied with it; and I will not any longer make you a reproach among the nations,

20 but I will remove the one from the north far from upon you, and I will drive him into a land of drought and desolation, with his face toward the eastern sea, and his rear toward the western sea. And his stench will come up, and his foul odour will ascend, for he will have grown great to perform."

21 Do not fear, land; rejoice and be glad, for Yahweh will be magnified at doing it.

22 Do not fear, beasts of the field, for the pastures of the wilderness will grow green; for the tree will bear its fruit, and the fig tree and the vine will give their strength.

23 So, sons of Zion, rejoice and be glad in Yahweh your God; for He has given to you the teacher of righteousness; and the rain will come down to you; the early rain, but at first the latter rain.

24 And the threshing floors will be full of grain, and the vats will overflow with new wine and oil.

25 "And I will restore to you the years which the swarming locust has eaten, the crawling locust and the caterpillar and the gnawing locust, My great army which I have sent among you.

26 And you will eat fully and be satisfied, and you will praise the name of Yahweh your God who will deal with you wondrously. Then My people will never be ashamed;

27 and you will know that I am in the midst of Israel, and I am Yahweh your God and there is not another. Yea, My people will never be ashamed.

28 And it will be afterward that I will pour out My Spirit on all flesh; and your sons and your daughters will prophesy, and your elders will dream dreams, and your youth will see visions.

29 And even on the servants and handmaids I will pour out My Spirit in those days."

The people of Israel will know discernment and learn insight, after hearing the words of the Branch's book, and after witnessing how wondrously God deals with Israel at that time.

ISAIAH THIRTY-TWO

1 Behold, by righteousness a King will reign, and rulers will rule with judgment.

2 And each will be as a hiding place from the wind, and a shelter from the storm; like channels of water in a dry place, like the shadow of a huge rock in a weary land.

3 And the eyes of those seeing will not look away, and the ears of those hearing will listen.

4 And the heart of the rash will discern knowledge, and the tongue of the inarticulate will hasten to speak clearly.

5 The fool will no longer be called noble, and the scoundrel will not be called generous.

6 For the fool speaks foolishness, and his heart works wickedness, to do ungodliness and to speak error against Yahweh, to make the soul of the hungry empty, and cause the drink of the thirsty to fail.

7 And the tools of the scoundrel are evil; he devises evil plans to destroy the afflicted with false words, even when the needy speaks what is right.

8 But the noble devise noble things, and by noble things will stand.

9 Rise up, women at ease; hear My voice, daughters who are secure.

10 Listen to My word of the days concerning the year you tremble, secure ones; when the vintage fails, and the harvest does not come.

11 Tremble, those at ease; be troubled, secure ones. Strip and make bare and bind a girdle on the loins.

12 Lament over the breasts, over the pleasant fields, over the fruitful vines.

13 The thorn and the brier will come up on the ground of My people, even on all the joyful houses of the jubilant city.

14 For the palace will be abandoned, the crowd of the city deserted; hill and watchtower will be for dens for a long duration, a joy of wild donkeys, the pasturage of flocks;

15 until the Spirit is poured out on us from on high, and the wilderness becomes a fruitful field, and the fruitful field is reckoned as a forest.

16 And justice will dwell in the wilderness, and righteousness will abide in the fruitful field.

17 And the work of righteousness will be peace, and the service of righteousness, quietness and security forever.

18 And My people will dwell in a habitation of peace, and in dwellings of refuge, and in secure resting places.

19 And it will hail when the forest comes down, and the city is made low in a low place.

20 Blessed you will be who will sow beside all waters, who will send out the feet of the ox and the donkey.

Isaiah chapter thirty-two gives us a glimpse of some important end time events and their sequence. The chapter opens by describing Christ's righteous reign, that will start at His second advent. Then verses 9—12 go back in time from Christ's righteous reign, to a time in which the people of Israel are dwelling securely in their land. Verse ten has been poorly translated by standard translations.

(802)pl 7600	6965 8085 (6963)pro	(1323)pl
Women at ease, rise up; hear My voice,		daughters

      982   238   (565)pro
that are secure. Listen to My word (of) (the)

(3117)pl   5921   8141 pro(7264)
  days   concerning (the) year you tremble,

    982   3588 3615   1210   625
secure ones; when fails (the) vintage, (the) harvest

1097   935
not   does come.

God warns the people of Israel that their security will be broken by harvest failure. God instructs them to listen to His Word concerning this time. God's Word describes this time more fully in Joel 1:1—20 and Joel 2:12—17, which describes that not only will their harvest fail, but Israel will also be invaded by a northern army. This army is not the army of locusts that also occurs at this time, but the northern army of Gog. For Gog will invade Israel at a time when Israel is dwelling securely (Ezek. 38:8; 38:11; 38:14), and at a time that is just before the pouring out of God's Spirit (Ezek. 39:29).

Verses 13—14 regress further in time to describe the abandonment of the land at the time of the Babylonian captivity. Verse fourteen describes the fact that the land of Israel will then be a wilderness for a long duration of time. Note that the land of Israel being a wilderness is describing the lack of God's Spirit in the land of Israel, not the lack of inhabited areas. For it is the pouring out of God's Spirit that changes the wilderness into a fruitful field, which is reckoned as a forest. Although God's Spirit was poured out on the day of Pentecost after Christ's resurrection, the number who received God's Spirit weren't sufficient to consider the wilderness to be changed into a fruitful field. The people of Israel who will have God's Spirit poured out upon them will be a fruitful field, given that the Spirit produces fruit (Gal. 5:22). In addition, they will be considered as a forest, being oaks of righteousness (Isaiah 61:3).

Isaiah twenty-nine also describes the transformation of the spiritual wilderness of Israel into a fruitful field.

Isaiah 29:17—19 (D. Israel)
17 Is it not a little while and Lebanon will be turned into a fruitful field, and the fruitful field will be reckoned as a forest?
18 And in that day the deaf will hear the words of a book, and the eyes of the blind will see out of gloom and out of darkness.
19 And the humble in Yahweh will increase in joy; and the poor of mankind will rejoice in the Holy One of Israel;

Here we are given additional information, the fact that the people of Israel will at this time hear the words of a book. Joel describes that God will give Israel the teacher of righteousness at the time of the harvest failure, just before the pouring out of God's Spirit (Joel 2:28—29); for the Branch is the teacher of righteousness who will write for Yahweh (Psalm 45:1; Isaiah 29:18; Isaiah 44:5), and who will help the people of Israel (Isaiah 44:2). He will give them the understanding necessary to accept Jesus as their Messiah. In addition, the Branch will give them the understanding that will open the flood gates of Heaven, that will result in the pouring out of God's Spirit upon them (Isaiah 44:3).

Verses 16—17 describe the peace and security of those who have God's Spirit poured out upon them. All those who receive the pouring out of God's Spirit will first be born again by belief in Jesus, and will have the security of knowing they have eternal life. Even if they die they will be given eternal life at the resurrection and rapture of the church.

Verse eighteen describes the three phases that those in Israel who accept Jesus will experience. The first phase is the dwelling in a habitation of peace, which describes the peace that stretches from the pouring out of God's Spirit until the time of the Antichrist. The second phase is the dwellings of refuge, which describes the refuge in Heaven from the events of the day of Yahweh, which stretches from the rapture at the mid-point of the seven year covenant to Jesus' second advent. The third phase is the secure resting places of Christ's millennial kingdom.

Verse nineteen reveals that it will hail when the forest comes down, when the city is laid low in a low place. The forest coming down is not describing the cutting down of a forest, but is describing the descending of believers (verse 15), who come down to earth with Christ at His second advent. The city that is laid low is the city of Jerusalem, which is laid low by an earthquake at the time of Jesus' second advent (Rev. 16:18—21).

> Revelation 16:18—21 (NAS)
> 18 And there were flashes of lightning and sounds and peals of thunder; and there was a great earthquake, such as had not been since man came to be upon the earth, so great an earthquake was it, and so mighty.
> 19 And the great city was split into three parts, and the cities of the nations fell. And Babylon the great was remembered before God, to give her the cup of wine of His fierce wrath.
> 20 And every island fled away, and the mountains were not found.
> 21 And huge hailstones, about one hundred pounds each, came down from heaven upon men; and men blasphemed God because of the plague of hail, because its plague was extremely severe.

One of the effects of an earthquake is that the land can decrease or increase in elevation. From verse nineteen, we are told that the earthquake will cause the elevation of Jerusalem to drop. However, it appears that additional seismic activity will then cause Jerusalem to rise to dwell in its place (Zech. 14:10).

ISAIAH 38:15-20

15 What I spoke, even He had said to me, and Himself did. I have gone humbly all my years because of the bitterness of my soul.

16 Lord, because of them, they live; yea, for all have in them my life, my Spirit. Therefore, You have restored me, even causing me to live.

17 Behold, for peace was bitter to me, bitter; but You loved my soul from the pit of destruction. Assuredly You have cast behind Your back all my sins.

18 For Sheol cannot thank You, nor death praise You; those descending to the pit cannot hope for Your living truth.

19 The living is he who can thank You, as I do today, Father. To sons He reveals, God, Your truth.

20 Yahweh is for delivering me; yea, my songs we will sing to stringed instruments all the days of our lives at the house of Yahweh.

The speaker of Isaiah 38:15—20 is not Hezekiah, as commonly believed. In Isaiah 38:14, Hezekiah asked God to be surety for him. Hezekiah's prayer triggered a prophetic utterance through him in verses 15—20. In verses 15—20, it is the Word who speaks as the Branch. In these verses, the Branch speaks of his separation from Jesus, and describes the fact that Jesus is our surety of eternal life. In verse fifteen, the Branch describes that what he spoke as Jesus' soul was spoken to him by Yahweh the Father, and what he performed as Jesus' soul was worked by Yahweh. Then in verses 15—16, the Branch describes that he has gone humbly all his years, because of the bitterness of his soul. He explains that because of all these years, all live who have his life, his Spirit, in them. The Branch's soul was Jesus' soul who was separated from Jesus' Spirit at Jesus' death, which freed Jesus' Spirit to indwell and give eternal life to whosoever believes in Him.

In Psalm seventy-three, the Branch also describes his embitterment, due to being separated from Jesus' Spirit.

Psalm 73:21—22 (D. Israel)
21 Indeed, my heart, even my kidneys had been embittered.
22 I had been pierced, but I was brutish and did not understand. I was like the animals toward You, but I was continually with You.

Psalm 73:21—22 describes the fact that the Branch didn't know his identity in his younger years. He didn't understand that he had been embittered, due to being separated from He who was his Spirit. He was like the animals toward God, not acknowledging God's existence; yet he was continually with God, in that He who was his Spirit sits at Yahweh's right hand.

Verse sixteen also describes the fact that Yahweh has restored him to life. The Branch will be restored to life in the latter years, given that he will be instrumental in the latter year pouring out of God's Spirit. In Psalm twenty-three, Jesus' soul speaks from the point of time of being in Sheol, during the three days and nights after Jesus' death. Jesus' soul looks ahead to lying down in pastures of grass, and to being led to the waters of rest of Heaven; then further ahead in time to being restored to life, and then being led in paths of righteousness, his Christian walk.

Psalm 23:1—3 (D. Israel)
1 Yahweh is my shepherd, I will not want.
2 He will make me lie down in pastures of grass; He will lead me to waters of rest;
3 He will restore my soul; He will lead me in paths of righteousness for His name's sake.

In Psalm 116:3—6, Jesus' soul describes being in Sheol after Jesus' death; then in Psalm 116:7 the resurrected Jesus tells His soul to return to his rest, his rest in Heaven; then in Psalm 116:8—9, Jesus' soul restored to life as the Branch's soul declares that because Jesus delivered his soul from death, he walks before Yahweh in the lands of the living.

Psalm 116:3—9 (D. Israel)

3 The cords of death encompassed me, the straits of Sheol have found me;

4 trouble and sorrow I have found; therefore, on the name of Yahweh I call: "I pray, Yahweh, deliver my soul."

5 Yahweh is gracious and righteous, and our God is merciful; Yahweh watches over the simple.

6 I have been brought low, but because of me He saves.

7 Return, My soul, to your rest, for Yahweh will deal bountifully on account of you.

8 Because You delivered my soul from death, my eyes from tears, and my feet from stumbling,

9 I walk before Yahweh in the lands of the living.

In verse seventeen, the Branch states that the peace of Heaven was bitter to him, even though Yahweh's love brought him up from Sheol, the pit of destruction. The Branch states that Yahweh has cast behind His back all his sins, due to the fact that he has repented of his sins and accepted Jesus as Lord. Those who go to Sheol upon death have no hope to receive God's living truth. God's living truth is God's Spirit. In verse nineteen, He who reveals God's truth to God's sons is God's Spirit, the Holy Spirit.

John 14:16—17 (NAS)

16 "And I will ask the Father, and He will give you another Helper, that He may be with you forever;

17 that is the Spirit of truth, whom the world cannot receive, because it does not behold Him or know Him, but you know Him because He abides with you, and will be in you."

John 14:26 (NAS) "But the Helper, the Holy Spirit, whom the Father will send in My name, He will teach you all things, and bring to your remembrance all that I said to you."

John 16:13 (NAS) "But when He, the Spirit of truth, comes, He will guide you into all truth; for He will not speak on His own initiative, but what He hears, He will speak; and He will disclose to you what is to come."

In verse twenty, the Branch states that Yahweh is for delivering him. The Branch knows that God will deliver him from his enemies, because God's vows are upon him to do so.

Psalm 56:11—12 (D. Israel)
11 In God I trust, I will not fear; what can man do to me? Upon me, God, are Your vows.
12 I will render thanksgiving to You, for You will snatch my soul from death.

The prophetic utterance ends with the Branch stating that his songs will be sung all the days of their lives in the house of Yahweh. This may be a reference to the songs that worship God with the truth of His plan of salvation. It will be the Branch who explains that the worshipping of God with the truth of His plan of salvation, will result in the latter year pouring out of His Spirit. In Psalm one hundred and nineteen, the Branch also describes his songs.

Psalm 119:54 (D. Israel) Songs of Your statutes are mine in the house of my pilgrimage.

Standard translations have fudged the translation of Psalm 119:54, to make it fit their understanding.

(2158)pl 1961 (3807a)pro   (2706)(pl)pro
Songs   are   ----- mine (of) Your statutes

preb(1004)   (4033)pro
in (the) house (of) my pilgrimage.

God's plan of salvation includes: what happened at Jesus' conception, death, and resurrection; and what happened at the interruption of the seventy weeks of years, and what will happen at the resumption of the seventy weeks of years. And of course, God's plan of salvation includes what happens when a person is born again, and the realization of eternal life at the resurrection and rapture.

Standard translations have poorly translated Isaiah 38:15—20.

4100 pro(1696)   2050a(559)   3807a)pro
What I spoke,   even (He) had said   to me,

2050a(1931)   6213   pro(1718)   3605
and Himself   did. I have gone humbly all

(8141)pro   5921   4751   (5315)pro
my years because of (the) bitterness (of) my soul.

136   (5921)pro   (2421)pro 2050a(3807a)3605
Lord, because of them, they live;   yea for all

          (preb)pro (2416)pro   (7307)pro
(have) in them   my life,   my Spirit.

          2050a(3807a)(2492)pro
Therefore, You have restored me,

          2050a(2421)pro
even having caused me to live.

2009   3807a(7965)   4843   (3807a)pro 4751
Behold, for peace   was bitter   to me,   bitter;

2050a(859) 2836 (5315)pro 4480(7845)
   but You loved   my soul from (the) pit (of)

   1097   3588   (7993)pro   310
destruction. Assuredly You have cast behind

(1460)pro 3605 (2399)pro
Your back all   my sin.

3588 3808 7585   (3034)pro   4194
For   not Sheol can thank You; (nor) death

(1984)pro   3808   7663   (3381)pl
praise You;   not can hope those descending (to)

    953   413 (571)pro   2416
(the) pit   for Your truth   living.

     2416 1931   (3034)pro   (prek)pro
(The) living he   can thank You,   as I   (do)

def(3117)   1   (3807a(1121)pl pro(3045) 410
   today, Father.   To sons   He reveals, God,

(571)pro
Your truth.

   3068   3807a(3467)pro   2050a(5058)(pl)pro
Yahweh (is) for delivering me;   yea, my songs

      pro(5059   3605   (3117)pl
we will sing to stringed instruments   all (the) days

     (2416)(pl)pro 5921   1004   3068
(of)   our lives   at (the) house (of) Yahweh.

ISAIAH 40:9

9 Go up upon the high mountain to Yourself, bearer of good
news to Zion. Lift up your voice with strength, bearer of good
news to Jerusalem. Lift up, do not fear, say to the cities of Judah,
"Behold your God!"

As a result of theologians not recognizing the identity of the Branch,
standard translations have destroyed Isaiah 40:9.

| 5921 | 2022 | 1364 | 5927 | (3807a)pro |
| Upon (the) | mountain | high | go up to Yourself, |

| 1319 | 6726 | 7311 | preb(3581) |
| bearer of good news (to) | Zion. Lift up with strength |

| (6963)pro | 1319 | 3389 | 7311 |
| your voice, bear of good news (to) | Jerusalem. Lift up |

| 408 3372 | 559 | 3807a(5892)pl | 3063 | 2009 |
| not do fear, say | to (the) cities (of) | Judah, "Behold |

(430)pro
your God!"

Isaiah 40:9 is Yahweh's instruction to the Branch, to go to Mount
Zion to be reunited with Jesus, just before being anointed with the fullness of Yahweh's Spirit. Isaiah 40:9 is one of several scriptures that describe the Branch going to Mount Zion for his glorification. The Branch

is the Lamb who shed his blood, his life giving Spirit, to take away the sins of the world. When it is time for the Branch's glorification, God commands that he be sent from his refuge in Sela to the mountain of the daughter of Zion.

Isaiah 16:1 (D. Israel) Send the Lamb who will rule the earth, from Sela of the wilderness to the mountain of the daughter of Zion.

Before the Branch's glorification, he bears the good news of salvation to Jerusalem (Psalm 116:12—14). When it is time for his glorification, he is directed to go up upon the high mountain to Himself, to be reunited with the resurrected Jesus, he who was his body and Spirit at Jesus' first advent.

When it is time to be glorified, the Branch is to act in faith and to declare to the people, "Behold Your God!" At his declaration, he will be reunited with Jesus by means of Jesus coming out of the midst of the church and indwelling his spirit. At that time, he will have reached the summit of the everlasting hill; and he will receive the blessing of Jacob (Gen. 27:29), that was passed on to Joseph (Gen. 49:26), the blessing of becoming ruler of the nations.

Genesis 27:29 (D. Israel) "May the nations serve you, and the peoples bow to you; become the ruler of your brothers, and may your mother's sons bow to you; may those who curse you be cursed, and may those who bless you be blessed."

Genesis 49:26 (D. Israel) "The blessings of your father have prevailed over the blessings of my progenitors; as far as the summit of the everlasting hill they will be for the head of Joseph, and for the crown of the head of the prince of his brothers."

At that time, he will be anointed with the fullness of Yahweh's Spirit on Zion, Yahweh's holy mountain.

In Psalm 2:6, Yahweh tells us why the nations rage during the last days, against Him and His anointed. The nations will rage, because Yahweh will have anointed His King on Mount Zion. Then in Psalm 2:7—9, the Branch who has become Jesus declares what Yahweh tells him on that day, the day of Jesus' super-natural birth, the day of the reunification of the Branch with Jesus.

Psalm 2:6—9 (D. Israel)

6   "Yea, I anointed My King on Zion, My holy mountain."

7   "I will declare concerning the statute of Yahweh: He said to Me, 'You are My Son, today I have begotten You.

8   Ask of Me and I will give the nations as Your inheritance, even the ends of the earth as Your possession.

9   You will break them with a rod of iron; You will dash them as a potter's vessel.'"

The Branch will have gone up upon the mountain of Yahweh, and stood up in Yahweh's holy place. He will have received the blessing of Jacob of becoming the ruler of the nations. He will have become Yahweh, the King of glory, since Yahweh is the ruler of the nations (Jer. 10:6—7).

Psalm 24:3—10 (D. Israel)

3   Who will go up upon the mountain of Yahweh, and who will stand up in His holy place?

4   One who will have clean hands and a pure heart, who will not have lifted up his soul to vanity, and will not have sworn to deceit.

5   He will lift up the blessing from Yahweh, and righteousness from the God of his salvation.

6   This one a generation will seek, those who will seek your face, Jacob.

7 Lift up your heads, O gates, and be lifted up, O everlasting doors, and the King of glory will come in.

8 Who is the King of glory? Yahweh powerful and mighty, Yahweh mighty in battle.

9 Lift up your heads, O gates, and be lifted up, O everlasting doors, and the King of glory will come in.

10 Who is He, this King of glory? Yahweh of hosts, He is the king of glory.

At becoming the King of glory, the Branch will become the ruler of the nations, and he will become Israel's ruler. The Word will become ruler of Israel and the nations at Jesus' super-natural birth and anointing. The Word is He who has existed from the days of eternity, who became Jesus' soul, who then becomes the Branch's soul, and who once again becomes Jesus' soul at Jesus' super-natural birth.

Micah 5:2—3 (D. Israel)

2 "And you, Bethlehem Ephrathah, small at being among the thousands of Judah, out of you He will go forth for Me to become ruler in Israel; and His goings forth have been from ancient times, from the days of eternity.

3 Therefore, He will give them up until the time when she who travails has brought forth; then the rest of His brothers will return to the sons of Israel."

On the day of the Branch's glorification, he will not only become ruler of Israel and the nations, but will once again become the Son of God (Psalm 2:7). On that day, the day of Jesus' super-natural birth, the Branch is reunited with the seed of God, the resurrected Jesus, the parts of Jesus that were conceived at Jesus' conception. Thus, Yahweh the Father will declare to him on that day, "You are My Son, today I have begotten You." On that day, the day of Jesus' super-natural birth, the Branch who becomes the King of glory is caught up to the throne of God.

Revelation 12:1—5 (NAS)

1   And a great sign appeared in heaven: a woman clothed with the sun, and the moon under her feet, and on her head a crown of twelve stars;

2   and she was with child; and she cried out, being in labor and in pain to give birth.

3   And another sign appeared in heaven: and behold, a great red dragon having seven heads and ten horns, and on his heads were seven diadems.

4   And his tail swept away a third of the stars of heaven, and threw them to the earth. And the dragon stood before the woman who was about to give birth, so that when she gave birth he might devour her child.

5   And she gave birth to a son, a male child, who is to rule all the nation with a rod of iron; and her child was caught up to God and to His throne.

ISAIAH 41:4

4 "Who wrought and did this, calling forth the generations from the beginning? I, Yahweh, am the First and with the last ones; I am He."

In Isaiah 41:4, Yahweh introduces the concepts of the First and the last ones, but standard translations have destroyed this verse by changing last ones to singular.

4310	6466	2050a(6213)	7121	def(1755)pl
Who wrought		and did (this),	calling the generations

4480(7218)	589	3068
from (the) beginning?	I,	Yahweh, (am) (the)

7223	2050a(854)	(314)pl	589	1931
First	and with (the)	last ones;	I (am)	He."

From Isaiah 44:5—7 and Revelation 1:7—8, we can deduce the concepts of the First, last ones, and Last. In Isaiah 44:6, Yahweh reveals that He is the First and the Last.

Isaiah 44:5—7 (D. Israel)
5 "This one will say, 'I am for Yahweh'; and this one will call out in the name of Jacob; and this one will write with his hand for Yahweh, and be named by the name of Israel."

6   Thus says Yahweh, the King of Israel and his redeemer, Yahweh
    of hosts: "I am the First and I am the Last, and apart from Me
    there is no God.
7   And who is as I am? He will proclaim and declare it; and He
    will set it in order for Me, from My placing the people of old.
    And things to come, even which will come, They will declare
    concerning them."

Jesus is also the First and the Last, as He reveals in the book of Revelation.

Revelation 1:7—8 (D. Israel)
7   Behold, He is coming with the clouds, and every eye will see
    Him, even those who pierced Him; and all the tribes of the
    earth will mourn over Him. Yes indeed. Amen.
8   "I am the First and the Last," says the Lord God who is, "even
    who was and who is to come, the Almighty."

At the time of Jesus' statement, He is the Lord God who is, and He is
also the First and the Last who was and who is to come. Jesus revealed
that the First and the Last is Yahweh, the Almighty. So, at the time
of making this statement, which is after His death and resurrection,
Jesus in not Yahweh the Almighty; but He was Yahweh the Almighty,
and He will once again become Yahweh the Almighty. The thing that
makes Jesus Yahweh the Almighty is being anointed with the fullness of
Yahweh's Spirit. It was during Jesus' first advent, from His baptism with
Yahweh's Spirit until Yahweh's Spirit left Him at His death, that Jesus
was Yahweh the Almighty, the First. It will be immediately after Jesus'
super-natural birth, that Jesus will once again be anointed with Yahweh's
Spirit; thus, He will again be Yahweh the Almighty, the Last. So, both
Yahweh and Jesus are the First, from Jesus' baptism with Yahweh's Spirit
until Jesus' death; and both Yahweh and Jesus are the Last, from Jesus
being anointed with Yahweh's Spirit, immediately after Jesus' super-natural birth to eternity. During the time that Jesus is anointed with the

fullness of Yahweh's Spirit, they are one. They are Yahweh the Almighty. Yahweh is one.

Isaiah 44:5 describes the First and the last ones. It was Jesus, the First, who said that He was for Yahweh (John 6:38). It is the resurrected Jesus, one of the last ones, who calls out in the name of Jacob. Jesus calls out to the church in the name, the authority of Jacob, given that the blessing to become ruler of the nations was originally given to Jacob. It is the Branch, the other last one, who writes with his hand for Yahweh, and who is named by the name of Israel (Psalm 45:1; Isaiah 49:3). The last ones will be reunited at Jesus' super-natural birth, and will become the Last at being anointed with Yahweh's Spirit. Isaiah 44:7 describes the First and the Last. From Jesus' baptism with Yahweh's Spirit until His death, Jesus is the First. Jesus as the First proclaimed that He was as Yahweh. He proclaimed that He and Yahweh the Father were one.

John 10:30 (NAS) "I and the Father are one."

After Jesus' super-natural birth, and after Jesus is once again anointed with Yahweh's Spirit, Jesus as the Last will set the world in order for Yahweh. Both Jesus as the First and as the Last proclaim concerning future events.

ISAIAH 41:25–29

25 "I will raise up one from the north, and he will come from the rising of the sun. He will call out in My name, and he will come upon rulers as on mortar, even as a potter tramples clay.

26 Who has declared this from the beginning that we might have known, or before now that we might have said, 'He is right'"? Yea, not one declares; yea, not one proclaims; yea, not one hears Your words; the First will say to Zion, "Behold, behold them!"

27 "Therefore, I will give to Jerusalem one bearing good news,

28 since I see that there is not a man, and especially from these, that there is not a counsellor, that I might ask them and they could answer a word.

29 Behold, all of them are evil; their works are nothing, wind and vanity are their cast images."

Most incorrectly understand that Isaiah 41:25 refers to king Cyrus, who is described at the beginning of chapter forty-one. Verse twenty-five is a two-legged double-step. Leg one describes the Branch before his glorification; who comes from the north, and who calls out in the name of Yahweh to the nation of Israel; whereas leg two describes the Branch after his glorification at him becoming Jesus, who comes from the east at the rapture (Matthew 24:27), and later comes upon rulers at Jesus' second advent.

leg 1 step 1   I will raise up one from the north,
leg 2 step 1   and he will come from the rising of the sun.

leg 1 step 2   He will call out in My name,

leg 2 step 2   and he will come upon rulers as on mortar, even as a
potter tramples clay.

It will be the Branch who comes from the north; exaltation coming not
from the east, nor from the west, nor from the south, but from the north
(Psalm 75:6). It will be the Branch who will be exalted at his glorification.

Psalm 75:6 (D. Israel) For exaltation will not come from the
east, nor from the west, nor from the south.

It will be the Branch who will call out to the nation of Israel in the name
of Yahweh. In Psalm one hundred and sixteen, it is the Branch who
vows to lift up and offer the cup of salvation to the people of Israel, and
call out in the name of Yahweh.

Psalm 116:12—14 (D. Israel)

12 What will I return to Yahweh for all His benefits to me?

13 The cup of salvation I will lift up, and in the name of Yahweh I
will call out.

14 My vow to Yahweh I will complete in front, I pray, of all His
people.

It will be the Branch who will call a nation he doesn't know, and who
doesn't know him. The nation of Israel will run to him at him being
glorified.

Isaiah 55:5 (D. Israel) "Behold, you will call a nation you do
not know; and a nation that does not know you will run to you
because of Yahweh your God, even because of the Holy One of
Israel, for He will glorify you."

The Branch will call out to Israel in the name, the authority of Yahweh,
in that he will be sent to Israel by God as God's messenger (Isaiah

42:19—21). The Branch will bring a message of good news to Israel, lifting up and offering to Israel the cup of salvation through belief in Jesus; and by so doing remove the stumbling blocks to salvation caused by poor teaching of God's Word.

After his glorification, the Branch will return to earth as Jesus, circling the globe from the east at the rapture (Matthew 24:27); later he will again return to earth at Jesus second advent, trampling upon rulers who will be under the command of the Antichrist. In Psalm two, Jesus declares what God tells Him on the day of His super-natural birth. God declares to Jesus that He will give Him the nations as His inheritance, and that Jesus will dash them as a potter's vessel.

Psalm 2:7—9 (D. Israel)

7   "I will declare concerning the statute of Yahweh: He said to Me, 'You are My Son, today I have begotten You.

8   Ask of Me and I will give the nations as Your inheritance, even the ends of the earth as Your possession.

9   You will break them with a rod of iron; You will dash them as a potter's vessel.'"

How people deal with the message of salvation given by the Branch will determine how the Branch deals with them after his glorification. He will either come and rescue them at the rapture, or deal with them at Jesus' second advent.

In verse twenty-six, Yahweh asks, Who has declared this from the beginning, or before now? Who has declared concerning the Branch from the creation of mankind, or before Yahweh speaks here through Isaiah? Yahweh's question is answered in verse twenty-seven, that no one declares or proclaims about the Branch, because no one hears Yahweh's words concerning the Branch. Scripture is riddled with God's words describing the Branch, but no one hears these words. Even though Jesus as the First said, Behold, behold them, still no one will hear Yahweh's words. No one will hear Yahweh's words concerning the Branch, until he is raised up. Jesus pointed out Yahweh's words concerning the Branch on two occasions.

In Matthew 21:42, Jesus quoted Psalm 118:22, which reveals what would happen on account of His death. Psalm 118:22 reveals that Jesus would become the head of the corner, of He who existed before His conception as the Word; given that the Word became Jesus' soul, and then becomes the Branch's soul. Jesus becomes the head of the corner at the Branch being born again, given that Jesus is the head of all the members of His church.

Psalm 118:22—24 (D. Israel)

22 The stone the builders rejected became the head of the corner;

23 this was from Yahweh, it is marvellous in our eyes.

24 Such was the day Yahweh made, we will rejoice and be glad in it.

Then in Matthew 23:39, Jesus quoted Psalm 118:26. Jesus stated that the people of Jerusalem would not see Him again until they say, Blessed is he who comes in the name of the Lord. It will be the Branch to whom the people of Jerusalem say, Blessed is he who comes in the name of Yahweh. They will say this just before they cry out to God for the reunification of the Branch with Jesus, when they cry out to God, "Bind the sacrificial feast with cords, even to the horns of the alter." Immediately thereafter, they will see Jesus at His super-natural birth.

Psalm 118:26—27 (D. Israel)

26 Blessed is he who comes in the name of Yahweh; we have blessed you from the house of Yahweh.

27 God is Yahweh, and He has given light to us. Bind the sacrificial feast with cords, even to the horns of the alter.

So, while Jesus was in Jerusalem He said twice to Zion, to behold God's words that described the existence of the Branch. However, no one has taken to heart the scriptures that Jesus pointed out.

Because no one will hear Yahweh's words concerning the Branch, Yahweh will send to Jerusalem the Branch, bearing the good news of salvation. Isaiah 40:9 describes the time of the Branch's glorification, and also describes the fact that the Branch will have borne good news to Jerusalem.

Isaiah 40:9 (D. Israel) Go up upon the high mountain to Yourself, bearer of good news to Zion. Lift up your voice with strength, bearer of good news to Jerusalem. Lift up, do not fear, say to the cities of Judah, "Behold your God!"

Yahweh finishes Isaiah chapter forty-one stating that there is not a man that can answer Him a word. There is not a man who can answer Yahweh concerning the Branch. There is not a counsellor that hears Yahweh's words concerning the Branch before he is raised up, especially from those who resort to cast images.

ISAIAH 42:19-21

19 Who is blind, yet My servant; or deaf as My messenger I send? Who is blind as he who is at peace, even blind as the servant of Yahweh?

20 You have seen many things, but have not taken heed. His ears are open, but he can not hear;

21 Yahweh is pleased on account of his righteousness; he magnifies the law and makes it honorable.

Isaiah 42:19—21 has been poorly translated by standard translations.

4310	5787	3588(518)	pro(5650)	2050a(2795)
Who (is) blind,		yet	My servant;	or deaf

prek(4397)pro	pro(7971)	4310	5787
as My messenger	I send?	Who (is) blind	

prek(7999)	2050a(5787)	prek(5650)
as (he) at peace,	even blind	as (the) servant (of)

3068
Yahweh?

(7200)pro	(7227)pl	2050a(3808)
You have seen	many things,	but not

8104	6491	(241)pl
have taken heed.	Open (are) (his)	ears

2050a(3808)   pro(8085)
but not   he can hear.

3068   2654   3807a(4616)
Yahweh is pleased on account of

(6664)pro   pro(1431)   8451
his righteousness; he magnifies (the) law

2050a(142)
and makes(it) honorable.

These verses are a two-legged double-step. Leg one refers to the nation of Israel, whereas leg two refers to the Branch.

leg 1 step 1   Who is blind, yet My servant;
leg 2 step 1   or deaf as My messenger I send?
leg 1 step 2   Who is blind as he who is at peace, even blind as the
               servant of Yahweh? You have seen many things, but
               have not taken heed.
leg 2 step 2   His ears are open, but he can not hear; Yahweh is
               pleased on account of his righteousness; he magnifies
               the law and makes it honorable.

Yahweh calls the nation of Israel His servant, a servant that is blind. The
people of Israel have seen many things performed by God, but have not
taken heed. The people of Israel have seen the great works that Jesus did
which were performed by Yahweh, but did not take heed. The people
of Israel also have seen the speaking in tongues by those who believed
in Jesus, but did not take heed. At the time that the Branch is sent to
Israel as God's messenger, Israel will be at peace with her neighbors. We
know from the book of Joel that the Branch will already be in Israel,
at the time of Israel being invaded by the northern army of Gog (Joel
2:19—23). And we know that before the invasion of Israel by Gog, that
Israel will be at peace (Ezekiel 38:8; 38:11; 38:14).

The Branch will be sent to Israel as God's messenger, a messenger who is deaf to God's voice. Even though the Branch will be deaf to God's voice, at the time of being sent to Israel, he will see. The Branch will see, and be satiated with his knowledge, because of his effort to understand.

Isaiah 53:10—11 (D. Israel)

10 But Yahweh will be pleased to crush Him, to make Him sick. When You make his soul guilty, he will see his seed, he will prolong his days, and the pleasure of Yahweh will prosper in his hands.

11 From the work of his soul he will see; he will be satiated with his knowledge.

Because of his effort, Yahweh will cause the Branch to see into His plan of salvation.

Psalm 91:14—16 (D. Israel)

14 "Because he will set his love on Me, even I will deliver him, I will set him on high. Because he will know My name, he will call on Me, and I will answer him.

15 I will be with him in distress; I will draw him out of it, and I will honor him.

16 I will have satisfied him with length of days, and I will have caused him to see into My salvation."

God's message that is delivered by the Branch will be precept with reference to precept from His Word, line with reference to line from His Word; a little here and a little there from God's Word.

Isaiah 28:9—10 (D. Israel)

9 Whom will He teach knowledge, and whom will He cause to understand the message? Those weaned from milk, those taken from the breasts?

10 For precept will be with reference to precept, precept with reference to precept; line with reference to line, line with reference to line; a little here, a little there.

Because the Branch will see into God's plan of salvation, He will lift up and offer it to the people of Israel.

Psalm 116:12—14 (D. Israel)
12 What will I return to Yahweh for all His benefits to me?
13 The cup of salvation I will lift up, and in the name of Yahweh I will call out.
14 My vow to Yahweh I will complete in front, I pray, of all His people.

The Branch will magnify God's law, God's Word, and make it honorable; he will correctly expound the scriptures that reveal God's plan of salvation.

ISAIAH 44:1-8

1   And now listen, Jacob My servant, even Israel: I have cho-
    sen him.

2   Thus says Yahweh, your maker and former from the womb, "He
    will help you. Do not fear, My servant Jacob, even Jeshurun, I
    have chosen him.

3   For I will pour water upon the thirsty, and floods upon dry
    ground; I will pour My Spirit upon your seed, and My blessing
    upon your offspring.

4   And they will spring up in among grass, as willows by streams
    of water.

5   This one will say, 'I am for Yahweh'; and this one will call out
    in the name of Jacob; and this one will write with his hand for
    Yahweh, and be named by the name of Israel."

6   Thus says Yahweh, the King of Israel and his redeemer, Yahweh
    of hosts: "I am the First and I am the Last, and apart from Me
    there is no God.

7   And who is as I am? He will proclaim and declare it; and He
    will set it in order for Me, from My placing the people of old.
    And things to come, even which will come, They will declare
    concerning them.

8   Do not fear nor be afraid; from that time will I not cause you
    to hear? Yea, I declare, even you are My witness. Is there a God
    apart from Me? Yea, there is not a rock, I know none."

Theologians have mistranslated sections of Isaiah 44:1—8, due to not recognizing the identity of the Branch, and due to not understanding the concepts of the First, last ones, and Last. Verses 1—2 have been destroyed by standard translations.

2050a(6258) 8085 3290   (5650)pro 2050a(3478)
And now listen, Jacob My servant, even Israel:

(977)pro   (preb)pro
I have chosen ---- him.

3541 559   3068   (6213)pro 2050a(3335)pro
Thus says Yahweh, your maker and your former

4480(990)   pro(5826)pro   408   3372
from (the) womb, "He will help you. Not do fear,

(5650)pro   3290   2050a(3484)   (977)pro
My servant Jacob, even Jeshurun, I have chosen

(preb)pro
----- him."

In verses 1—2, Yahweh addresses the seed of Israel living during the latter years, near the time of the latter year poring out of His Spirit. In verses 1—2, it is not Israel whom God has chosen, but it is the Branch. He will help the people of Israel regarding salvation and the latter year pouring out of God's Spirit. Genesis 49:25 also describes the fact that the Branch will help Israel.

Genesis 49:22—25 (D. Israel)
22 "Joseph will be a fruitful branch, a fruitful branch on account of a spring;
23 his branches will go over the wall, and the masters of arrows will vex him, and shoot at and hate him;

24 but his bow will abide with strength, and the arms of his hands will be agile from the hands of the Mighty One of Jacob; from there will be the Shepherd, the Stone of Israel,

25 from the God of your father; and he will help you; then together with the Almighty, even He will bless you with the blessings of the heavens above, the blessings of the deep lying below, and the blessings of the breasts and the womb."

In verses 3—7, Yahweh addresses the people of Israel who are Isaiah's contemporaries, linking he who helps Israel in verse two with the latter year pouring out of His Spirit. In verse three, we are told that Yahweh will pour out water upon the thirsty, floods upon dry ground, and that He will pour out His Spirit upon the descendants of Israel. Water is sometimes used to symbolize God's Spirit, but not in verse three; for Joel reveals that the latter year pouring out of God's Spirit will occur after God pours out rain to end a severe drought.

Joel 2:23—29 (D. Israel)

23 So, sons of Zion, rejoice and be glad in Yahweh your God; for He has given you the teacher of righteousness; and the rain will come down to you; the early rain, but at first the latter rain.

24 And the threshing floors will be full of grain, and the vats will overflow with new wine and oil.

25 "And I will restore to you the years which the swarming locust has eaten, the crawling locust and the caterpillar and the gnawing locust, My great army which I have sent among you.

26 And you will eat fully and be satisfied, and you will praise the name of Yahweh your God who will deal with you wondrously. Then My people will never be ashamed;

27 and you will know that I am in the midst of Israel, and I am Yahweh your God and there is not another. Yea, My people will never be ashamed.

28 And it will be afterward that I will pour out My Spirit on all flesh; and your sons and your daughters will prophesy, and your elders will dream dreams, and your youth will see visions.

29 And even on the servants and handmaids I will pour out My Spirit in those days."

In Joel 2:23, the teacher of righteousness is the Branch. The Branch will explain that Jesus is the believer's righteousness, by means of indwelling the believer's spirit and making the believer's spirit righteous, even unable to sin. It is the believer's spirit that is made righteous, and it is the believer's soul that is still capable of sin. The Branch will teach the people of Israel to worship God with the truth of His salvation. The result of this worship will be the latter year pouring out of God's Spirit upon the people of Israel.

To understand Isaiah 44:5—8, we must first understand the concepts of the First, last ones, and Last. Because theologians don't yet understand these concepts, standard translations have poorly translated these verses.

    2088   559   3807a(3068) 589
"This one will say, 'for Yahweh   I (am)'

2050a(2088)   7121   preb(8034)   3290
and this one will call out in (the) name (of) Jacob;

2050a(2088)   3789   (3027)pro 3807a(3068)
and this one will write (with) his hand   for Yahweh,

2050a(preb)(8034)   3478   3655
and by (the) name (of) Israel will be named."

3541 559   3068   4428   3478
Thus says Yahweh (the) King (of) Israel

2050a(1350)pro   3068   (6635)pl 589
and his redeemer, Yahweh of hosts: I (am) (the)

7223 2050a(589)   314 2050a(4480)(1107)pro
First   and I (am) (the) Last,   and apart from Me

    369   430
there is no God.

2050a(4310)   (prek)pro   pro(7121)
   And who (is) as I am?   He will proclaim

2050a(5046)pro   2050a(pro)(6186)pro
and declare it;   and He will set it in order for Me

4480(7760)pro   5971   5769
from My placing (the) people (of) old.

    2050a(857)pl   2050a(834)   935
And things to come, even which will come,

    (5046)pro   (3807a)pro
They will declare concerning them.

408 6342   2050a(408)   7297   int(3808)
Not do fear   and not   be afraid. Will not

    4480(227)   (8085)(pro)pro
since that time I cause you to hear? ——"

God introduces the concepts of the First and the last ones in
Isaiah 41:4.

Isaiah 41:4 (D. Israel) "Who wrought and did this, calling forth
the generations from the beginning? I, Yahweh, am the First
and with the last ones; I am He."

The First refers to both Jesus and Yahweh during Jesus' first advent, from Jesus' baptism with the fullness of Yahweh' Spirit until Jesus' death. During this period of time both Yahweh and Jesus are Yahweh the Almighty, due to Jesus being anointed with the fullness of Yahweh's Spirit. Upon Jesus' death, Jesus is no longer anointed will the fullness of Yahweh's Spirit; thus, He is no longer as Yahweh. However, Jesus will once again be anointed with the fullness of Yahweh's Spirit, immediately after being reunited with the Branch at Jesus' super-natural birth. (Psalm 2:6—7).

Psalm 2:6—7 (D. Israel)
6   "Yea, I anointed My King on Zion, My holy mountain."
7   "I will declare concerning the statute of Yahweh: He said to Me, 'You are My Son, today I have begotten You.'"

From Jesus' death to His super-natural birth, the resurrected Jesus and Jesus' soul who becomes the Branch's soul are the last ones. So, now that we understand the concepts of the First, last ones, and Last, we can understand Isaiah 44:5—7. Isaiah 44:5 gives a description of the First and the last ones, that were introduced in Isaiah 41:4. God describes the First by stating that He would say He was for Yahweh. This is a description of Jesus during His first advent, who said He came to do the will of Yahweh the Father (John 6:38). Then verse five describes one who will call out in the name of Jacob. This is a description of the resurrected Jesus, one of the last ones, who calls out to the church (Revelation chapters two-three). Jesus calls out in the name, the authority of Jacob, because the blessing of being set over the nations was originally given to Jacob (Genesis 27:29), and then passed on to Judah (Genesis 49:10) and Joseph (Genesis 49:26). Then verse five describes one who will write for Yahweh, being named by the name of Israel. This is a description of the Branch who will be from the tribe of Joseph, the other last one, who will write for Yahweh (Psalm 45:1), and who will be named by the name of Israel (Isaiah 49:3).

In Isaiah 44:6, Yahweh declares that He is the First and the Last, and apart from Him there is no God. Yahweh is the First because of the anointing of Jesus with the fullness of His Spirit during Jesus' first advent; and Yahweh is the Last because He will anoint Jesus once again at the resumption of the seventy weeks of years, immediately after Jesus' super-natural birth on Mount Zion. Apart from Yahweh, there is no God. Jesus is also God due to coming from Yahweh, being conceived the Son of God. Jesus is not always Yahweh the Almighty, due to not always being anointed with the fullness of Yahweh's Spirit, but Jesus is always God.

In Isaiah 44:7, Yahweh asks the question, Who is as I am? Yahweh then describes He who is as He is. He first describes Jesus during His first advent as the First, who declared that He was as Yahweh (John 14:6—11). Yahweh then describes Jesus after His second advent as the Last, who will set the world in order for Yahweh at that time (Isaiah 9:6—7). Yahweh then reveals that Jesus as both the First and the Last will declare concerning future events.

In verse 8a, Yahweh again addresses the seed of Israel living in the latter years, indicating that at the time of the Branch's ministry, Israel will hear God's words. Yahweh again tells the people of Israel not to fear, not to fear the teaching of the Branch, whom God has chosen to help the nation. The people of Israel are not to fear what the Branch writes for Yahweh. Yahweh then asks the question, Will I not cause you to hear from that time? The people of Israel will hear the words of the book written by the Branch for Yahweh, which in turn will cause them to hear Yahweh's words as contained in Scripture. In verses 8b—20, Yahweh speaks of the fact that there is no God other than from Him, and that idols are worthless. Israel is God's witness.

Sometimes Lebanon is used to symbolize that which is great or glorious. In Isaiah 29:17—19, Lebanon refers to the nation of Israel, who will become spiritually great and glorious at the latter year pouring out of God's Spirit. Israel will hear the words of a book written by the Branch, and as a result Israel will see and understand.

Isaiah 29:17—19 (D. Israel)

17 Is it not a little while and Lebanon will be turned into a fruitful field, and the fruitful field will be reckoned as a forest?

18 And in that day the deaf will hear the words of a book, and the eyes of the blind will see out of gloom and out of darkness.

19 And the humble in Yahweh will increase joy, and the poor of mankind will rejoice in the Holy One of Israel;

The spiritual wilderness of Israel will be turned into a fruitful field at the latter year pouring out of God's Spirit. The book written by the Branch for Yahweh will cause the people to hear and understand God's words as contained in Scripture. As a result, the people of Israel will understand God's plan of salvation and worship God with the truth. And as a result of this understanding and worship, God will pour out His Spirit.

Isaiah 32:13—14 describes the desolation of Judah on account of the Babylonian captivity, and Isaiah 32:15 describes Israel becoming a fruitful field at the latter year pouring out of God's Spirit.

Isaiah 32:13—15 (D. Israel)

13 The thorn and the brier will come up on the ground of My people, even on all the joyful houses of the jubilant city.

14 For the palace will be abandoned, the crowd of the city deserted; hill and watchtower will be for dens for a long duration, a joy of wild donkeys, the pasturage of flocks;

15 until the Spirit is poured out on us from on high, and the wilderness becomes a fruitful field, and the fruitful field is reckoned as a forest.

To sum up, God will pour out His Spirit in the latter years on the nation of Israel, on account of the Branch's teaching. The result of God pouring out His Spirit is that Israel will become a fruitful field. Genesis 49:22 reveals that the Branch becomes fruitful, when Israel becomes a fruitful field, on account of the spring of God's Spirit.

ISAIAH 49:1-9

1   Listen to Me, coasts, and pay attention, peoples from afar. Since the womb Yahweh called Me, since the belly of My mother bringing to remembrance My name.

2   And He made My mouth like a sharp sword, in the shadow of His hand He hid Me. Even He made Me a choice arrow, in his quiver He hid Me.

3   And He said to Me, "You are My servant, Israel, You in whom I will be glorified."

4   And I said, "I have labored in vain, for nothing and vainly I have spend My strength. But indeed, My judgment is with Yahweh and My work with My God."

5   And from now on, said Yahweh who formed Me from the womb to be a servant to Him, to bring back Jacob to Him; though Israel was not gathered, yet I would be honoured in the eyes of Yahweh, and My God would be My strength.

6   And He said, "It is too little that You be My servant to raise up the tribes of Jacob and to restore the preserved of Israel, so I give You for the light of the nations, to be My salvation as far as the end of the earth."

7   Thus says Yahweh, the Redeemer of Israel, his Holy One, to the despised soul, to the one hated by the nation, to the servant of rulers, "Kings will see and stand up, leaders also will bow down on account of Yahweh who is faithful, the Holy One of Israel, even He has chosen you."

8　Thus says Yahweh, "At the time of acceptance I will answer you, and in the day of deliverance I will help you. For I will keep you and give you for a covenant of the people to restore the earth, to cause to inherit the desolated heritages;

9　to say to the prisoners, 'Go forth,' to those in darkness, 'Show yourselves.' —"

In verses 1—3, the Word speaks as Jesus, speaking from a point in time that is after Jesus' second advent. Jesus addresses the peoples of the world, and He refers back to when His soul became the Branch's soul. Jesus relates that as the soul of the Branch, Yahweh called him since being in the belly of his mother. Yahweh brought to his remembrance his name, caused him to understand his identity. Verse two skips ahead in time to the Branch's glorification, when Yahweh makes the Branch's mouth like a sharp sword. At his glorification, he is reunited with Jesus, and it is Jesus' Spirit that makes his mouth like a sharp sword. Similarly in Psalm forty-five, Yahweh commands the Branch to gird on his sword, his glory and his majesty.

Psalm 45:3—4 (D. Israel)

3　Gird your sword on your thigh, Mighty One, your glory and your majesty.

4　And in Your majesty prosper; ride on the matter of truth and meekness and righteousness, and Your right hand will teach You fearful things.

In Revelation, we see the Word wielding the sword of His Spirit, given that it was the Word who became Jesus' soul, who then becomes the Branch's soul in the latter years, and then once again becomes Jesus' soul at the Branch's glorification.

Revelation 19:11—15 (NAS)

11　And I saw heaven opened; and behold, a white horse, and He who sat upon it is called Faithful and True; and in righteousness He judges and wages war.

12 And His eyes are a flame of fire, and upon his head are many diadems; and He has a name written upon Him which no one knows except Himself.

13 And He is clothed with a robe dipped in blood; and His name is called the Word of God.

14 And the armies which are in heaven, clothed in fine linen, white and clean, were following Him on white horses.

15 And from His mouth comes a sharp sword, so that with it He may smite the nations; and He will rule them with a rod of iron; and he treads the wine press of the fierce wrath of God, the Almighty.

At the Branch's glorification and rapture, Yahweh will hide him in the shadow of His hand in Heaven, making him a choice arrow to be used at Jesus' second advent. Yahweh will be glorified through the Branch who becomes Jesus, first at the resurrection and rapture of the church, and then at Jesus' second advent. Yahweh addresses the Branch as Israel, because it is the Branch who writes for Yahweh, who is named by the name of Israel. Isaiah 44:5 describes the First and the last ones; Jesus during His first advent being the First, whereas the resurrected Jesus and the Branch are the last ones.

Isaiah 44:5 (D. Israel) "This one will say, 'I am for Yahweh'; and this one will call out in the name of Jacob; and this one will write with hand for Yahweh, and be named by the name of Israel."

In verses 4—6, the Word speaks as Jesus. Jesus is again speaking from a point in time that is after His second advent, and addresses the peoples of the world. In these verses, Jesus is referring back to a point in time that is just after the cross, and He is describing the dejection that His Spirit felt at that time. Yahweh encouraged Him by telling His Spirit that He would not only raise up the tribes of Jacob, but that He would also be Yahweh's salvation to the end of the earth; He would be God's salvation to all humankind.

In verses 7—9, Yahweh addresses Jesus' soul through His Word, who has become the Branch's soul. Standard translations have muddied verse seven, by not translating "soul" as soul.

3541 559   3068   1350   3478
Thus says Yahweh, (the) Redeemer (of) Israel,

(6918)pro   3807a(960)   5315
His Holy (one), to (the) despised soul,

    3807a(8581)   1471   3807a(5650)
to (the) (one) hated (by) (the) nation, to (the) servant

    (4910)pl (4428)pl   7200   2050a(6965) (8269)pl
(of) rulers, "Kings   will see and stand up,   leaders

    2050a(7812)   3807a(4616)   3068   834
also will bow down on account of Yahweh who

    539   6918   3478
is faithful; (the) Holy (One) (of) Israel,

    2050a(pro)(977)pro
even He has chosen you."

It is Jesus who is despised and hated by the nation of Israel, for being a false Messiah; thus, it is the Branch who is the despised soul, in that he is born having Jesus' soul.

Similar to Isaiah 44:1-2, in verse seven Yahweh states that He has chosen the Branch.

Isaiah 44:1—2 (D. Israel)

1 And now listen, Jacob My servant, even Israel: I have chosen him.

2 Thus says Yahweh, your maker and former from the womb, "He will help you. Do not fear, My servant Jacob, even Jeshurun, I have chosen him."

Yahweh has chosen the Branch to be His messenger of salvation to the nation of Israel. In verse eight, Yahweh states that in the time of acceptance He will answer the Branch. The time of acceptance is the day that the nation of Israel officially accepts Jesus as her Messiah and King. The time of acceptance is also the day of deliverance of the Branch from his enemies; it is the day of his glorification and rapture to the throne of God. In Psalm 118:17—21, it is the Branch who speaks of Yahweh answering him and being his deliverance. Yahweh will answer him on the day of acceptance, by glorifying him and delivering him, at his rapture through the gates of righteousness of Heaven.

Psalm 118:17—21 (D. Israel)

17 I will not die; indeed, I will live and I will recount the works of Yah.

18 Chastening, Yah has chastened me, but He will not give me to death.

19 Open to me the gates of righteousness; I will enter into them, I will thank Yah.

20 This is the gate to Yahweh; the righteous will enter into it.

21 I thank You, for You will answer me and be my deliverance.

In Psalm ninety-one, Yahweh states that He will answer and deliver the Branch, that He will set the Branch on high.

Psalm 91:14—15 (D. Israel)

14 "Because he will set his love on Me, even I will deliver him, I
   will set him on high. Because he will know My name, he will
   call on Me, and I will answer him.

15 I will be with him in distress; I will draw him out of it, and I will
   honor him."

On the day of acceptance on Mount Zion, the nation of Israel will
officially accept Jesus as her Messiah. Israel's acceptance of Jesus will
result in Jesus' super-natural birth, when the people of Israel cry out to
God for the reunification of the Branch with Jesus; when they cry out
to God, "Bind the sacrificial feast with cords, even to the horns of the
alter."

Psalm 118:26—27 (D. Israel)

26 Blessed is he who comes in the name of Yahweh; we have blessed
   you from the house of Yahweh.

27 God is Yahweh, and He has given light to us. Bind the sacrificial
   feast with cords, even to the horns of the alter.

At the Branch's glorification, he will be Jesus, and Jesus will restore the
earth after His second advent.

ISAIAH FIFTY-THREE

1 Who has believed our message, and to whom has the arm of Yahweh been revealed,

2 that He came up as a shoot before Him, and as a root out of ground of drought? There was no form to Him nor glory that we saw Him, and there was no appearance that we desired Him.

3 He was despised and rejected of men; being a man of sorrows and known by sickness.

4 And at the time of the hiding of faces from Him, He was despised and we did not esteem Him.

5 Nevertheless our sickness He has lifted up, and our sorrows He has carried, though we regarded Him stricken by God and afflicted; but He was wounded on account of our transgressions, crushed on account of our iniquities, chastening for our completeness was upon Him, and with His wound it is healed for us.

6 All of us like sheep have gone astray; we have turned, every man to his way, but Yahweh has caused the iniquity of us all to meet with Him.

7 He will be oppressed and He will be afflicted, but He will not open His mouth. As a lamb to the slaughter He will be brought, and as a sheep before her shearers is dumb so He will not open His mouth.

8 From restraint and from justice He will be taken; and with His generation, who will consider that He was cut off from the land of the living on account of the trespass of My people?

9   The stroke will be for them, and He will make His grave with
the wicked and be with the rich in His deaths, on account of He
will have done no injustice and no deceit will have been in His
mouth.

10 But Yahweh will be pleased to crush Him, to make Him sick.
When You make his soul guilty, he will see his seed, he will
prolong his days, and the pleasure of Yahweh will prosper in his
hands.

11 From the work of his soul he will see; he will be satiated with his
knowledge.

12 My righteous servant will justify many, but their iniquities he
will bear. Therefore, I will divide to him with the many, and
he will divide the spoil with the strong; because he will have
stripped bare his soul to death, and will be counted with transgressors; and the sin of many He will lift up, and for transgressors He will reach the mark.

Isaiah chapter fifty-three opens and closes with a two-legged double-step. The opening double-step describes the origin of Jesus and the
origin of the Branch, whereas the closing double-step describes the destiny of Jesus' Spirit and the destiny of Jesus' soul. Verses 1—6 are spoken
by Israelis who are contemporaries of the Branch. They have turned to
believe in Jesus due to the Branch's teaching.

Isaiah 53:1—3 (D. Israel)
Who has believed our message, and to whom has the arm of Yahweh
been revealed,
leg 1 step 1   that He came up before Him as a shoot,
leg 2 step 1   and as a root out of ground of drought?
leg 1 step 2   There was no form to Him nor glory that we saw Him,
and no appearance that we desired Him.
leg 2 step 2   He was despised and rejected of men; a man of sorrows and known by sickness

Jesus came from the stem of Jesse, being a shoot from the stem of Jesse, and being from the tribe of Judah (Isaiah 11:1). The Branch comes from the roots of Jesse, being from Jesse's root, Jacob; and being from Jacob's branch, Joseph (Isaiah 11:1; Gen. 49:22—24). Jesus came from God, but the people didn't see God's glory upon Him, and they didn't desire Him to be their Messiah and King. The Branch came from being rejected and despised as the soul of Jesus; and because the Branch is born of normal parents, he is a man of sorrows and known by sickness, as a result of being born a sinner. Verse five describes the fact that he who believes in Jesus has the sickness of the sin of his spirit removed, and the sin of his spirit is healed for him. The Hebrew word #7965 can be appropriately translated as completeness or as peace. Standard translations have poorly translated verse five.

> 403   (2483)pro   1931   5375
> Nevertheless our sickness   He   has lifted up
>
> 2050a(4341)(pl)pro   5445   2050a(853)pro
> and our sorrows (He) has carried, though --- we
>
> (2803)pro   5060   5221   430 2050a(6031)
> regarded Him stricken, smitten (by) God and afflicted;
>
> 2050a(1931)   2490
> but He   was wounded
>
> 4480(6588)(pl)pro   1792
> on account of our transgressions; crushed
>
> 4480(5771)(pl)pro   4148
> on account of our iniquities; chastening (for)
>
> (7965)pro   (5921)pro
> our completeness (was) upon Him,
>
> 2050a(preb)(2250)   7495   (3807a)pro
> and with His wound (it) is healed   for us.

The believer is born again by means of Jesus' Spirit indwelling the believer's spirit; thus, his spirit is made alive and righteous, even unable to sin. It is the believer's soul that still capable of sin. So, he who is born again is made complete, and he is at peace with God.

> I John 3:9 (J. P. Green) Everyone who has been begotten of God does not sin, because His seed abides in him, and he is not able to sin, because he has been born of God.

It was not Jesus' scourging that heals us, but the wound of His death. Jesus' death is described as a wound, because His death was not permanent. In Psalm 69:26, Jesus' soul speaks from the point in time of being in Sheol, during the three days and nights after His death. Jesus' soul refers to himself as God's wounded one, being wounded at being separated from his Spirit at his death. Because of the wound of Jesus soul at being separated from his Spirit, the sickness of the believer's spirit is healed for him, because the separation of Jesus' soul and Spirit freed His Spirit to indwell and make righteous the spirit of the believer.

> Psalm 69:26 (D. Israel) For whom You smote they persecuted, and they gossip to the pain of Your wounded one.

Verse six describes the fact that at being indwelt by Jesus' Spirit, the sin of the believer's spirit meets with Jesus' Spirit. The result is that Jesus removes the sin of the believer's spirit, reaching the mark of being without sin for the believer.

> Isaiah 53:12 (D. Israel) —— and the sin of many He will lift up, and for transgressors He will reach the mark.

Jesus abiding in the believer justifies him, makes his spirit righteous (Isaiah 53:12). It is the believes soul that is still capable of sin.

> Isaiah 53:12 (D. Israel) My righteous servant will justify many, ——

Verses 7—8 are spoken by Yahweh the Father, from the point in time of being penned by Isaiah. Yahweh describes Jesus before the Jewish priests on the morning of the day of His crucifixion. The Jewish priests unjustly delivered up Jesus to death.

Mark 14:60—64 (NAS)

60 And the high priest stood up and came forward and questioned Jesus, saying, "Do You make no answer? What is it that these men are testifying against You?"

61 But He kept silent, and made no answer. Again the high priest was questioning Him, and saying to Him, "Are You the Christ, the Son of the Blessed One?"

62 And Jesus said, "I am; and you shall see the Son of Man sitting at the right hand of power, and coming with the clouds of heaven."

63 And tearing his clothes, the high priest said, "What further need do we have of witnesses?

64 "You have heard the blasphemy; how does it seem to you?" And they all condemned Him to be deserving of death.

Verses 9—11 are spoken by the Word. Standard translations have incorrectly linked, "the stroke will be for them," to the previous verse. Verse nine describes the stroke of death being to Jesus for the people of Israel. The stroke was not for the purpose of punishing sin, but in order to provide the means for the believer in Jesus to pass out of spiritual death into spiritual life. Verse nine is not stating that Jesus was with the rich in His death, on account of He had done no injustice and was not deceitful. Jesus would not have considered it an honor to be laid in a rich man's tomb. Rather, verse nine is stating that the stroke of dearth was to Jesus, because He had done no injustice, and because there was no deceit in His mouth. In other words, Jesus was without sin; He was the unblemished lamb. Therefore, Jesus had a live righteous Spirit, that which is necessary to indwell and make righteous the spirit of whosoever believes in Him. Verse nine describes that Jesus experienced two deaths. Unlike a normal person, Jesus suffered soul death at being separated from His live Spirit, His soul making His grave with the wicked in Sheol (Psalm 16:10; Psalm 116:3); and similar to a normal person, His body suffered physical death at being separated from His soul, His body being laid in a rich man's tomb (Mat. 27:57—60).

Standard translations have destroyed verse ten, by interpreting the Hebrew adjective #818 as the Hebrew noun #817.

2050a(3068)   2654   (1792)pro
But Yahweh will be pleased to crush Him,

(2470)pro   518   pro(7760)   818 (5315)pro
to make Him sick. When You make guilty his soul,

pro(72900)   2233   pro(748)   (3117)pl
he will see (his) seed, he will prolong (his) days,

2050a(2656)   3068   preb(3027)pro
and (the) pleasure (of) Yahweh   in his hand

6743
will prosper

Both these Hebrew words have the same consonantal spelling. So, standard translations have incorrectly translated this word as "offering for sin, or as "guilt offering," whereas it should be translated as "guilty." Verse ten describes that Yahweh gave Jesus' soul the sickness of sin, as also described by Paul.

II Corinthians 5:21 (D. Israel) For He not knowing sin, for the sake of us He gave sin, so that we might become the righteousness of God in Him.

3588 1063 3361   1097   266   5228
He   For   not   knowing   sin, for the sake of

2257 266   4160   2443 2449   1096
us sin   He gave, so that   we might become (the)

   1343   2316 1722   846
righteousness (of) God   in   Him.

How is it possible for someone who has been given sin by God to make anyone righteous? God gives Jesus' soul sin at his re-entry into life as the soul of the Branch. However, it was because Yahweh crushed Jesus at His death, that His live righteous Spirit was freed from His soul, freed to indwell and make righteous the spirit of whosoever believes in Him. The spirit of whosoever believes in Jesus becomes the righteousness of God, becomes the righteousness of Jesus, due to Jesus' Spirit indwelling the spirit of the believer. The believer is justified, made righteous, due to his spirit being made righteous by Jesus.

Verse ten contains Yahweh's promise to Jesus' soul. Yahweh promised that when He makes Jesus' soul guilty as the soul of the Branch, that the Branch would see his children, that he would live a long life, and that Yahweh's pleasure would prosper in his hands. The fact that the Branch will see his seed is also described in Psalm forty-five. In Psalm 45:10—16, Yahweh addresses the Branch's bride to be. She will bear the Branch a daughter (verse 13) and sons (verse 16). Psalm 45:12—16 is spoken from a point in time that is after the Branch's glorification, a point in time that is during the millennium, when the Branch has become his bride's Lord.

Psalm 45 10—16 (D. Israel)
10 Listen, daughter, and consider and incline your ear, and forget
     your people and your father's house;

11 even the king desires your beauty; indeed, he will be your Lord and you will bow down to him.

12 And the daughter of Tyre will come with a gift; the rich of the people will entreat your face.

13 All glorious within will be the daughter of the King; her clothing will be out of braided gold.

14 She will be led to the King in embroidered work, after her the virgins, her companions, will be brought to you.

15 They will be led with gladness and rejoicing, they will enter into the King's palace.

16 Your sons will be in place of your fathers; you will set them for rulers in all the earth.

The fact that the Branch will live a long life before his glorification and rapture is also described in Psalm ninety-one. Yahweh will answer the Branch's cry for Yahweh to deliver him, setting him on high and honouring him at his rapture to the throne of God.

Psalm 91:14—16 (D. Israel)

14 "Because he will set his love on Me, even I will deliver him, I will set him on high. Because he will know My name, he will call on Me, and I will answer him.

15 I will be with him in distress; I will draw him out of it, and I will honor him.

16 I will have satisfied him with length of days, and I will have caused him to see into My salvation."

The pleasure of Yahweh will prosper in the Branch's hands to some degree during the Branch's ministry to the nation of Israel, but more fully after his glorification at being reunited with Jesus and then anointed with the fullness of Yahweh's Spirit. God will raise up the Branch to David, to become the Davidic King. As the Davidic King, the Branch will have become Jesus, and will reign and prosper.

Jeremiah 23:5—6 (D. Israel)

5 "Behold, days are coming," says Yahweh, "that I will raise up to David a righteous Branch; and a King will reign and prosper, and will do justice and righteousness in the earth.

6 In His days Judah will be saved, and Israel will dwell safely; and this will be His name by which He will be called, Yahweh our righteousness."

In verse eleven, translators have incorrectly linked "with his knowledge" to "My righteous servant." In verse twelve, standard translations have inappropriately translated "with the many" as "with the great," and have adulterated it by adding "a portion."

4480(5999)   (5315)pro   pro(7200)
From (the) work (of) his soul   he will see;

pro(7646)   preb(1847)pro
he will be satiated with his knowledge.

6663   6662   (5650)pro   3807a(7227)
Will justify righteous my servant   ------ many,

2050a(5771)(pl)pro 1931   5445   3807a(3651)
but their iniquities   he   will bear.   Therefore,

pro(2505)   (3807a)pro   preb(7227) 2050a(854)
I will divide   to him   with (the) many and with

6099   pro(2505)   7998   8478 834
(the) strong he will divide (the) spoil;   because (he)

6168   3807a(4194) (5315)pro
will have stripped bare   to death   his soul,

2050a(854)   (6586)pl   4487   2050a(1931)
and with   transgressors will be counted; and He

```
2399      7227      5375      2050a(3807a)
(the) sin (of) many will lift up,      and for
```

```
(6586)pl                  pro(6293)
transgressors       He will reach the mark.
```

Jesus does not justify the many by His knowledge, but by His righteous-ness. It is Jesus' live righteous Spirit indwelling the spirit of the believer who justifies him by means of making his spirit righteous, even unable to sin. It is the Branch who will be satiated with his knowledge, the knowledge he gains from the work of his soul. From the Branch's effort and with the help of God, the Branch will see; he will see into God's plan of salvation. Yahweh clarifies the fact that He will cause the Branch to see into His salvation in Psalm 91:14—16 above.

Verse twelve is spoken by Yahweh the Father. Isaiah chapter fif-ty-three opens and closes with a two-legged double-step. The opening two-legged double-step in verses 2—3 describes the origin of Jesus and the origin of the Branch; whereas the closing two-legged double-step in verse twelve describes the destiny of Jesus' Spirit and the destiny of Jesus' soul.

leg 1 step1   My righteous servant will justify many,
leg 2 step1   but their iniquities he will bear.
leg 2 step 2 Therefore, I will divide to him with the many, and he will divide the spoil with the strong; because he will have stripped bare his soul to death, and will be counted with transgressors;
leg 1 step 2 and the sin of many He will lift up, and for transgres-sors He will reach the mark.

Leg one describes the destiny of Jesus' Spirit, whereas leg two describes the destiny of Jesus' soul. Leg-one step-one describes that Jesus' Spirit jus-tifies whosoever believes in Him. Jesus' Spirit justifies, makes righteous, the believer by indwelling the believer's spirit. The resurrected Jesus consists of His glorified spiritual body and His Spirit, the parts of Jesus that came into being at His conception. It was the Word who existed before Jesus' conception, and who became flesh, became Jesus' soul. In I John 3:9, the seed of God consists of the parts of Jesus that were conceived, and which make up the resurrected Jesus. I John 3:9 confirms that Jesus justifies the believer, causing the believer to be unable to sin by means of indwelling him. It is the believer's spirit that is made righteous, even unable to sin. It is the believer's soul that is still capable of sin.

Leg-two step-one describes that Yahweh God will divide justification to Jesus' soul, along with the many that Jesus justifies. When Jesus' soul re-enters life as the soul of the Branch, he will be born a sinner. The Branch will be guilty of being a transgressor of God; therefore, when the Branch becomes a born again Christian, Jesus will become his head, just as Jesus is the head of all members of the church (Eph. 1:22—23). At the Branch being born again, the stone rejected by the builders became the head of the corner.

Psalm 118:22—23 (D. Israel)
22 The stone the builders rejected became the head of the corner;
23 this was from Yahweh, it is marvellous in our eyes.

Psalm 118:22—23 is spoken by a contemporary of the Branch, who receives understanding of God's plan of salvation through the Branch's teaching. Jesus was rejected by the Jewish priests for claiming to be the Son of God. The Son of God, that which was conceived, consists of Jesus' glorified spiritual body and His Spirit, the parts of Jesus that make up the resurrected Jesus. It was Jesus' soul who existed before Jesus' conception as the corner or cornerstone. So, at the Branch being born again, the stone rejected by the builders became the head of the corner. After the Branch is glorified by being reunited with Jesus, the Branch will be Jesus. And as Jesus, the Branch will divide the spoil with the strong.

After Jesus' second advent He will divide the spoil with the people of Israel, who rise up and join Him against the armies gathered against Him at His second advent.

In verse twelve, translators have inappropriately translated the Hebrew verb #6168 as poured out. This verb is in the hiphil form, and should be translated as stripped bare. Jesus stripped bare His soul to death. At Jesus' death He stripped bare His soul of His life giving Spirit. The purpose of Jesus' death was to free His live righteous Spirit from His soul, in order that His Spirit be freed to indwell and make righteous the spirit of whosoever believes in Him. Theologians understand that being counted with transgressors refers to Jesus being crucified with two transgressors of the Roman state. However, the fuller meaning of this verse refers to after Jesus' death, when Jesus' soul becomes a transgressor of God at becoming the Branch's soul. Nevertheless, when the Branch becomes a born again Christian, Jesus will reach the mark for him, just as Jesus reaches the mark for all who are born again. Jesus lifts up and removes the sin of the believer's spirit, causing his spirit to be incapable of sin (I John 3:9). Jesus reaches the mark of being without sin for the believer. Even though the believer's soul is still capable of sin, he is no longer considered a transgressor of God.

In verse twelve, translators have translated the Hebrew verb #6293 as "made intercession." It is true that Jesus did make intercession for transgressors. However, a more appropriate translation would be to translate this verb as "to reach the mark," similar to how the NAS has translated #6293 in Job 36:32. Reaching the mark of being without sin for transgressors is what Jesus does when he justifies them. Jesus reaches the mark of being without sin for whosoever believes in Him. To be justified is to be made righteous. It is Jesus' live righteous Spirit indwelling the believer's spirit that makes him righteous, even unable to sin. It is the believer's soul that is still capable of sin.

ISAIAH 55:1–5

1   "Ho, all who are thirsty come to the water; and he who doesn't have silver, come buy food and eat; yea, come, buy food without silver, and wine and milk without price.

2   Why do you weigh out silver for what is not bread, and your labor without satisfaction? Listen carefully to Me, and eat the good thing, and your soul will delight in fatness.

3   Incline your ear to Me; hear and your soul will live; and I will cut to you the everlasting covenant of the faithful mercies of David.

4   Behold, I will give him as a witness of the peoples, as the leader and commander of the peoples.

5   Behold, you will call a nation you do not know; and a nation that does not know you will run to you because of Yahweh your God, even because of the Holy One of Israel, for He will glorify you."

In verses 1—4, Yahweh gives an invitation to all those in need to come to Him for salvation and eternal life. In the latter years, Yahweh will call the nation of Israel and all the nations through the Branch (verse 5). In Jeremiah 15:16, it is the Branch who finds and eats God's words.

Jeremiah 15:16 (D. Israel) Your words were found and I ate them, and Your words were to me joy and gladness of heart; for Your name is called upon me, Yahweh God of hosts.

Because of eating God's words, the Branch will see and be satiated with his gained knowledge.

Isaiah 53:10—11 (D. Israel)

10 But Yahweh will be pleased to crush Him, to make Him sick. When You make his soul guilty, he will see his seed, he will prolong his days, and the pleasure of Yahweh will prosper in his hands.

11 From the work of his soul he will see; he will be satiated with his knowledge.

Because of his effort, Yahweh will cause the Branch to see into His plan of salvation.

Psalm 91:14—16 (D. Israel)

14 "Because he will set his love on Me, even I will deliver him, I will set him on high. Because he will know My name, he will call on Me, and I will answer him.

15 I will be with him in distress; I will draw him out of it, and I will honor him.

16 I will have satisfied him with length of days, and I will have caused him to see into My salvation."

The Branch's ministry is to point out God's words regarding His plan of salvation, so that whosoever hears God's words will also eat and be satisfied, and accept Jesus as Lord. In so doing, they will be cut the everlasting covenant of the faithful mercies of David, which consists of God's faithful mercy of eternal life. The mercies of David are not the mercies of king David, but of the Davidic King, the Messiah. Those who come to God must accept Jesus as their Messiah and Lord, and then they will be given the everlasting faithful mercies of David. God will give them everlasting life. It is the Branch who will be raised up to be the Davidic King. The Branch will become the Davidic King at his glorification, when he is reunited with Jesus and once again becomes Jesus' soul.

Jeremiah 23:5—6 (D. Israel)

5   "Behold, days are coming," says Yahweh, "that I will raise up to David a righteous Branch; and a King will reign and prosper, and will do justice and righteousness in the earth.

6   In His days Judah will be saved, and Israel will dwell safely; and this will be His name by which He will be called, Yahweh our righteousness."

In verse four, it is the Branch whom God will give as a witness to the peoples during his ministry, and then as the leader and commander of the peoples after his glorification. The Branch will not be from Israel, but will be sent to Israel as God's messenger (Isaiah 42:19—21), who comes from the north (Psalm 75:6; Isaiah 41:25). The nation of Israel will run to the Branch at his glorification. At the Branch's glorification, he will be Jesus, so those who run to the Branch at his glorification will be running to Jesus. Similarly, Micah describes the rest of Jesus' brothers returning to the sons of Israel at the Branch's glorification, at Jesus' super-natural birth.

Micah 5:2—3 (D. Israel)

2   "And you, Bethlehem Ephrathah, small at being among the thousands of Judah, out of you He will go forth for Me to become ruler in Israel; and His goings forth have been from ancient times, from the days of eternity.

3   Therefore, He will give them up until the time when she who travails has brought forth; then the rest of His brothers will return to the sons of Israel."

However, those who wait until the Branch's glorification, to accept Jesus as Lord will cause trouble for themselves. For the Branch's glorification is what causes the resumption of the seventy weeks of years, and those who accept Jesus as Lord during this period of time will not be born again at this time; thus, they will not be raptured. They will have to endure the entire great tribulation; and then after Jesus' second advent, those of the age of accountability will be judged by their deeds as to whether or not they receive eternal life (Mat. 25:31—46). During the seventieth week of years, salvation is no longer received by grace through belief in Jesus, but salvation is received after being judged to have been obedient to the law.

ISAIAH 57:13–19

13 "—— But one who will take refuge in Me will possess the earth, and he will inherit My holy mountain";

14 and will say, "Raise up, raise up, prepare the way, lift up the stumbling block from the way of My people." For thus says the high and exalted One, "He will abide forever, and holy will be his name.

15 I dwell in a high and holy place, also with the contrite and humble of spirit, to make live the spirit of the humble and to quicken the heart of the contrite.

16 For I will not contend forever, and I will not always be angry, for the spirit before Me would faint, even the spirits I have made.

17 In the iniquity of his unjust gain, I will be angry and strike him; I will hide Myself and be angry, but he will go turning away in the way of his heart.

18 His ways I see, but I will heal him and lead him and restore comforts to him; and for his mourning create the fruit of the lips.

19 Peace, peace to him who is far off and to him who is near," says Yahweh; "and I will heal him."

Verse thirteen is referring to the Branch, who will take refuge with Yahweh at his glorification and rapture, as also described in Psalm 57:1 and 71:1—2.

Psalm 57:1 (D. Israel) Be merciful to me, God, be merciful to me for my soul seeks refuge with you; even in the shadow of Your wings I seek refuge until the destruction passes.

Psalm 71:1—2 (D. Israel)

1 With You, Yahweh, I seek refuge: I will eternally not be confounded.

2 With Your righteousness snatch me away, and cause me to escape. Incline Your ear to me and deliver me.

At Jesus' super-natural birth at the Branch's reunification with Jesus, the Branch will become Jesus (Psalm 2:7), and immediately after this Jesus will be anointed with the fullness of Yahweh's Spirit (Psalm 2:6), and immediately after this Jesus as Yahweh will be raptured to the throne of God (Psalm 24:7—10; Rev. 12:5).

Psalm 2:6—7 (D. Israel)

6 "Yea, I anointed My King on Zion, My holy mountain."

7 "I will declare concerning the statute of Yahweh: He said to Me, 'You are My Son, today I have begotten You.'"

The Branch who becomes Jesus will possess the earth starting at Jesus' second advent, as also described in Psalm 2:8—9.

Psalm 2:8—9 (D. Israel)

8 "Ask of Me and I will give the nations as Your inheritance, even the ends of the earth as Your possession.

9 You will break them with a rod of iron; You will dash them as a potter's vessel."

In verse fourteen, it is the Branch who removes the stumbling block to the people of Israel of Christ crucified. Paul pointed out that Christ crucified was a stumbling block to the Jews.

I Corinthians 1:22—24 (NAS)

22 For indeed Jews ask for signs, and Greeks search for wisdom;

23 but we preach Christ crucified, to Jews a stumbling block, and to Gentiles foolishness,

24 but to those who are the called, both Jews and Greeks, Christ the power of God and the wisdom of God.

The people of Israel were expecting a Messiah who would take back the nation from the Roman occupation. So, Christ crucified was a stumbling block to them. The people of Israel didn't understand the purpose of Jesus' death. Up to the present day, even Christians can not give a logical and scriptural explanation for the purpose of Jesus' death. It is because God will cause the Branch to see into His plan of salvation, that the Branch is able to remove the stumbling block of Christ crucified.

In Psalm 91:14—16, Yahweh reveals that He will deliver the Branch by setting him on high. Yahweh will set the Branch on high at his glorification and rapture to the throne of God. In addition, Yahweh reveals that He will cause the Branch to see into His salvation.

Psalm 91:14—16 (D. Israel)

14 "Because he will set his love on Me, even I will deliver him, I will set him on high. Because he will know My name, he will call on Me, and I will answer him.

15 I will be with him in distress; I will draw him out of it, and I will honor him.

16 I will have satisfied him with length of days, and I will have caused him to see into My salvation."

God crushed Jesus at His death, and God will make Jesus' soul guilty as the soul of the Branch, giving him the sickness of sin. However, with God's help, and through his effort he will see; he will see into God's plan of salvation.

Isaiah 53:10—11 (D. Israel)

10 But Yahweh will be pleased to crush Him, to make Him sick. When You make his soul guilty, he will see his seed, he will prolong his days, and the pleasure of Yahweh will prosper in his hands.

11 From the work of his soul he will see; he will be satiated with his knowledge.

The Branch will correctly explain to the people of Israel how Jesus' death was the means by which whosoever believes in Him has eternal life. The Branch will explain that the purpose of Jesus' conception was for Jesus' life giving Spirit to be conceived, explaining that it was Jesus' soul who existed before Jesus' conception as the Word. The Branch will explain that the purpose of Jesus' death was to free His Spirit from His soul, in order that His life giving Spirit might indwell and give eternal life to whosoever believes in Him. As Isaiah reveals, Jesus stripped bare His soul to death on the cross. Jesus stripped bare His soul of His life giving Spirit.

Isaiah 53:12 (D. Israel) —— Therefore, I will divide to him with the many, and he will divide the spoil with the strong, because he will have stripped bare his soul to death, ——

In verse fourteen, Yahweh reveals that the Branch will abide forever, and that his name will be holy. The Branch will abide forever, because he will be glorified by being reunited with Jesus. At his glorification, the Branch will be raised up to David, to become the Davidic King. At being reunited with Jesus and then anointed with Yahweh's Spirit, the Branch will be Jesus and be as Yahweh; and he will be called Yahweh our righteousness. Thus, his name will be holy.

Jeremiah 23:5—6 (D. Israel)

5 "Behold, days are coming," says Yahweh, "that I will raise up to David a righteous Branch; and a King will reign and prosper, and will do justice and righteousness in the earth.

6 In His days Judah will be saved, and Israel will dwell safely; and this will be His name by which He will be called, Yahweh our righteousness."

In verse fifteen, Yahweh states that He dwells in a high and holy place, but also with those having a contrite and humble spirit. Yahweh dwells in the high and holy place of Heaven, but also with those who humble themselves and accept God's rule. The Branch will teach the people of Israel God's plan of salvation, and why Jesus is their Lord. Whoever humbles themselves and accepts Jesus, will have his spirit made alive by being indwelt by Jesus. He will be born again and have the surety of eternal life.

Verses 16—17 describe Yahweh's anger with Judah, because of the iniquity of its covetousness or unjust gain. These verses refer to Yahweh's anger with Judah due to its covetousness, that resulted in God causing Judah to go into captivity to Babylon (Jer. 6:13; 8:10; Ezek. 22:13; 33:31).

Jeremiah 6:13 (King James) For from the least of them even unto the greatest of them every one is given to covetousness; and from the prophet even unto the priest every one dealeth falsely.

Due to Judah's sin that resulted in him going into captivity, Yahweh has hidden His face from the people of Israel (Isaiah 64:7—11; Ezek. 39:23—24).

Ezekiel 39:23—24 (King James)
23 And the heathen shall know that the house of Israel went into captivity for their iniquity: because they trespassed against me, therefore hid I my face from them, and gave them into the hand of their enemies: so fell they all by the sword.

24 According to their uncleanness and according to their transgressions have I done unto them, and hid my face from them.

Verse eighteen refers to the fact that Yahweh will heal Israel from
the sickness of sin. Yahweh will heal Israelis as a result of the Branch's
teaching. The Branch will remove the stumbling block of Christ crucified, by correctly and logically explaining how Jesus' death gives eternal
life to whosoever believes in Him. As a result of the Branch's teaching,
many Israelis will be healed by being born again. Isaiah 53:5 describes
our healing from sin and being made complete, due to the wound of
Jesus' death. Jesus' death was for our correction.

Isaiah 53:5 (D. Israel) Nevertheless our sickness He has lifted
up, and our sorrows He has carried, though we regarded Him
stricken by God and afflicted; but He was wounded on account
of our transgressions, crushed on account of out iniquities,
chastening for our completeness was upon Him, and with His
wound it is healed for us.

In addition, the Branch's teaching will cause Israel to worship God
in a manner that will result in the latter year pouring out of God's Spirit
(Joel 2:28—29), in which God will create the fruit of the lips for the
believer, giving the oil of joy instead of mourning (Isaiah 61:3). At the
latter year pouring out of God's Spirit, God will no longer hide from
the people of Israel.

Ezekiel 39:29 (D. Israel) "And I will not hide My face any more
from them, for I will pour out My Spirit on the house of Israel,"
says the Lord Yahweh.

Isaiah 44:1—5 reveals that the Branch will be instrumental in the latter
year pouring out of God's Spirit.

Isaiah 44:1—5 (D. Israel)

1 And now listen, Jacob My servant, even Israel: I have chosen him.

2 Thus says Yahweh, your maker and former from the womb, "He will help you. Do not fear, My servant Jacob, even Jeshurun, I have chosen him.

3 For I will pour out water upon the thirsty, and floods upon dry ground; I will pour out My Spirit upon your seed, and My blessing upon your offspring.

4 And they will spring up in among grass, as willows by streams of water.

5 This one will say, 'I am for Yahweh'; and this one will call out in the name of Jacob; and this one will write with his hand for Yahweh, and be named by the name of Israel."

In Isaiah 44:1—2, it is the Branch whom God has chosen to help Israel. In Isaiah 44:5, it is the Branch who will write for Yahweh, and who will be named by the name of Israel.

Genesis chapter forty-nine also describes the Branch helping Israel. The Branch will become fruitful on account of the spring of God's Spirit. The Branch is of the branch of Joseph, who will help Israel receive eternal life through belief in Jesus; and he will help Israel to worship God with the truth, that will result in the latter year pouring out of God's Spirit.

Genesis 49:22—25 (D. Israel)

22 "Joseph will be a fruitful branch, a fruitful branch on account of a spring;

23 his branches will go over the wall, and the masters of arrows will vex him, and shoot at and hate him;

24 but his bow will abide with strength, and the arms of his hands will be agile from the hands of the Mighty One of Jacob; from there will be the Shepherd, the Stone of Israel,

25 from the God of your father; and he will help you; then together
with the Almighty, even He will bless you with the blessings of
the heavens above, the blessings of the deep lying below, and the
blessings of the breasts and the womb."

Isaiah 44:3 indicates that the latter year pouring out of God's Spirit
will occur just after God pours out rain on dry ground. Joel describes
more fully this time of severe drought in Israel, that is ended by God
sending rain, and is followed by the pouring out of God's Spirit. Joel
indicates that it is not only a time of severe drought, but it is also the
time that Israel is invaded by the northern army of Gog (Joel 2:20), as
also described in Ezekiel chapters thirty-eight and thirty-nine. In Joel
2:23, at this point in time of drought, God indicates that He has given
Israel the teacher of righteousness. It is the Branch who is the teacher
of righteousness, who will correctly explain to the people of Israel why
Jesus is the believer's righteousness; he will explain that whosoever believes in Jesus has his spirit made righteous, by being indwelt by Jesus'
righteous life giving Spirit.

Joel 2:15—29 (D. Israel)

15 Blow a trumpet in Zion, consecrate a fast, call an assembly,

16 gather the people, sanctify the congregation, assemble the elders, gather the children and those sucking the breasts. Let
the bridegroom come out of his room, and the bride from her
chamber.

17 Let the priests weep at the porch and toward the alter, ministers of Yahweh; and let them say, "Have pity, Yahweh, on Your
people, and do not give Your inheritance to reproach, that the
nations should rule over them. Why should they say among the
peoples, 'Where is their God?'"

18 Then Yahweh will be jealous for His land, and will have pity on
His people.

19 And Yahweh will answer and say to His people, "Behold, I will send grain to you, and new wine and fresh oil, and you will be satisfied with it; and I will not any longer make you a reproach among the nations,

20 but I will remove the one from the north far from upon you, and I will drive him into a land of drought and desolation, with his face toward the eastern sea, and his rear toward the western sea. And his stench will come up, and his foul odour will ascend, for he will have grown great to perform."

21 Do not fear, land; rejoice and be glad, for Yahweh will be magnified at doing it.

22 Do not fear, beasts of the field, for the pastures of the wilderness will grow green; for the tree will bear its fruit, and the fig tree and the vine will give their strength.

23 So, sons of Zion, rejoice and be glad in Yahweh your God; for He has given you the teacher of righteousness; and the rain will come down to you; the early rain, but at first the latter rain.

24 And the threshing floors will be full of grain, and the vats will overflow with new wine and oil.

25 "And I will restore to you the years which the swarming locust has eaten, the crawling locust and the caterpillar and the gnawing locust, My great army which I have sent among you.

26 And you will eat fully and be satisfied, and you will praise the name of Yahweh your God who will deal with you wondrously. Then My people will never be ashamed;

27 and you will know that I am in the midst of Israel, and I am Yahweh your God and there is not another. Yea, My people will never be ashamed.

28 And it will be afterward that I will pour out My Spirit on all flesh; and your sons and your daughters will prophesy, and your elders will dream dreams, and your youth will see visions.

29 And even on the servants and handmaids I will pour out My Spirit in those days."

Isaiah 57:19 describes the fact that those who are healed of sin have peace with God. In Isaiah 53:5, completeness can also be translated as peace. Chastening for our completeness or peace was upon Jesus; and with the wound of His soul at being separated from His Spirit at His death, the sickness of being a sinner is healed for us. The sickness of sin is healed through belief in Jesus.

JEREMIAH 15:16-19

16 Your words were found and I ate them, and Your words were to me joy and gladness of heart; for Your name is called upon me, Yahweh God of hosts.

17 I did not sit in the circle of merrymakers, nor did I exalt. I sat alone because of the presence of Your hand; for You have filled me with indignation.

18 Why has my pain been continual and my wound incurable? It has refused to be healed. Surely You have become to me as deceitful water that is not faithful.

19 Therefore, thus says Yahweh, "If you restore, then I will restore you; you will stand before Me; yea, if you bring out the precious from the worthless, you will be as My mouth."

Similar to Isaiah 38:15:20, Jeremiah contains a prophetic utterance that is triggered by a descriptive phrase of a prayer. The speaker of Jeremiah 15:16—18 is not Jeremiah, but is a prophetic utterance made through him. In Jeremiah 15:15, Jeremiah asked God to take vengeance for him on his persecutors, and pointed out that for God's sake he has endured reproach. So, in Jeremiah 15:16—18, God responds to Jeremiah's prayer by giving a prophetic utterance in which the Branch is the speaker, he whose soul bore reproach for God's sake as the soul of Jesus. Psalm 69:19—21 is spoken by Jesus' soul, from the point in time of the three days and nights that he spent in Sheol after Jesus' death. Jesus' soul describes the reproach that he felt at the time of Jesus' death.

Psalm 69:19—21 (D. Israel)

19 You know of my reproach and my shame and my disgrace; my
adversaries are before You.

20 Reproach broke my heart, and I was full of heaviness; and I
looked for sympathy, but there was none; and for comforters,
but I found none.

21 But they gave me gall as my food, and for my thirst they gave
me vinegar to drink.

In Jeremiah 15:16, the Branch describes finding God's words and
eating them. The Branch will find God's words, particularly regarding
God's plan of salvation. Because of the Branch' effort, he will see and be
satiated with his knowledge from God's Word.

Isaiah 53:10—11 (D. Israel)

10 But Yahweh will be pleased to crush Him, to make Him sick.
When You make his soul guilty, he will see seed, he will prolong
his days, and the pleasure of Yahweh will prosper in his hands.

11 From the work of his soul he will see; he will be satiated with his
knowledge.

With God's help, the Branch will see into God's plan of salvation as
contained in His Word.

Psalm 91:14—16 (D. Israel)

14 "Because he will set his love on Me, even I will deliver him, I
will set him on high. Because he will know My name, he will
call on Me, and I will answer him.

15 I will be with him in distress; I will draw him out of it, and I will
honor him.

16 I will have satisfied him with length of days, and I will have
caused him to see into My salvation."

In Jeremiah 15:16, the Branch states that God's words were to him joy and gladness of heart, because God's name is called upon him. From Isaiah 44:5 and Isaiah 49:3, we know that God's name of "Israel" is named upon the Branch.

Isaiah 44:5 (D. Israel) "This one will say, 'I am for Yahweh'; and this one will call out in the name of Jacob; and this one will write with his hand for Yahweh, and be named by the name of Israel."

Isaiah 49:1—3 (D. Israel)
1   Listen to me, coasts, and pay attention, people from afar. Since the womb Yahweh called Me; since the belly of My mother bringing to remembrance My name.
2   And He made My mouth like a sharp sword, in the shadow of His hand He hid Me. Even He made Me a choice arrow, in His quiver He hid Me.
3   And He said to Me, "You are My servant, Israel, You in whom I will be glorified."

Israel is God's name that He gave to Jacob. Strong's concordance gives the meaning of the name Israel as, "he will rule as God." The Branch will rule as God starting at his glorification, at his mouth being made a sharp sword.

In verse seventeen, the Branch relates that he didn't sit with merry-makers, nor did he exalt. The presence of God's hand upon him will set him on a path that will lead to him being born again, and eventually seeing into God's plan of salvation. However, the presence of God's hand will also result in him sitting alone and being filled with indignation. He will feel that the presence of God's hand, that has resulted in him sitting alone has done an injustice to him.

In verse eighteen, the Branch questions why his pain has been continual, and his wound incurable. The Branch also states that God has become to him as deceitful water that is not faithful. His pain and wound is an affliction placed upon him by God, in order that he learn God's statutes (Psalm 119:67—71).

Psalm 119:67—71 (D. Israel)

67 Before I was afflicted I went astray, but now I keep Your word.

68 You are good and do good; teach me Your statutes.

69 The proud have forged a lie against me; I with all my heart will keep Your precepts.

70 Insensitive like fat are their hearts; I delight in Your law.

71 It was good for me that I was afflicted, so that I might learn Your statutes.

In Psalm seventy-three, similar to Jeremiah 15:17—18, the Branch complains about his affliction from the hand of God. He states that he has washed his hands in innocence, yet he is still stricken by his chastisement.

Psalm 73:13—14 (D. Israel)

13 Surely in vain I have cleansed my heart; yea, I have washed my hands in innocence,

14 but I am stricken all the day, and my chastisement is toward the mornings.

The Branch's complaint that God has become to him as deceitful water that is not faithful, may be a reference to the fact that he is deaf to God's voice. Isaiah 42:19—21 describes that the Branch is God's deaf messenger sent to the nation of Israel. The Branch will be deaf to the voice of God, but is able to be God's messenger, due to seeing into God's plan of salvation. The Branch may have expected God to baptize him with His Spirit; thus, cause him to hear His voice.

In verse nineteen, God responds to the Branch's complaints. Yahweh states that if the Branch restored, then He would restore the Branch, and that the Branch would stand before Him. If the Branch brings out the precious from the worthless, then the Branch would become as Yahweh's mouth. Yahweh is describing the Branch's work for Him. God afflicted the Branch in order that he learn God's statutes. As a consequence of his affliction, the Branch has found God's words regarding His plan of salvation. Yahweh's condition for healing the Branch is for the Branch to restore God's words that he has found, to bring out God's precious words from the worthless words that cover over God's words. The Branch is not to keep God's words that he has found to himself, but to restore them and present them to the people of Israel and to the world.

Much of God's plan of salvation as contained in Scripture has been destroyed by poor translation. In addition, poor teaching has further distorted the truth of God's plan of salvation. The Branch's work is to set straight God's precepts that deal with God's plan of salvation.

Psalm 119:126—128 (D. Israel)
126 It is time to work for Yahweh; they have made void Your law.
127 Therefore I love Your commandments more than gold, even more than fine gold.
128 Therefore, all the precepts, the totality, I will make straight; every way of falsehood I hate.

The Branch will set straight the totality of God's precepts, by setting straight the foundation. The foundation of God's word is the truth of His plan of salvation. In Psalm forty-five, the Branch also describes his work for Yahweh in which his tongue is the stylus of a rapid writer, the stylus of a modern day computer.

Psalm 45:1 (D. Israel) My heart is astir with a good matter. I speak my work for the King, my tongue being the stylus of a rapid writer.

JEREMIAH 23:5-6

5   "Behold, days are coming," says Yahweh, "that I will raise up to David a righteous Branch; and a King will reign and prosper, and will do justice and righteousness in the earth.

6   In His days Judah will be saved, and Israel will dwell safely; and this will be His name by which He will be called, Yahweh our righteousness."

In Jeremiah 23:5—6, David does not refer to king David, but to the Davidic King and Messiah. Yahweh will raise up the Branch to become the Davidic King, at his glorification at being reunited with Jesus. At being reunited with Jesus, the Branch will once again become Jesus. He will once again be Jesus' soul. Immediately after Jesus' super-natural birth, Jesus once again will be anointed with the fullness of Yahweh's Spirit. In Psalm 2:7—9, Jesus describes His super-natural birth on Mount Zion, and what Yahweh declares to him on that day, the day that he is also once again anointed with the fullness of Yahweh's Spirit. In Psalm 2:6, Yahweh describes the fact that He anoints Jesus on Mount Zion on the day of Jesus' reunification with the Branch, the day of Jesus' super-natural birth at the resumption of the seventy weeks of years.

Psalm 2:6—9 (D. Israel)

6   "Yea, I anointed My King on Zion, My holy mountain."

7   "I will declare concerning the statute of Yahweh: He said to Me, 'You are My Son, today I have begotten You.

8 Ask of Me and I will give the nations as Your inheritance, even the ends of the earth as Your possession.

9 You will break them with a rod of iron; You will dash them as a potter's vessel.'"

After the Branch's glorification and anointing with Yahweh's Spirit, he will be called Yahweh our righteousness. The Branch who will have become Jesus will be as Yahweh, because of being anointed with the fullness of Yahweh's Spirit; and Jesus is our righteousness, making righteous the spirit of whosoever believes in Him. So, the Branch who will be raised up to become the Davidic king will appropriately be called, Yahweh our righteousness.

JOEL 2:15-29

15 Blow a trumpet in Zion, consecrate a fast, call an assembly,

16 gather the people, sanctify the congregation, assemble the elders, gather the children and those sucking the breasts. Let the bridegroom come out of his room, and the bride from her chamber.

17 Let the priests weep at the porch and toward the alter, ministers of Yahweh; and let them say, "Have pity, Yahweh, on Your people, and do not give Your inheritance to reproach, that the nations should rule over them. Why should they say among the peoples, 'Where is their God?'"

18 Then Yahweh will be jealous for his land, and will have pity on His people.

19 And Yahweh will answer and say to His people, "Behold, I will send grain to you, and new wine and fresh oil, and you will be satisfied with it; and I will not any longer make you a reproach among the nations,

20 but I will remove the one from the north far from upon you, and I will drive him into a land of drought and desolation, with his face toward the eastern sea, and his rear toward the western sea. And his stench will come up, and his foul odour will ascend, for he will have grown great to perform."

21 Do not fear, land; rejoice and be glad, for Yahweh will be magnified at doing it.

22 Do not fear, beasts of the field, for the pastures of the wilderness
    will grow green; for the tree will bear its fruit, and the fig tree
    and the vine will give their strength.

23 So, sons of Zion, rejoice and be glad in Yahweh your God; for
    He has given to you the teacher of righteousness; and the rain
    will come down to you; the early rain, but at first the latter rain.

24 And the threshing floors will be full of grain, and the vats will
    overflow with new wine and oil.

25 "And I will restore to you the years which the swarming locust
    has eaten, the crawling locust and the caterpillar and the gnaw-
    ing locust, My great army which I have sent among you.

26 And you will eat fully and be satisfied, and you will praise the
    name of Yahweh your God who will deal with you wondrously.
    Then My people will never be ashamed;

27 and you will know that I am in the midst of Israel, and I am
    Yahweh your God and there is not another. Yea, My people will
    never be ashamed.

28 And it will be afterward that I will pour out My Spirit on all
    flesh; and your sons and your daughters will prophesy, and your
    elders will dream dreams, and your youth will see visions.

29 And even on the servants and handmaids I will pour out My
    Spirit in those days."

Joel 2:15—20 describes a crisis that will occur in Israel in the latter
years. It describes a severe drought, and Israel being invaded by a northern army (verse 20). This time of crisis will occur shortly before the
latter year pouring out of God's Spirit (verses 28—29). The invasion by
this army is described in more detail in Ezekiel chapters 38—39, which
describe Israel being invaded by Gog and her allies, just before the latter
year pouring out of God's Spirit. Ezekiel describes that at the time of the
invasion, Israel will be at rest and dwelling securely (Ezek. 38:8; 38:11;
38:14; 39:26).

Isaiah chapter forty-two describes the Branch being sent to Israel as God's messenger, at a time that Israel is at peace. Isaiah 42:19—21 is a two-legged double-step, in which leg one describes the nation of Israel, and leg two describes the Branch.

Isaiah 42:19—21 (D. Israel)

leg 1 step 1　Who is blind, yet My servant;

leg 2 step 1　or deaf as My messenger I send?

leg 1 step 2　Who is blind as he who is at peace, even blind as the servant of Yahweh? You have seen many things, but have not taken heed.

leg 2 step 2　His ears are open, but he can not hear; Yahweh is pleased on account of his righteousness; he magnifies the law and makes it honorable.

So, the Branch will be in Israel when Israel is at peace with her neighbors and the Palestinians, which will be when the northern armies of Gog invade Israel.

In Joel 2:23, Yahweh reveals that He has given Israel the teacher of righteousness for this time of crisis. Standard translations have translated the teacher of righteousness out of Joel 2:23. At one time, the NIV translation had correctly translated the teacher of righteousness, but have since then changed their translation. The confusion comes from the fact that the Hebrew word #4175 can mean "early rain" or "teacher."

2050a(1121)pl　　6726　1523　　2050a(8055)
So, sons　　(of) Zion, rejoice　　and be glad

preb(3068)　　(430)pro 3588　　　　5414　(3807a)pro
in Yahweh　　your God; for (He) has given　　to you

853 def(4175) 3807a(6666)　　　　2050a(3381)
--- the teacher of righteousness; and will come down

(3807a)pro   1653   4175
to you (the) rain; (the) early rain,

2050a(4456)   preb(7223)
but (the) latter rain   at first.

The Branch will be sent to Israel as God's messenger, in particular God's messenger of His plan of salvation. With his effort and God's help, the Branch will see (Isaiah 53:10—11). With God's help, the Branch will see into God's plan of salvation (Psalm 91:14—16). The Branch will correctly explain to the people of Israel why Jesus is the righteousness of whosoever believes in Him. The Branch will explain that it is Jesus who indwells and makes righteous the spirit of the believer, and by so doing gives him eternal life. The Branch will explain that Jesus is the seed of God who indwells the believer, rendering his new born spirit incapable of sin.

I John 3:9 (J. P. Green) Everyone who has been begotten of God does not sin, because His seed abides in him, and he is not able to sin, because he has been born of God.

The Branch will explain that it is the believer's spirit that is born again, whereas it is the believer's soul that is still capable of sin.

At the height of this latter year crisis in Israel, God will deal wondrously with Israel. God will send rain to end the drought, and He will remove the northern army of Gog; and He will send His message of salvation through the Branch, the teacher of righteousness. The Branch will not only teach the people of Israel God's plan of salvation, but he will also teach them how to worship God in a manner that will result in the latter year pouring out of God's Spirit. Isaiah 44:1—5 reveals that God has chosen the Branch to help Israel, and that he will be instrumental in the latter year pouring out of God's Spirit. Isaiah 44:3 is in agreement with Joel 2:23—29, in that God will send rain to end a drought shortly before He pours out His Spirit.

Isaiah 44:1—5 (D. Israel)

1 And now listen, Jacob My servant, even Israel: I have chosen him.

2 Thus says Yahweh, your maker and former from the womb, "He will help you. Do not fear, my servant Jacob, even Jeshurun, I have chosen him.

3 For I will pour out water upon the thirsty, and floods upon dry ground; I will pour out My Spirit upon your seed, and My blessing upon your offspring.

4 And they will spring up in among grass, as willows by streams of water.

5 This one will say, 'I am for Yahweh'; and this one will call out in the name of Jacob; and this one will write with his hand for Yahweh, and be named by the name of Israel."

MICAH 5:2-3

2   "And you, Bethlehem Ephrathah, small at being among the thousands of Judah, out of you He will go forth for Me to become ruler in Israel; and His goings forth have been from ancient times, from the days of eternity.

3   Therefore, He will give them up until the time when she who travails has brought forth; then the rest of His brothers will return to the sons of Israel."

Theologians value Micah 5:2—3, because it predicted Bethlehem to be the place of Jesus' birth. However, they have missed the most important revelation of these verses. Micah 5:2—3 reveals the event that will cause the resumption of the seventy weeks of years. Daniel 9:24—26 predicted that the Messiah would appear to Israel sixty-nine weeks of years after the decree to rebuild Jerusalem. Sixty-nine weeks of years were completed when Jesus appeared before the Jewish priests on the morning of the day of His death. It was Jesus' death that made atonement available; thus, it interrupted the Jewish dispensation and started the age of grace or church age. Jesus gave up the nation of Israel at His death, but Micah reveals that Jesus will once again take up the nation of Israel, when a woman gives birth to a child. Revelation 12:1—5 reveals that the woman is the nation of Israel (Genesis 37:9—10), and that the child is Jesus.

Revelation 12:1—5 (NAS)

1   And a great sign appeared in heaven: a woman clothed with the sun, and the moon under her feet, and on her head a crown of twelve stars;

2   and she was with child; and she cried out, being in labor and in pain to give birth.

3   And another sign appeared in heaven: and behold, a great red dragon having seven heads and ten horns, and on his heads were seven diadems.

4   And his tail swept away a third of the stars of heaven, and threw them to the earth. And the dragon stood before the woman who was about to give birth, so that when she gave birth he might devour her child.

5   And she gave birth to a son, a male child, who is to rule all the nations with a rod of iron; and her child was caught up to God and to His throne.

This birth is not Jesus' natural birth at Bethlehem to Mary, but Jesus' super-natural birth on Mount Zion to the nation of Israel. In Psalm 2:6, Yahweh reveals what will cause the nations to rage at the time of the end. It will be His anointing of His King on Mount Zion, which will occur at the resumption of the seventy weeks of years, immediately after Jesus' super-natural birth. In Psalm 2:7—9, on the day of Jesus' super-natural birth, Jesus speaks of what Yahweh declares to Him on that day.

Psalm 2:6—9 (D. Israel)

6   "Yea, I anointed My King on Zion, My holy mountain."

7   "I will declare concerning the statute of Yahweh: He said to Me, 'You are My Son, today I have begotten You.

8   Ask of Me and I will give the nations as Your inheritance, even the ends of the earth as Your possession.

9   You will break them with a rod of iron; You will dash them as a potter's vessel.'"

Jesus stated just before His death, that Jerusalem would not see Him again until they say, Blessed is he who comes in the name of the Lord (Mat. 23:39). It will be the Branch who will come in the name of Yahweh at the time of his glorification. At that time, the people of Israel will cry out to God for the reunification of the Branch with Jesus. They will cry out to God, "Bind the sacrificial feast with cords, even to the horns of the alter."

Psalm 118:26—27 (D. Israel)
26 Blessed is he who comes in the name of Yahweh; we have blessed you from the house of Yahweh.
27 God is Yahweh, and He has given light to us. Bind the sacrificial feast with cords, even to the horns of the alter.

At their cry, God will glorify the Branch by reuniting him with Jesus. Jesus will come out of the midst of the church and indwell the spirit of the Branch. At that point in time, the Branch will once again be Jesus, whom the people of Jerusalem will see.

Bethlehem was appointed to be the place of Jesus' natural birth, whereas Jerusalem is appointed to be the place of Jesus' super-natural birth (Micah 6:9).

Micah 6:9 (D. Israel) The voice of Yahweh will call out to the city, and he having wisdom will see Your name; hear the Branch, and what is appointed her.

6963   3068   3807a(5892)   7121
(The) voice (of) Yahweh to (the) city will call out,

2050a(8454)   7200   (8034)pro 8055
and (he) (of) wisdom will see Your name; hear (the)

4294   2050a(4310)   (3259)pro
Branch,   and what   is appointed her.

It is the Branch who will call out to the city of Jerusalem (Psalm 116:12—14), Yahweh making the Branch as His mouth (Jeremiah 15:19). Those having wisdom will see God's name of Israel upon the Branch (Isaiah 44:5; 49:3). The Branch will lift up the cup of salvation and offer it to the people of Jerusalem and Israel, and he will also explain that Jerusalem is the site of the people of Israel giving birth to Jesus at His super-natural birth. The people of Israel will give birth to Jesus, when they the cry out to God for the reunification of the Branch with Jesus.

ZECHARIAH CHAPTER TWO

1   And I lifted up my eyes and looked, and behold a man with a measuring line in his hand.

2   And I said, "Where are you going?" And he said to me, "To measure Jerusalem, to see what its breath is and what its length is."

3   And behold, the angel who was speaking with me went forth, and another went forth to meet him,

4   and said to him, "Run, speak to this young man, saying, 'Jerusalem will be inhabited unwalled from the multitude of men and cattle in her midst.'"

5   "And I will be for her a wall of fire," says Yahweh, "and I will be the glory in her midst."

6   "Ho, ho, even flee from the land of the north," says Yahweh, "for I have scattered you as the four winds of the heavens," says Yahweh.

7   "Ho, Zion, escape, who dwells with the daughter of Babylon."

8   For thus has said Yahweh of hosts, "After the glory He will send Me to the nations who plunder you; for he who touches you touches the center of His eye.

9   For behold, I will wave My hand over them, and they will be plunder for their servants; and you will know that Yahweh of hosts has sent Me."

10 "Sing and rejoice, daughter of Zion; for behold, I am coming and will dwell in your midst," says Yahweh.

11 And many nations will be joined to Yahweh in that day, and they will be for a people to Me; and I will dwell in your midst, and you will know that Yahweh of hosts has sent Me to you.

12 And Yahweh will possess Judah, His portion in the holy land, and again will choose Jerusalem.

13 Be silent, all flesh, before Yahweh, when He is aroused from His holy habitation.

Zechariah 2:1—5 describes Jerusalem during Jesus' millennial reign. It describes that Yahweh will be Jerusalem's protection. He will be a wall of fire for her. In Zechariah 2:4—13, the angel who speaks is the Word. Theologians are confused as to what "the glory" refers to in verse eight. They have no hope of understanding this verse, because they don't understand who the Branch is. They don't understand that the Word will become the Branch's soul, and that the glory refers to the glory that will be given the Branch at the resumption of the seventy weeks of years. Psalm twenty-one describes that the Branch's glory will be great at being delivered by Yahweh.

Psalm 21:5 (D. Israel) His glory will be great in Your deliverance, honor and majesty You will lay upon him.

Psalm forty-five describes that the Branch's glory is Jesus, the Branch's sword. The Branch will be glorified at being reunited with Jesus.

Psalm 45:3—4 (D. Israel)

3 Gird your sword on your thigh, Mighty One, your glory and your majesty.

4 And in Your majesty prosper; ride on the matter of truth and meekness and righteousness, and Your right hand will teach You fearful things.

Psalm seventy-three reveals that after the glory, the water of Yahweh's Spirit will take the Branch to Heaven.

Psalm 73:24—26 (D. Israel)

24 And after the glory You will take me, the water for me in Heaven.

25   And beside You, I will desire nothing on earth.

26   My flesh and my heart will be complete; God will be the rock of
     my heart and my portion forever.

The Branch will be raptured through the everlasting doors of
Heaven, after becoming Yahweh, the King of glory. It is the Branch who
will stand up in Yahweh's place on Mount Zion. He is addressed as Jacob
in Psalm 24:6, because the blessing of becoming the ruler of the nations
was originally given to Jacob.

Psalm 24:3—10 (D. Israel)

3   Who will go up upon the mountain of Yahweh, and who will
     stand up in His holy place?

4   One who will have clean hands and a pure heart, who will not
     have lifted up his soul to vanity, and will not have sworn to deceit.

5   He will lift up the blessing from Yahweh, and righteousness
     from the God of his salvation.

6   This one a generation will seek, those who will seek your face,
     Jacob.

7   Lift up your heads, O gates, and be lifted up, O everlasting
     doors, and the King of glory will come in.

8   Who is the King of glory? Yahweh powerful and mighty, Yahweh
     mighty in battle.

9   Lift up your heads, O gates, and be lifted up, O everlasting
     doors, and the King of glory will come in.

10   Who is He, this king of glory? Yahweh of hosts, He is the King
     of glory.

At the time of the Branch's glorification, he will go up to Mount Zion
and will be reunited with Jesus, and then he as Jesus will be anointed
with Yahweh's Spirit (Psalm 2:6—10).

After the Branch's glory, he will be Jesus, and Yahweh will send him
to confront the nations gathered against Him at His second advent.

In verse ten, the Word reveals that Yahweh will dwell in the midst of Jerusalem, during Jesus' millennial reign. In verse eleven, the Word states that many nations will be joined to Yahweh, and that they will be the Word's people; for the Word will once again be Jesus' soul at the Branch's glorification. In verses nine and eleven, the Word states that the people of Jerusalem will know that Yahweh has sent Him. They will know this at Jesus' second advent, at the start of Jesus' millennial reign. By this time, the Word will have once again become Jesus' soul, and there will be no doubt then that Jesus is God and sent by Yahweh.

However, there will be a time when there is doubt as to whether or not Yahweh has sent he who was the Word. The Word will become the Branch's soul, and the Branch will be sent to Israel as God's messenger (Isaiah 42:19—21). Isaiah forty-eight also describes that Yahweh will send the Branch to Israel. Isaiah 48:16 is spoken from a point in time that is after God has brought the Branch to Israel, and a point in time that is after the latter year pouring out of God's Spirit. So, in Isaiah 48:16 the Word speaking as the Branch states that Yahweh has sent him and His Spirit. In Isaiah 48:14, it is the Branch who will declare concerning Yahweh being the First and the Last, and concerning creation. After the Branch's glorification he will be Jesus, and Jesus will do His pleasure on Babylon and the Chaldeans.

Isaiah 48:12—16 (D. Israel)

12 "Listen to Me, Jacob and Israel My called; I am He; I am the First, I am also the Last.

13 Indeed, My hand founded the earth, and My right hand spread out the heavens; I called to them, they stood up together.

14 All of you assemble and hear. Who among them has declared these things? Yahweh loves him; he will do his pleasure on Babylon, and his arm will be on the Chaldeans.

15 I, I have spoken; yea, I have called him; I have brought him, and will make prosper his way."

16 Draw near to me, hear this, from the beginning I did not speak in secret; from the time of its being there I was, and now the Lord Yahweh has sent me and His Spirit.

Standard translations have poorly translated Isaiah 48:16.

7126	(413)pro	8085 2063 3808
Draw near	to me,	hear this, not

4480(7218)	preb(5643)	(1696)pro
from (the) beginning	in secret	I did speak;

4480(6256)	(1961)pro 8033 589	2050a(6258)
from (the) time (of) its being	there I (was), and now	

136	3068	(7971)pro	2050a(7307)pro
the Lord Yahweh has sent me			and His Spirit.

ZECHARIAH CHAPTER THREE

1   And he showed me Joshua the high priest standing before the angel of Yahweh, and Satan standing at his right hand to oppose him.

2   And Yahweh said to Satan, "Yahweh rebukes you, Satan; yea, Yahweh who has chosen Jerusalem rebukes you. Is this not a brand snatched from he fire?"

3   And Joshua was clothed with filthy garments, and stood before the angel.

4   And he spoke and said to those standing before him, saying, "Remove the filthy garments from him." And he said to him, "See, I have removed your iniquity, and will clothe you with stately robes";

5   and said that they should put a clean turban on his head. So they put the clean turban on his head, and clothed him with clothes. And the angel of Yahweh stood by.

6   And the angel of Yahweh admonished Joshua, saying,

7   "Thus says Yahweh of hosts, 'If you walk in My way, and if you keep My charge, then you will also govern My house and keep My court; and I will give you access among these who stand by.

8   Hear now, Joshua the high priest, you and your fellows who sit before you, for they are the men in the sign; for behold, I will bring forth My servant the Branch.

9   For behold, the stone that I have set before Joshua, on one stone are seven eyes. Behold, I have engraved its engravings,'

says Yahweh of hosts, 'and I will remove the iniquity of the land in one day.

10 In that day,' says Yahweh of hosts, 'you will call each man his neighbor, to sit under his vine and under his fig tree.'"

Zechariah chapter three is a vision that is given to Zechariah from God. In the vision, Joshua the high priest and his fellows are symbols. Joshua symbolizes the Branch, and his fellows symbolize those who stand before Yahweh in Heaven. In the vision, Joshua has his filthy garments exchanged for clean ones by the angel of Yahweh. This symbolizes the removal of Joshua's iniquity. Just as Joshua had need for his iniquity to be removed, so will the Branch need to have his iniquity removed. The Branch will have his iniquity removed at becoming a born again Christian, at the stone rejected by the builders becoming the head of the corner. Joshua is admonished to walk in Yahweh's way and to keep Yahweh's charge. If he does so, Joshua would govern Yahweh's house, and keep God's court. Similarly, if the Branch walks in Yahweh's way and keeps His charge, he will govern God's house and keep His court. The Branch will receive this promise, after the glory at being reunited with Jesus. The Branch's charge, his task, is to speak for Yahweh through the medium of print.

Psalm 45:1 (D. Israel) My heart is astir with a good matter. I speak my work for the King, my tongue being the stylus of a rapid writer.

The stone that is set before Joshua symbolizes Jesus, and the seven eyes symbolize the seven spirits of Yahweh. The stone set before Joshua indicates the Branch's destiny. At the Branch's glorification he will be reunited with Jesus; thus, he will be Jesus. Immediately after being reunited with Jesus, the Branch who has become Jesus is anointed with the fullness of Yahweh's Spirit. In addition, the Branch who will have become Jesus and anointed with Yahweh's Spirit, will receive all seven of the spirits of Yahweh (Rev. 5:6). Jesus will have the six spirits of Yahweh that are listed in Isaiah 11:2, plus the spirit of judgment. So, the seven spirits of Yahweh that the Branch will have after becoming Jesus and anointed with the fullness of Yahweh's Spirit are: the spirit of wisdom, the spirit of understanding, the spirit of counsel, the spirit of might, the spirit of knowledge, the spirit of the fear of Yahweh, and the spirit of judgment.

Joshua also symbolizes the Branch in Zechariah 6:11—13.

Zechariah 6:11—13 (D. Israel)

11 "And take silver and gold, and make crowns and set them on the head of Joshua the son of Jehozadak, the high priest.

12 And speak to him, saying, 'Thus says Yahweh of hosts, "Behold a man, the Branch is his name; and from his place he will spring up; and he will build the temple of Yahweh.

13 Even he will build the temple of Yahweh; and he will lift up the glory, and will sit and rule on his throne; and he will be a priest on his throne, and the counsel of peace will be between the two offices."'

It will be the Branch who will lift up the glory at his glorification, the glory to sit on his throne as priest and King.

ZECHARIAH 9:6-14

6 And a mongrel race will dwell in Ashdod, and I will cut off the
   pride of the Philistines.
7 And I will remove the blood from his mouth, and his abomina-
   tions from between his teeth. But he that remains, even he will
   be for our God. And he will be as a chief in Judah, and Ekron
   as a Jebusite.
8 And I will encamp about My house, because of an army from
   he who will have passed through, even from he who will have
   returned; and an oppressor will not pass over them again, for
   then I will see with My eyes.
9 Rejoice greatly, daughter of Zion! Shout, daughter of Jerusalem!
   Behold, your King comes to you, righteous and having salvation, He will be humble and riding on an ass, even on a colt, the
   foal of an ass.
10 And I will cut off the chariot from Ephraim, and the horse from
   Jerusalem; and the battle bow will be cut off. And He will speak
   peace to the nations; and His dominion will be from sea to sea,
   from the river to the ends of the earth.
11 Also You, by the blood of Your covenant I will send forth Your
   captives from the waterless pit.
12 Return to the stronghold, captives of the hope; even today I
   declare that I will restore double to you,
13 when I have bent for Me Judah, a bow I will fill with Ephraim.
   And I will stir up your sons, Zion, against your sons, Greece,
   and make you as the sword of a mighty man.

14 And Yahweh will appear over them, and His arrow will go forth
    as lightning, and the Lord Yahweh will blow the trumpet, and
    will go forth with the storms of the south.

Zechariah 9:6—14 goes back and forth between the time of Jesus second advent, and the time of His first advent. Verses 6—8 describe end
time events and the result of Jesus' second advent. Regarding end time
events, verse thirteen gives us the most precise indication of the home-
land of the Antichrist. We know that the Antichrist will become the
leader of a ten state federation that will come out of the territory of
the former Roman empire (Daniel 7:19—25). We also know that the
Antichrist will come out of the territory of the former Grecian empire
which overlapped the Roman empire, but whose western boundary
was Greece (Daniel 8:5—9). In addition, we know that the beast of
Revelation is the Antichrist, the beast pre-existing as one of the leaders
of the major empires of history: the Egyptian empire, the Assyrian empire, the Babylonian empire, the Persian empire, the Grecian empire, or
the Roman empire (Revelation 17:8—11).

The fact that the beast pre-exists the Antichrist, and that he comes
up out of the abyss indicates that the beast is a demon. He can not be
Satan himself, for Satan is the prince of the air who is not in the abyss.
However, Satan does give the beast his power (Revelation 13:2). So, we
can see that the Antichrist, the beast from the abyss, and Satan com-
bine to form a counterfeit to the Branch, Jesus, and Yahweh. When
the Branch is reunited with Jesus, he becomes Jesus; and then when he
as Jesus is anointed with the fullness of Yahweh's Spirit he becomes as
Yahweh, as he is described in Zechariah 9:14 and 14:5. The counterfeit
to God is formed when the Antichrist is indwelt by the beast; thus,
he becomes the beast, the Antichrist as the beast being empowered by
Satan.

Of all the leaders of the former six empires, the most impressive in
conquering territory was Alexander the Great, the leader of the former

Grecian empire. This is an indication that it was Alexander the Great who was the former emperor, that was empowered by the beast from the abyss. Zechariah 9:13 does not refer to the time of the former divided Grecian empire, as commonly believed; but it is a confirmation that the Antichrist will come out of Greece. The last conqueror to oppress Israel will be the Antichrist. Zechariah 9:8 describes that the last oppressor will first pass through Israel, but then he will return. The Antichrist will first pass through Israel to conquer Egypt (Daniel 11:40—43), then he will return to lay siege and conquer Jerusalem at the mid-point of the seven year covenant (Zech. 14:2; Rev. 11:2).

We know that the Antichrist will conquer three nations before going on to control the entire world (Daniel 7:8). Daniel chapter eleven describes the leader of Egypt as the king of the south, and describes the leader of Syria as the king of the north. These kings conducted wars against each other during the time of the divided Grecian empire. It is understood that Daniel 11:40—43 describes the Antichrist as the king of the north, who during the end time wages war with Egypt, the king of the south. In addition, Daniel 8:9 describes the Antichrist growing exceedingly great toward the south, toward the east, and toward Israel, the beautiful land. Daniel 11:40—43 tells us that the Antichrist wages war against Egypt with land forces and with ships, that he overflows countries and passes through them, that one of the countries he enters is Israel, and that the end result is that he conquers Egypt. So, it appears that the Antichrist will first grow exceedingly great toward the south, going to war with Egypt which lies directly south of Greece; then he will grow exceedingly great toward the east, conquering Turkey which is directly east of Greece; then he will grow exceedingly great toward the beautiful land, conquering Syria which is directly toward the beautiful land from Turkey; then he passes through Israel and conquers Egypt. Thus, the three nations that the Antichrist conquers to start his world dominion appears to be Turkey, Syria, and Egypt. By conquering Syria, he more fully becomes the king of the north, who then passes through Israel and conquers Egypt, the king of the south.

Zechariah 9:6—8, 9:10, and 9:13—14 refer to the time of Jesus' second advent. Verse nine is recognized as referring to Jesus' triumphant entry into Jerusalem at His first advent, five days before His death. On the day of His death, Jesus confirmed to the Jewish priests that He was the Son of God (Mat. 26:63—64). It was this confirmation that gave the Jewish priests their excuse to insist that Pilate crucify Him. In verse nine, Jesus is described as being righteous and having salvation. It was because Jesus was the Son of God that He was righteous, having a live righteous Spirit. It was because Jesus was the Son of God that salvation became available upon His death to whosoever believes in Him. Before Jesus' death, God provided for the forgiveness of sins. After Jesus' death, God not only forgives sins; but He provides salvation by justifying the believer, making the believer righteous. Upon Jesus' death, salvation was made available, because Jesus' live righteous Spirit was freed from His soul. Jesus' Spirit was enabled to indwell and thus make righteous the spirit of the believer.

In verses eleven and twelve, there is confusion regarding the waterless pit, the prisoners of the hope, and the stronghold. Standard translations have poorly translated these verses.

1571 859   preb(1818)   (1285)pro
Also You, by (the) blood (of) Your covenant

    (7971)pro   (615)(pl)pro   4480(953)
I will send forth Your captives from (the) pit

        369   4325 (preb)pro
not there is water   in it.

7725   3807a(1225)   (615)pl   def(8615)
Return to (the) stronghold, captives (of) the hope.

Many believe that these verses refer to the time of the Babylonian captivity. They believe that the waterless pit refers to the Babylonian captivity being like a waterless pit, and that the Jews held captive were the prisoners of the hope. They had the hope of returning to Jerusalem, the stronghold. However, these verses clearly refer to the time of Jesus' death, the time of the shedding of His blood. It refers to the time of the coming into being of the covenant by Jesus' blood. The covenant states that whosoever believes in Jesus will have eternal life. Jesus' covenant in His blood came into effect upon His death, because upon His death His righteous Spirit was freed to indwell and make righteous the spirit of whosoever believes in Him. The waterless pit refers to Sheol or Hades, the abode of the dead. It was because of the blood of Jesus' covenant, that God was able to send forth Jesus' captives from Sheol to the stronghold of Heaven. The captives of the hope included all the souls of those who were obedient to God up to Jesus' death.

Because Jesus' death freed His Spirit from His soul, He was able to lead captivity captive out of Sheol to the stronghold of Heaven, after His resurrection.

Psalm 68:18 (D. Israel)
18 You will ascend on high, You will lead captivity captive; You will bring gifts into men, and even those having been rebellious, that Yah God may dwell among them.

Ephesians 4:8-10 (D. Israel)
8 Therefore it says, He ascended on high, He led captive captivity. And gave gifts to men.
9 Now He who ascended, what is this except that He also had first descended into the lower parts of the earth?
10 The One descending Himself is also the one ascending high above all the heavens, that He might fill all things.

Upon Jesus' death, Jesus' Spirit was freed to give life to the spirits of the captives; thus, He was able to bring them out of Sheol to the stronghold of Heaven. And as stated in verse eleven, Jesus Himself would also be among Jesus' captives that He would take out of the waterless pit to Heaven. That is, the resurrected Jesus consisting of His glorified spiritual body and His Spirit took His soul out of the heart of the earth (Mat. 12:40), along with the rest of captives of the hope.

> Matthew 12:40 (King James) For as Jonah was three days and three nights in the whale's belly; so shall the Son of man be three days and three nights in the heart of the earth.

Jesus being in the heart of the earth does not refer to his body being in a tomb on the surface of the earth, but to His soul being in Sheol in the heart of the earth. Jesus' body was resurrected on Sunday, the third day (Mat. 17:22—23). However, after three days and three nights; thus, on Monday on the day after Jesus' resurrection, the resurrected Jesus told his soul who was in Sheol to return to his rest, the rest that would be his at returning to the stronghold of Heaven.

Psalm 116:3—6 describes Jesus' soul in Sheol after Jesus' death. In Psalm 116:7, the resurrected Jesus tells His soul to return to his rest, to return to Heaven. Then in Psalm 116:8—9, Jesus' soul describes his restoration to life as the soul of the Branch, which occurs in the latter years. As stated in Psalm 22:30, all who die will bow before Yahweh, even Jesus' soul who was not revived at Jesus' resurrection; but he would become a seed, would re-enter life through the process of conception and birth.

> Psalm 116:3—9 (D. Israel)
> 3 The cords of death encompassed me, the straits of Sheol have found me;
> 4 trouble and sorrow I have found; therefore, on the name of Yahweh I call: "I pray, Yahweh, deliver my soul."

5   Yahweh is gracious and righteous, and our God is merciful;
    Yahweh watches over the simple.
6   I have been brought low, but because of me He saves.
7   Return, My soul, to your rest, for Yahweh will deal bountifully
    on account of you.
8   Because You delivered my soul from death, my eyes from tears,
    and my feet from stumbling,
9   I walk before Yahweh in the lands of the living.

Psalm 22:30 (D. Israel) All those going down to the dust will
bow before Him, even His soul not being revived. A seed will
serve Him, he will declare concerning the Lord to a generation.

REVELATION 12:1-5 (NAS)

1   And a great sign appeared in heaven: a woman clothed with the sun, and the moon under here feet, and on her head a crown of twelve stars;

2   and she was with child; and she cried out, being in labor and in pain to give birth.

3   And another sign appeared in heaven: and behold, a great red dragon having seven heads and ten horns, and on his heads were seven diadems.

4   And his tail swept away a third of the stars of heaven, and threw them to the earth. And the dragon stood before the woman who was about to give birth, so that when she gave birth he might devour her child.

5   And she gave birth to a son, a male child, who is to rule all the nations with a rod of iron; and her child was caught up to God and to His throne.

Revelation 12:1—5 is the center piece of the book of Revelation, yet we do not understand its significance. It is easy to see that the woman is the nation of Israel (Genesis 37:9—10), and the child is Jesus (Psalm 2:7—9). However, these verses are not describing Jesus' natural birth at Bethlehem to Mary. Before we can fully understand this scripture, we must understand God's plan of salvation. We must understand that Jesus' soul and Spirit were separated at His death, and were not reunited at Jesus' resurrection. We haven't even made the effort to understand that the birth of Jesus as described here, is the event that causes the resumption of the seventy weeks of years. This fact can easily be deduced from Micah which also describes this birth.

Micah 5:2—3 (D. Israel)

2   "And you, Bethlehem Ephrathah, small at being among the thousands of Judah, out of you He will go forth for Me to become ruler in Israel; and His goings forth have been from ancient times, from the days of eternity.

3   Therefore, He will give them up until the time when she who travails has brought forth; then the rest of His brothers will return to the sons of Israel."

Jesus gave up the nation of Israel at His death, and His death is the event that caused the interruption of the seventy weeks of years of the Jewish dispensation. It was Jesus' death that enabled the finishing of transgression, the sealing up of sin, and the atoning for iniquity. It was Jesus' death that freed His live righteous Spirit to indwell and make righteous the spirit of the believer, creating the age of grace or church age. Jesus gave up Israel at His death, which caused the interruption of the seventy weeks of years. So, it can be deduced that Jesus once again taking up the nation of Israel at this birth, will cause the resumption of the seventy weeks of years.

It will be this birth of Jesus that will bring in Jesus' everlasting righteous reign at the resumption of the seventy weeks of years, followed by the sealing up of vision and the prophet at the mid-point of the seventieth week of years, and then the anointing of the most holy place at the end of the seventieth week of years.

Daniel 9:24—26 (D. Israel)

24   "Seventy weeks will be divided concerning your people and concerning your holy city, to finish the transgression and to seal up sins, even to make atonement for iniquity; then to bring in

everlasting righteousness, and to seal up vision and the prophet, and to anoint the most holy place.

25 Therefore, know and understand, from the issuing of the word to restore and rebuild Jerusalem until the Messiah, the Ruler, will be seven weeks and sixty-two weeks. It will be rebuilt with plaza and ditch, even in the distress of the times.

26 And after the sixty-two weeks the Messiah will be cut off, and there will be nothing for Him. …"

This birth of Jesus as described in Micah 5:2—3 and Revelation 12:1—5 is not Jesus' natural birth at Bethlehem to Mary, but His super-natural birth on mount Zion to the nation of Israel. This birth of Jesus is the re-unification of the Branch with Jesus, the reunification of he who is born having Jesus' soul with the resurrected Jesus. This event is described as Jesus' birth, because the same thing happens at Jesus' super-natural birth as at His natural birth. That is, at Jesus' natural birth the Word became flesh, became Jesus' soul, and was united with His conceived body and Spirit (John 1:14; 1:18); whereas at Jesus' super-natural birth Jesus' soul who has become the Branch's soul is reunited with He who was his body and Spirit. The resurrected Jesus consists of His glorified spiritual body and His Spirit, but not His soul.

At the time of the Branch's glorification he will go to Mount Zion to be reunited with Jesus. It is the Branch who will come in the name of Yahweh at the time of his glorification. At that time, the people of Israel will cry out to God for the reunification of the Branch with Jesus. They will cry out, "Bind the sacrificial feast with cords, even to the horns of the alter." The sacrificial feast symbolizes Jesus' soul, who has become the Branch's soul, and the blood smeared on the horns of the alter symbolizes Jesus' life giving Spirit.

Psalm 118:26—27 (D. Israel)

26 Blessed is he who comes in the name of Yahweh; we have blessed you from the house of Yahweh.

27 God is Yahweh, and He has given light to us. Bind the sacrificial feast with cords, even to the horns of the alter.

At the people's cry for the reunification of the Branch with Jesus, Jesus will come out of the midst of the church, and will indwell the Branch's spirit.

In II Thessalonians 2:1—8, Paul explains that the day of Christ, the rapture, will not come before the end time falling away and the revelation of the Antichrist. Jesus is He who is restraining the man of sin, the Antichrist, until He comes out of the midst of the church. At Jesus coming at His second advent, He will destroy the Antichrist with His Spirit. The Word who became Jesus' soul, who becomes the Branch's soul, who once again becomes Jesus' soul at Jesus' super-natural birth, will wield the sword of His reacquired Spirit at Jesus' second advent (Rev. 19:11—15).

II Thessalonians 2:1—8 (D. Israel)

1 Now we request you brethren, concerning the coming of our Lord Jesus Christ, and our gathering together to Him,

2 that you not be quickly shaken in mind, nor be troubled; not by a spirit, nor by a message, nor by a letter, as by us, as that the day of Christ is at hand.

3 Let no one by any means deceive you, since it will not come unless the falling away comes first, and the man of sin is revealed, the son of destruction;

4 who opposes and exalts himself over all that is called God or object of worship, so that he sits in the temple of God as God.

5 Do you not remember that while I was still with you, I told you these things?

6 And what restrains him now you know, for him to be revealed in his time.

7   For the mystery of lawlessness already works; only He is re-
    straining him now until He comes out of the midst.

8   And then the lawless one will be revealed, whom the Lord will
    consume with the Spirit of His mouth, and will destroy by the
    appearance of His coming;

When Jesus comes out of the midst of the church, the church age will
end. Even though the church will not be raptured for about another
eight months, the church will cease from being the body of Christ. Jesus
will cease from working through the church. Immediately after coming
out of the midst of the church, Jesus will reunite with His soul by indwelling the spirit of the Branch. This will cause the resumption of the
seventy weeks of years, and bring in Jesus' everlasting righteous reign.
Immediately after Jesus' super-natural birth, the Branch who will once
again be Jesus will be anointed with Yahweh's Spirit (Psalm 2:6), and
then caught up to the throne of God (Rev. 12:5).

Revelation 12:3—4 describes a great red dragon who will attempt
to kill Jesus, the new born child on Mount Zion. Revelation 12:9 identifies the dragon as Satan. In verse three, the dragon casts a third of the
stars of Heaven to earth. This is a description of the end time falling
away mentioned by Paul in II Thessalonians 2:3. The Antichrist will
come empowered by Satan, with lies and deception.

II Thessalonians 2:9—12 (D. Israel)

9   this one is coming according to the working of Satan, with all
    power and signs and lying wonders,

10 and with all the deception of unrighteousness to those who per-
    ish, because they did not receive the love of the truth for them
    to be saved.

11 And because of this God will send them the working of deceit,
    that they might believe a lie;

12 in order that all might be judged who did not believe the truth, but took pleasure in unrighteousness.

Ephesians 2:6 describes Christians being seated with Jesus in heavenly places. Satan working through the Antichrist will cause some of the stars to fall; he will cause some Christians seated in heavenly places to fall. Those Christians that have no firm root will be caused to fall, by lies and false wonders worked by Satan through the Antichrist.

Daniel 8:8—10 also describes the little horn, the Antichrist, causing some of the stars to fall to earth. Daniel 8:8 describes the former Grecian empire headed by Alexander the Great. After Alexander's death his empire was divided between four generals. The Antichrist, the little horn, will come out of one section of the former Grecian empire.

Daniel 8:8—10 (D. Israel)

8   And the he goat became exceedingly great. But at his becoming mighty the great horn was broken; and in its place came up four notable ones toward the four winds of heaven.

9   And out of one of them came forth a little horn, and it became exceedingly great toward the south, and toward the east, and toward the beautiful land.

10 And it became great even to the host of the heavens; and it caused to fall to the earth some of the host and from the stars, and it trampled them.

Part III
THE PUTTING FORTH OF LEAVES
BY THE FIG TREE

Part III reveals the event that causes the fig tree, the nation of Israel, to put forth leaves. It reveals that shortly after the fig tree puts forth leaves, God will pour out His Spirit on the nation of Israel, and then on all the nations. In addition, Part III reveals the catylst necessary for the latter year pouring out of God's Spirit, and that the pouring out of God's Spirit will cause a great world wide revival.

THE PUTTING FORTH OF LEAVES
BY THE FIG TREE

Jesus gave the parable of the fig tree in the gospels. In Matthew 24:3, Jesus' disciples asked Him, What will be the sign of Your coming and the end of the age? So, in Matthew 24:4—31, Jesus described end time events, starting from the opening of the first seal. These events will stretch to the opening of the sixth seal, when He comes on the clouds to rapture the church. Then in Matthew 24:32—34, Jesus gave the parable of the fig tree.

Matthew 24:32—34 (NAS)

32 "Now learn the parable of the fig tree: when its branch has already become tender, and puts forth leaves, you know that summer is near;

33 even so you too, when you see all these things, recognize that He is near, right at the door.

34 "Truly I say to you, this generation will not pass away until all these things take place."

It is recognized that the fig tree symbolizes the nation of Israel. So, many have incorrectly understood that the putting forth of leaves by the fig tree occurred at the reestablishment of the nation of Israel in 1948. As time has passed, most have come to understand that this understanding is incorrect.

So, when will the fig tree put forth leaves? We know that the opening of the first seal will occur after the resumption of the seventy weeks of years, which occurs less than a year before Jesus comes on the clouds at the rapture of the church; and we know from Matthew 24:34 that the generation that sees all these things described in Matthew 24:4—34 will not pass away, until all these things have taken place. So, the putting forth of leaves by the fig tree must be the event that starts the list of events; and it will occur approximately, but not more than a generation before Jesus comes on the clouds at the rapture of the church. The question arises, how long is a generation? There are several different opinions as to the length of a generation. Technically, a generation is the average time between the birth of a person and the birth of the first child of that person.

So, what event marks the putting forth of leaves by the fig tree? To understand this it is helpful to understand the symbolism of the un-fruitful fig tree. Jesus told the parable of the unfruitful fig tree in Luke 13:6—9.

Luke 13:6—9 (NAS)

6 —— "A certain man had a fig tree which had been planted in his vineyard; and he came looking for fruit on it, and did not find any.

7 "And he said to the vineyard keeper, 'Behold, for three years I have come looking for fruit on this fig tree without finding any. Cut it down! Why does it even use up ground?'

8 "And he answered and said to him, 'Let it alone, sir, for this year too, until I dig around it and put in fertilizer;

9 and if it bears fruit next year, fine; but if not, cut it down.'"

Jesus came to Jerusalem, the place of God's temple, for three successive years; but He didn't see any fruit, particularly from the Jewish leaders and priests. In the fourth year, Jesus came again to Jerusalem, and once again He found no fruit. So, in the fourth year that Jesus came to Jerusalem, He caused a fig to die.

Matthew 21:18—19 (NAS)

18 Now in the morning, when He returned to the city, He became hungry.

19 And seeing a lone fig tree by the road, He came to it, and found nothing on it except leaves only; and he said to it, "No longer shall there be any fruit from you." And at once the fig tree withered.

Since that day the fig tree, the nation of Israel, has not produced fruit for God, because the nation of Israel rejected Jesus. Jesus has told us that unless we abide in Him and He in us, we can bear no fruit.

John 15:5 (NAS) "I am the vine, you are the branches; he who abides in Me, and I in him, he bears much fruit; for apart from Me you can do nothing.

So, the putting forth of leaves by the fig tree has nothing to do with the physical reestablishment of the nation of Israel in 1948. It has to do with Israel showing signs of life by belief in Jesus. When a tree puts forth leaves, it has done what is necessary to sustain life; and when a person believes in Jesus he has done what is necessary to have spiritual life. The born again believer has spiritual life, because Jesus' live righteous Spirit abides in his spirit. It is the Branch who will correctly explain to the nation of Israel the purpose of Jesus' death. It will be through the Branch's teaching, that the nation of Israel will start to put forth leaves by accepting Jesus as her Messiah. Once the nation of Israel returns to God by believing in Jesus, it will once again bear fruit.

Israel becoming fruitful will be greatly accelerated by the latter year pouring out of God's Spirit. Israel will be considered by God a spiritual wilderness until the time of the latter year pouring out of His Spirit, at which time the fig tree will become a fruitful field. Isaiah 32:13—14 describes the desolation of Judah caused by the Babylonian captivity, then Isaiah 32:15 describes Israel becoming a fruitful field, on account of the latter year pouring out of God's Spirit.

Isaiah 32:13—15 (D. Israel)

13 The thorn and the brier will come up on the ground of My people, even on all the joyful houses of the jubilant city.

14 For the palace will be abandoned, the crowd of the city deserted; hill and watchtower will be for dens for a long duration, a joy of wild donkeys, the pasturage of flocks;

15 until the Spirit is poured out on us from on high, and the wilderness becomes a fruitful field, and the fruitful field is reckoned as a forest.

It will be the Branch who will teach God's plan of salvation to Israel, which will result in the fig tree putting forth leaves. From the Branch's effort and with the help of God, he will see; he will see into God's plan of salvation.

Isaiah 53:10—11 (D. Israel)

10 But Yahweh will be pleased to crush Him, to make Him sick. When You make his soul guilty, he will see his seed, he will prolong his days, and the pleasure of Yahweh will prosper in his hands.

11 From the work of his soul he will see; he will be satiated with his knowledge.

Psalm 91:14—16 (D. Israel)

14 "Because he will set his love on Me, even I will deliver him, I will set him on high. Because he will know My name, he will call on Me, and I will answer him.

15 I will be with him in distress; I will draw him out of it, and I will honor him.

16 I will have satisfied him with length of days, and I will have caused him to see into My salvation."

In order to give back to God, the Branch vows to lift up the cup of salvation and offer it to the people of Israel; given that God has caused him to see into His salvation.

Psalm 116:12—14 (D. Israel)

12 What will I return to Yahweh for all His benefits to me?

13 The cup of salvation I will lift up, and in the name of Yahweh I will call out.

14 My vow to Yahweh I will complete in front, I pray, of all His people.

The Branch will discover God's words as contained in Scripture, that reveal the truth concerning His plan of salvation. He will discover that many key scriptures have been made void by poor translation (Psalm 119:126—128). In Jeremiah 15:16, it is the Branch, not Jeremiah, who finds God's words and eats them. It is the Branch who will have God's name of Israel called upon him (Isaiah 44:5; 49:3).

Jeremiah 15:16—19 (D. Israel)

16 Your words were found and I ate them, and Your words were to me joy and gladness of heart; for Your name is called upon me, Yahweh God of hosts.

17 I did not sit in the circle of merrymakers, nor did I exalt. I sat alone because of the presence of Your hand; for You have filled me with indignation.

18 Why has my pain been continual and my wound incurable? It has refused to be healed. Surely You have become to me as deceitful water that is not faithful.

19 Therefore, thus says Yahweh, "If you restore, then I will restore you; you will stand before Me; yea, if you bring out the precious from the worthless, you will be as My mouth."

The Branch complains about the things that occur to him as a result of God's hand being on him. God reveals in Jeremiah 15:19 that He will restore the Branch, if the Branch restores, bringing out the precious from the worthless. The Branch has discovered God's words, but much of God's words concerning His plan of salvation have been distorted by poor translation and teaching, making them void and worthless. In order for the Branch to be restored, he must first restore God's Word, by bringing out God's precious words from those which have been made void and worthless. In Psalm 119:126—128, the Branch describes his work for Yahweh of setting straight God's words that have been made void.

Psalm 119:126—128 (D. Israel)

126 It is time to work for Yahweh; they have made void Your law.

127 Therefore I love Your commandments more than gold, even more than fine gold.

128 Therefore, all the precepts, the totality, I will make straight; every way of falsehood I hate.

The Branch will find God's words and eat them (Jeremiah 15:16; thus, he will see (Isaiah 53:11); he will see into God's plan of salvation (Psalm 91:16), and he will be satiated with his knowledge (Isaiah 53:11). As a result, he vows to God to lift up the cup of salvation to the people of Israel (Psalm 116:12—14); and as a result of this the meek of the earth will also eat God's words that the Branch has found, and they too will be satiated (Psalm 22:26). Psalm 22:25—29 is spoken by the Branch, in which he describes fulfilling his vow of lifting up God's salvation to the people of Israel, by correctly explaining God's salvation to them. He then describes the latter year world wide revival.

Psalm 22:25—29 (D. Israel)

25 From You is my praise in the great assembly. I will pay my vow before those fearing Him.

26 The meek will eat and be satiated; those seeking Yahweh will praise Him. Your heart will live forever.

27 All the ends of the earth will remember and return to Yahweh; and all the families of the nations will worship before You.

28 For the kingdom is Yahweh's, and He rules among the nations.

29 All the fat ones of the earth will have eaten and will worship.

Once we recognize that it is the Branch who is the speaker of Psalm 22:25—29, we can see that it gives the general outline for what is required of humankind, in order that God pour out His Spirit in the latter years. We know that the Branch's vow is to lift up and offer the cup of salvation to the people of Israel (Psalm 116:12—14), and that he will be instrumental in the latter year pouring out of God's Spirit (Isaiah 44:1—5). From the Branch's effort and with God's help, he will see into God's plan of salvation. He will eat God's words from Scripture regarding God's plan of salvation, and he will be satiated with this knowledge. So, the Branch vows to lift up the cup of salvation and offer it to the people of Israel, and as a result of this the meek will also eat God's words regarding God's plan of salvation, and they too will be satiated with this knowledge. Then those who seek Yahweh will praise Him; they will praise God with the truth of His plan of salvation; and as a result of this praise God will reveal Himself by pouring out His Spirit (Ezekiel 39:29). The meek, those who humble themselves by accepting Jesus as Lord, will praise and worship God with the truth of His plan of salvation and become fat; they will become fat with the oil of joy of God's Spirit. Not only will God pour out His Spirit on the people of Israel, but He will follow this by pouring out His Spirit on all the nations, who worship Him with the truth of His plan of salvation. As a result of the pouring out of God's Spirit, all the families of the nations will return to Yahweh God. The latter year pouring out of God's Spirit will cause a great world wide revival. The catalyst for the latter year pouring out of God's Spirit will be worshipping Him with the truth of His plan of salvation.

God has hidden His face from the people of Israel (Isaiah 57:17); but He will heal those who turn to Him through belief in Jesus, and He will reveal Himself to them by pouring out His Spirit. In Ezekiel 39:29, God describes revealing Himself to Israel by pouring out His Spirit upon them, after He removes the northern armies of Gog from their land.

> Ezekiel 39:29 (D. Israel) "And I will not hide My face any more from them, for I will pour out My Spirit on the house of Israel," says the Lord Yahweh.

The latter year pouring out of God's Spirit will not be just for the fig tree, but for all the nations (Luke 21:29—31; Psalm 22:25—29). As Psalm 22:29 indicates, those who have eaten God's words regarding the truth of His plan of salvation will worship God with that truth; and they will become fat, they will become fat with the oil of joy of God's Spirit. Isaiah 61:3 describes the pouring out of God's Spirit, which provides the oil of joy instead of mourning. Isaiah 57:17 describes that God has hidden His face from Israel, but then describes that God will heal Israel, and for his mourning God will create the fruit of the lips. The healing of Israel will occur when the nation starts accepting Jesus as her Messiah, and the fruit of the lips will come from worshipping God with the truth of His salvation, which will result in the pouring out of God's Spirit.

> Isaiah 57:17—18 (D. Israel)
> 17 "In the iniquity of his unjust gain, I will be angry and strike him; I will hide Myself and be angry, but he will go turning away in the way of his heart.
> 18 His ways I see, but I will heal him and lead him and restore comforts to him; and for his mourning create the fruit of the lips."

Psalm 45:1, Isaiah 29:18, and Isaiah 44:5 all describe the Branch's work for Yahweh, that work consisting of writing for Yahweh. Isaiah 44:1—5 indicates that God has chosen the Branch to help Israel, and will be instrumental in the latter year pouring out of God's Spirit. Isaiah 44:5 describes the First and the last ones, Yahweh introducing these concepts in Isaiah 41:4.

Isaiah 44:1—5 (D. Israel)

1 And now listen, Jacob My servant, even Israel: I have chosen him.
2 Thus says Yahweh, your maker and former from the womb, "He will help you. Do not fear, My servant Jacob, even Jeshurun, I have chosen him.
3 For I will pour out water upon the thirsty, and floods upon dry ground; I will pour out My Spirit upon your seed, and My blessing upon your offspring.
4 And they will spring up in among grass, as willows by streams of water.
5 This one will say, 'I am for Yahweh'; and this one will call out in the name of Jacob; and this one will write with his hand for Yahweh, and be named by the name of Israel."

Isaiah 29:17—18 indicates that the nation of Israel will become a fruitful field, at the time of hearing the words of the Branch's book; and Isaiah 29:19 indicates that the Branch's message that he delivers for God will spread world wide. In Isaiah 29:17, Israel is symbolized by Lebanon, because Lebanon is sometimes used to denote something that is great or glorious. Israel will become great and glorious at the latter year pouring out of God's Spirit. Note that the humble in Yahweh must first accept Jesus to be in Yahweh, given that he who does not have the Son, neither has the Father. The humble in Yahweh will increase joy by having God's Spirit, the oil of joy, poured out upon them.

Isaiah 29:17—19 (D. Israel)

17 Is it not a little while and Lebanon will be turned into a fruitful field, and the fruitful field will be reckoned as a forest?

18 And in that day the deaf will hear the words of a book, and the eyes of the blind will see out of gloom and out of darkness.

19 And the humble in Yahweh will increase joy; and the poor of mankind will rejoice in the Holy One of Israel;

He who abides in Jesus, and who has Jesus abiding in him bears much fruit (John 15:5). He who is born again bears much fruit by helping to bring people into God's kingdom. However, when God pours out His Spirit in the latter years, the bearing of fruit will be greatly accelerated. Isaiah 11:1 reveals that the Branch will bear fruit, and Genesis 49:22 reveals that the Branch will bear fruit on account of a spring. The Branch will become fruitful, because of the spring of God's Spirit. He will share credit for the fruit borne as a result of the latter year pouring out of God's Spirit, because it will be the Branch who teaches the people to worship God with the truth of His salvation; and it will be this worship that will be the catylst for the pouring out of God's Spirit.

The parable of the fig tree indicates that Israel will start to turn to God through belief in Jesus, about a generation before the rapture of the church. And the pouring out of God's Spirit, because of worshipping God with the truth of His salvation will occur shortly thereafter. Isaiah 42:19—21 reveals that the Branch will be sent to Israel as God's messenger, when Israel is at peace. This indicates that Israel will have made peace with her neighbors and the Palestinians by the time the Branch is sent to Israel. Isaiah 42:19—21 is a two-legged double-step, in which leg one refers to the nation of Israel, and leg two refers to the Branch.

Isaiah 42:19—21 (D. Israel)

leg 1 step 1   Who is blind, yet My servant;

leg 2 step 1   or deaf as My messenger I send?

leg 1 step 2   Who is blind as he who is at peace, even blind as the servant of Yahweh? You have seen many things, but have not taken heed.

leg 2 step 2   His ears are open, but he can not hear; Yahweh is
                pleased on account of his righteousness; he magnifies
                the law and makes it honorable.

The Branch will magnify the law and make it honorable, by setting straight the scriptures that reveal God's plan of salvation. Many of the these key scriptures have been made void by poor teaching and translation.

Some incorrectly understand that the seven year covenant between Israel and the Antichrist is what establishes peace between Israel and the Palestinians. However, the seven year covenant has nothing to do with the Palestinians. Isaiah 28:14—15 reveals that the seven year covenant is an agreement that stops further aggression by the Antichrist against Israel. In return Israel allows the Antichrist's armies to pass through Israel on their way to conquer Egypt (Daniel 11:40—42). Ezekiel 38:11—14 indicates that Gog and her allies will invade Israel when Israel dwells securely, and Ezekiel 39:29 indicates that the invasion will occur just before the latter year pouring out of God's Spirit. Israel will be dwelling securely at the time of this invasion, due to being at peace with her neighbors and the Palestinians.

God reveals in Joel that the invasion by Gog and her allies will occur when Israel is experiencing a severe drought; and reveals that the Branch, the teacher of righteousness, will be in Israel at the time of God's promise to Israel that He will remove Gog, the one from the north; and God reveals that He will send rain to end the drought. God goes on to reveal that it will be after these events, that He will pour out His Spirit on the people of Israel.

Joel 2:15—29 (D. Israel)
15 Blow a trumpet in Zion, consecrate a fast, call an assembly,
16 gather the people, sanctify the congregation, assemble the el-
    ders, gather the children and those sucking the breasts. Let

the bridegroom come out of his room, and the bride from her chamber.

17 Let the priests weep at the porch and toward the alter, ministers of Yahweh; and let them say, "Have pity, Yahweh, on Your people, and do not give Your inheritance to reproach, that the nations should rule over them. Why should they say among the peoples, 'Where is their God?'"

18 Then Yahweh will be jealous for His land, and will have pity on His people.

19 And Yahweh will answer and say to His people, "Behold, I will send grain to you, and new wine and fresh oil, and you will be satisfied with it; and I will not any longer make you a reproach among the nations,

20 but I will remove the one from the north far from upon you, and I will drive him into a land of drought and desolation, with his face toward the eastern sea, and his rear toward the western sea. And his stench will come up, and his foul odour will ascend, for he will have grown great to perform."

21 Do not fear, land, rejoice and be glad, for Yahweh will be magnified at doing it.

22 Do not fear, beasts of the field, for the pastures of the wilderness will grow green; for the tree will bear its fruit, and the fig tree and the vine will give their strength.

23 So, sons of Zion, rejoice and be glad in Yahweh your God; for He has given to you the teacher of righteousness; and the rain will come down to you; the early rain, but at first the latter rain.

24 And the threshing floors will be full of grain, and the vats will overflow with new wine and oil.

25 "And I will restore to you the years which the swarming locust has eaten, the crawling locust and the caterpillar and the gnawing locust, My great army which I have sent among you.

26 And you will eat fully and be satisfied, and you will praise the name of Yahweh your God who will deal with you wondrously. Then My people will never be ashamed;

27 and you will know that I am in the midst of Israel, and I am Yahweh your God and there is not another. Yea, My people will never be ashamed.

28 And it will be afterward that I will pour out My Spirit on all flesh; and your sons and your daughters will prophesy, and your elders will dream dreams, and your youth will see visions.

29 And even on the servants and handmaids I will pour out My Spirit in those days."

Isaiah 44:1—5 parallels Joel 2:23—29. Isaiah 44:1—5 describes the Branch, he whom God has chosen to help Israel, and reveals that God will pour out water on the thirsty and floods on dry ground, and reveals that after this God will pour out His Spirit on the people of Israel. Similarly, Joel 2:23—29 describes the Branch, he who is the teacher of righteousness whom God has given to Israel, then God reveals that the rain will come down to Israel to end a severe drought, and that after this He will pour out His Spirit on all flesh.

Many believe that the latter year pouring out of God's Spirit will occur after the rapture of the church. However, Scripture reveals that the latter year pouring out of God's Spirit will start about a generation before the rapture. In addition, Scripture reveals that the latter year pouring out of God's Spirit will cause a world wide revival. Scripture indicates that the meek will eat God's words, that reveal the truth concerning His plan of salvation. Scripture indicates that the meek are those who have humbled themselves by accepting Jesus as their Lord; thus, they will be given eternal life. The meek who seek God will praise Him; they will praise God with the truth of His plan of salvation. In response to this worship, God will pour out His Spirit. Those who have God's Spirit poured out upon them will become fat; they will become fat with the oil of joy of God's Spirit.

CONCLUSION

The bad news is that the church doesn't properly understand the major themes of God's Word. The consequence of the church's poor understanding is that all of humankind doesn't understand these themes. The good news is that those who seek the truth can quickly come to understand these themes of God's Word. The consequence of this will be a great world wide revival, at the latter year pouring out of God's Spirit. These major themes include creation, which includes when God created the heavens and the earth, and when He created humankind; God's plan of salvation, which includes the purpose of Jesus' conception and death, what happens when a person is born again, and the time of the resurrection and rapture; the seventy weeks of years, which includes the events that cause the interruption and the resumption of the seventy weeks of years; and the fact that God is one, which includes the concepts of the First, last ones, and Last. To properly understand God's plan of salvation, we must also understand the seventy weeks of years and that God is one. The seventy weeks of years and the fact that God is one are intertwined with God's plan of salvation, given that the interruption and the resumption of the seventy weeks of years, and the First, last ones, and Last come into being due to the execution of God's plan of salvation.

In order to properly understand these major themes of God's Word, we must be willing to make the effort to think logically. God is logical, and He has composed His Word in a manner, that requires us to use logical thinking to discover the full truth of these themes. God gives us enough information straight up, so that we can have some understanding of these major themes, but the full truth of them is veiled in logic. God has composed His Word in a manner that requires us to make logical choices, in order to discover the full truth of these themes. We could say that God has placed a logical lock on the full truth of the major themes of His Word. However, we have not yet made the necessary effort that logic requires to unlock the full truth of these themes.

We have made two blunders regarding creation. The first blunder has to do with when God created the heavens and the earth. God has provided us with two options regarding when He created the heavens and the earth. We have chosen the illogical option, an option that clearly contradicts Scripture. We have chosen that God created the heavens and the earth during the first six earth days, even though Genesis chapter one clearly reveals that God created the heavens and the earth an indefinite period of time before He made the first earth day. God provided two options regarding the time of the creation of the heavens and the earth, by calling both the universe and the earth's sky "heavens," and by calling both our entire planet and the dry land "earth." We have chosen the wrong option by plugging in the inappropriate meanings of these Hebrew words into the translation of Exodus 20:11. As a result, we incorrectly believe that God created the heavens, earth, seas, and all that is in them during the first six earth days; whereas this verse is stating that God created the sky, the dry land, and the seas, and all that was in them during the first six earth days.

The second blunder that we have made regarding creation has to do with whether God made one or two creations of humankind. In Genesis chapters one and two, God has given us two accounts of the creation of humankind. With these two accounts, God has provided us with a choice. Are these two accounts both describing the creation of Adam and Eve, or is the first account describing a creation of humankind before the creation of Adam and Eve? Again we have chosen the illogical option. We have chosen that these two accounts are both describing the creation of Adam and Eve. There are two main scriptural reasons why these two accounts of the creation of humankind must be describing two different creations. The most obvious reason why these are two different creations is because of God's standard of morality. In Leviticus, God clearly forbids incest. He regards incest wicked and lewd. You would think that God would have created multiple couples, so that their offspring wouldn't have to commit incest to reproduce. In fact that is exactly what Scripture indicates that He did. The first creation of humankind consisted of multiple couple to avoid the necessity of incest, and these couples provided descendants that were taken for mates by the offspring of Adam and Eve. As Genesis 6:1—2 reveals, the sons of God took the daughters of men for wives. The sons of Adam and Eve were called the sons of God, because they had a remnant of the breath of the Spirit of life; whereas the offspring of the first creation were called the sons and daughters of men, because they did not have the breath of the Spirit of life.

The second scriptural reason why the two accounts are two creations of humankind, has to do with what they were permitted and forbidden to eat. In the first account, both male and female are forbidden nothing in regards to what they were permitted to eat. However, in the second account before the creation of Eve, God forbids Adam to eat from the tree of knowledge of good and evil. If the first account were referring to the creation of Adam and Eve, then God wouldn't have told them that they could eat anything. So, why did God give the green light to the first creation of humankind to eat anything, but forbid Adam and Eve to eat from the tree of knowledge of good and evil? Adam and Eve were created with the potential of eternal life, whereas the first creation were not. Adam and Eve were given the breath of the Spirit of live, whereas the first creation were not. Adam and Eve spiritually died the very day they ate from the tree of knowledge of good and evil; whereas the first creation of humankind could not spiritually die even if they ate from the tree of knowledge, given that they were not created having the breath of the Spirit of life.

Summing up creation, Genesis chapter one reveals that God created the heavens and the earth an indefinite period of time before He made the first earth day, and reveals that He created the first creation of humankind of multiple couples during the sixth earth day. Genesis chapter two reveals that God created Adam and Eve an indefinite period of time after the seventh day. We do not know whether science is correct in its estimate that the universe is billions of years old. What we do know is that Scripture does not contradict this estimate. However, the estimate that humankind has existed for millions of years seems to be incorrect, according to Scripture. From Bible genealogy, we know that Adam and Eve were created about 4000 BC; and Genesis 6:1—2 reveals that the descendants of the first creation of humankind began to be many or multiplied, at the time of the sons of God taking the daughters of men for wives. It certainly wouldn't have taken millions of years for the first creation of humankind to be multiplied or many. So, it appears from Scripture that science is incorrect in its estimate, that humankind has existed for millions of years. As creationist point out, science had to make certain assumptions to make these estimates. From Scripture, it seems more likely that science is in error in regards to its estimate that humankind has existed for millions of years, than to its estimate that the universe is billions of years old. The estimate that science has for the existence of the first human is flawed by its theory of evolution. The theory of evolution requires that humans have existed for millions of years. The majority of scientists have not yet deduced that humans were created.

In regards to God's plan of salvation and the purpose of Jesus' death, we have chosen an illogical fallacy. We have incorrectly concluded that the purpose of Jesus' death was to satisfy justice by means of paying the penalty of humankind's sins. Even though it is recognized that this is an illogical fallacy, we still cling to this falsehood. We haven't made the necessary effort to reason out the truth as contained in Scripture. We should be able to reason out and understand that the purpose of Jesus' death was not to satisfy justice. We should be able to understand that if Jesus' death paid the penalty of humankind's sins, then God can no longer punish sin. In fact, we would no longer need to ask for forgiveness for our sins, given that the penalty for our sins would have already been paid. A debt that has been paid does not need to be forgiven, given that the penalty has already been paid. However, we do need to ask for forgiveness for our sins, because the purpose of Jesus' death was not to pay the penalty for humankind's sins.

In John 12:24, Jesus gave us an analogy that indicates the purpose of His death. Jesus said that unless a grain of wheat falls to the earth and dies, it remains alone, but if it dies it bears much fruit. This analogy indicates that Jesus' death was not to fulfill a moral requirement, such as to satisfy justice by means of paying the penalty of sin. It indicates that Jesus would bear fruit at His death in accordance with His physiology, His natural functioning. In order for the seed of a plant to reproduce it must be separated from the rest of the plant and die. Similarly, in order for Jesus to bear fruit, the part of Jesus that is the seed of God had to be separated from the rest of Jesus at His death. The seed of God consists of Jesus' body and Spirit, those parts of Jesus that were conceived at Jesus' conception. It was Jesus' soul who existed as the Word before Jesus' conception. So, at Jesus' death His physiology resulted in the seed of God being separated from His soul. The resurrected Jesus, consisting of His glorified spiritual body and His Spirit, is the seed of God who bears much fruit; He bears fruit by means of indwelling and making righteous the spirit of the believer. As I John 3:9 states, everyone who has been born of God does not sin, because His seed abides in him, and he is not able to sin, because he has been born of God. It is the spirit of the believer that is made righteous and unable to sin, because of being indwelt by Jesus, the seed of God; and it is the soul of the believer that is still capable of sin.

In order to fully understand God's plan of salvation and the purpose of Jesus' death, we must make the effort to understand what happened at Jesus' conception, death, and resurrection. When we do this we will discover that it was Jesus' soul who existed before Jesus' conception as the Word, and that both Jesus' body and live righteous Spirit were conceived. We will discover that at Jesus' death His body, soul, and Spirit were all separated from each other. Jesus' Spirit ascended to the Father, Jesus' soul descended to Sheol, and Jesus' body was laid in a tomb. We will discover that the resurrected Jesus consists of His glorified spiritual body and His Spirit, but not His soul. So, from this information we can understand how the physiology of Jesus enabled Him to bear fruit at His death. Jesus' death separated the seed of God, Jesus' body and Spirit, from His soul. Jesus' death freed the seed of God from His soul, enabling Him to bear fruit by indwelling and making righteous the spirit of whosoever believes in Him. As II Corinthians 5:21 reveals, God gave Jesus' soul sin, as the soul of the Branch, that the believer might become the righteousness of God in Jesus' Spirit. Jesus is our righteousness.

Jesus' death was not for the purpose of paying the penalty of humankind's sins, but for the purpose of bearing much fruit by giving the gift of righteousness and eternal life, His live righteous Spirit. Because Jesus' death was not for the purpose of paying the penalty of our sins, we must repent of our sins and believe in Him, so that we can be forgiven our sins and have eternal life. As Isaiah 42:3 indicates, Jesus brought forth judgment to faithfulness. That is, Jesus' death brought forth the judgment of God that was already upon humankind due to the fall of humankind, and that resulted in the spiritual death of all humankind, to the faithfulness of God to whosoever believes in Jesus, that results in eternal life. Jesus' death was not for the purpose of executing judgment, in order to pay the penalty of humankind's sins. It was for the exact opposite purpose. Jesus' death was for the purpose of bringing forth the judgment of God already upon humankind, that resulted in the spiritual death of all humankind, to the faithfulness of God to who-soever believes in Jesus, that results in the believer having spiritual life.

Regarding the time of the rapture we are confused. One of our main problems concerns Jesus' description in Matthew chapter twenty-four and Mark chapter thirteen, of Him returning to the earth and appearing on the clouds. We have failed to correctly answer a multiple choice problem. We are given the choice of two tribulations that this event could follow. We must also choose whether this return of Jesus is His return to rapture the church, or His return at His second advent. We have illogically chosen that this return of Jesus occurs after the great tribulation, rather than after the tribulation of the fifth seal. So, we have incorrectly concluded that this return of Jesus is His return at his second advent. These mistakes are illogical due to the fact that Revelation chapter six describes this same event, and reveals that it occurs at the sixth seal, the event that follows the tribulation of the fifth seal. The sixth seal occurs well before the end of the great tribulation.

Another problem that we have with the time of the rapture, is our failure to search out all six sets of scriptures that reveal the time of its occurrence. We have almost totally ignored the three sets of scriptures in the Old Testament, and they give the most exact time of the rapture; and they are all in agreement as to when the rapture will occur. We have squandered the opportunity to magnify God's word, by our failure to properly explain the six sets of scriptures that reveal the time of the rapture. These six sets of scriptures were given by five different people, but are in agreement as to the time of the rapture. So, this fact should be used to illustrate that the Bible was indeed inspired by God.

As for the seventy weeks of years, theologians have made illogical choices regarding the event that interrupts the seventy weeks of years, and regarding the event that causes the resumption of the seventy weeks of years. Daniel 9:24—26 describes seventy weeks of years regarding the people of Israel and Jerusalem, which is interrupted by the church age or age of grace. Theologians have made the conclusion that it was Jesus' triumphant entry into Jerusalem five days before His death, that marks the time of the arrival of Israel's Messiah and King, at the completion of sixty-nine weeks of years. With this conclusion, theologians caused for themselves a problem. From the book of Revelation, they have seen that a full week of years has yet to be completed. So, they have the problem of what to do with the five days from Jesus' triumphant entry into Jerusalem until His death. They have concluded that Jesus' triumphant entry interrupted the seventy weeks of years at the end of the sixty-ninth week of years, and have placed the five days from Jesus' triumphant entry to His death in the age of grace or church age. This is illogical reasoning, given that it was Jesus' death that provided the atonement necessary for the church age to begin. It is true that Jesus' triumphant entry marked the coming of Israel's Messiah and King. However, at Jesus' triumphant entry He was just at the gates of the city, and had not yet reached His destination. At the gates of the city, the crowds accepted Jesus as the son of David, their Messiah and King. However, the crowds didn't have the authority to accept or reject Jesus as Israel's Messiah and King. It was the Jewish priests who had the authority to accept or reject Jesus as Israel's Messiah and King. So, it was Jesus' appearance before the Jewish priests on the morning of the day of His death, that marked the arrival of Israel's Messiah and King, and marked the end of the sixty-ninth week of years.

Jesus confirmed to the Jewish priests that He was the Son of God, and confirmed to Pilate that He was the King of the Jews. The Jewish priests chose to reject Jesus as Israel's Messiah and King, using Jesus' claim of being the Son of God for their justification. What the Jewish priests didn't understand is that it was because Jesus was the Son of God that He was without sin, and therefore had a live righteous Spirit; a live righteous Spirit being that which is necessary to cleanse the believer's spirit of sin, and give him eternal life. Jesus was the unblemished lamb who was sacrificed that we might have eternal life. The sixty-ninth week of years may well have ended, when the Jewish priests stirred up the crowd to call out to Pilate for Jesus' crucifixion. At that time, the rejection of Jesus as Israel's Messiah and King was complete. His fate was sealed for death. It was Jesus' death that interrupted the seventy weeks of years a few hours into the seventieth week of years. It was Jesus' death that provided atonement for whosoever believes in Him, and caused the age of grace or church age to begin. There were a few hours from Jesus' rejection at the end of the sixty-ninth week of years until His death. So, the seventieth week of years that is yet to be completed is a few hours short of a full week of years, but rounding off to the nearest day there is still $360(7) = 2520$ days to be completed.

Regarding the event that causes the seventy weeks of years to resume, theologians have illogically concluded that it is the seven year covenant between Israel and the Antichrist, as described in Daniel 9:26—27. In these verses, God has informed us of this covenant that has the right length of time required to fulfill the seventy weeks of years, but doesn't fit the description given for the final portion of the seventy weeks of years. Nevertheless, we have accepted that the seven year covenant is the seventieth week of years, rather than make the necessary effort to search out the scripture that reveals the event that causes the resumption of the seventy weeks of years.

In Daniel 9:24, theologians have inappropriately translated "divided" as "determined" or as "decreed". By this mistranslation, they have made the finishing of transgression, the sealing up of sin, and the atonement for iniquity to fall within the seventy weeks of years. We should be able to understand that these things do not fall within the seventy weeks of years, but describe the church age, which is the interval between the two portions of the seventy weeks of years. We should be able to understand that the finishing of transgression, the sealing up of sin, and the making of atonement for iniquity divided the weeks of years. These things began at Jesus' death and the kick off of the age of grace or church age, and occur throughout the church age whenever a person is born again. So, we should be able to understand that the bringing in of everlasting righteousness, the sealing up of vision and the prophet, and the anointing of the most holy place describe the remaining portion of the seventieth week of years. These things have nothing to do with the covenant between Israel and the Antichrist.

To fully understand the event that causes the resumption of the seventy weeks of years, we must first understand God's plan of salvation. We must understand that the birth of the child described in Micah 5:3 and Revelation 12:5 describes Jesus' super-natural birth on Mount Zion, the reunification of Jesus with the Branch. However, even without this understanding we still should be able to understand that Micah 5:3 describes the event that kicks off the remainder of the seventy weeks of years. Micah describes that Jesus would give up the people of Israel until the birth of this child. We should be able to understand that Jesus gave up the people of Israel at His death, and we should be able to understand that it was Jesus' death that interrupted the seventy weeks of years. So, we should be able to understand that Jesus will once again take up the nation of Israel at the birth of this child, and that it is the birth of this child that kicks off the remainder of the seventy weeks of years. It is the birth of this child that brings in everlasting righteousness, and causes the resumption of the seventy weeks of years.

At Jesus' super-natural birth, the Branch is first reunited with Jesus and becomes Jesus, then Jesus is once again anointed with the fullness of Yahweh's Spirit, and then Jesus as Yahweh is caught up to the throne of God. Revelation 11:17—18 describes this time when Jesus as Yahweh the Almighty has taken His great power and has begun to reign. It describes the fact that the nations will be enraged at this time. Psalm chapter two describes this rage by the nations, and describes it as occurring on the day of Jesus' birth, His super-natural birth on Mount Zion, and on the day of Jesus being anointed by Yahweh. So, the bringing in of everlasting righteousness at Jesus' super-natural birth describes the bringing in of Jesus' everlasting righteous reign as Yahweh the Almighty.

Regarding the fact that Yahweh is one, we should be able to understand that Yahweh being one implies something more than that He is the one and only God. We know that Jesus was baptized by Yahweh' Spirit during His first advent. So, we should be able to understand why

Jesus claimed to be one with the Father; that reason being because Jesus was anointed with the fullness of Yahweh's Spirit. Both Yahweh and Jesus call themselves the First and the Last. To understand these concepts we must fully understand God's plan of salvation, which reveals that Jesus is not always anointed with the fullness of Yahweh's Spirit. We need to recognize that Jesus ceased from being anointed by the fullness of Yahweh's Spirit at His death, but will once again be anointed by the fullness of Yahweh's Spirit at the resumption of the seventy weeks of years. At this point in understanding, we can reason out that both Yahweh and Jesus are the First, Yahweh the Almighty, during Jesus' first advent, from the time of His baptism with the fullness of Yahweh's Spirit until His death. And we can reason out that both Yahweh and Jesus are the Last, Yahweh the Almighty, starting when Jesus is once again anointed by the fullness of Yahweh's Spirit, at the resumption of the seventy weeks of years.

Isaiah 44:7 is one scripture that that gives us insight into the First and the Last. In Isaiah 44:7, Yahweh asks the question, Who is as I am? He then describes Jesus at His first advent who proclaimed that He was as Yahweh; then Yahweh describes Jesus at His second advent who will set the world in order for Him at that time; and then Yahweh states that They, both Jesus as the First and the Last, will declare concerning future events. However, theologians have covered over these truths by mistranslating Isaiah 44:7.

We must conclude that the church is stunted, because of the false doctrine taught regarding the major themes of God's Word. The consequence of this is that fewer of the lost have found salvation through belief in Jesus. Theologians study many books to receive their diplomas. However, despite the many books studied, they are still incompetent, in regards to handling the major themes of God's Word. They could become competent by the thorough study of just Part I of this book. However, we know that is not likely to happen any time soon. Theologians are rigid in their beliefs, even if those beliefs are illogical and contradict God's Word. They feel pressure from both lay people and those higher in authority to continue teaching the standard doctrine, even if that doctrine is false. It appears that it will be up to lay people to get the ball moving, in regards to correctly teaching these major themes of God's Word. If enough lay people make the effort to thoroughly understand these major themes, theologians would be compelled to start teaching and preaching the truth. The logical truth that agrees with Scripture is far superior to illogical fallacy that contradicts Scripture. So, teaching and preaching the logical truth that lines up with Scripture should cause the church to grow. However, worshipping God with the truth of His plan of salvation will result in rapid growth of the church. For it is worshipping God with the truth of His plan of salvation, that is the catylst for the latter year pouring out of God's Spirit. And it will be the pouring out of God's Spirit that will rapidly grow the church.

Theologians have not made the necessary effort to properly understand the major themes of God's Word. As a consequence of their lack of understanding, theologians are silent, speak nonsense, or contradict God's Word regarding these themes. So, lay people, rise up to the truth. It is up to you learn the truth of the major themes of God's Word. If enough lay people learn the truth, theologians will make the transition to the truth. People of Israel, God is waiting to pour out His Spirit upon you. However, for this to happen you must first worship God with the truth of His plan of salvation. People of all the other nations, God will follow this by pouring out His Spirit upon you also, if you worship Him with the truth of His plan of salvation. Many Christians believe that the rapture could occur at any time. However, Scripture reveals that there are many things yet to be fulfilled before the time of the rapture. One of the most important of these things is the latter year pouring out of God's Spirit, for the latter year pouring out of God's Spirit will cause a great world wide revival.